Against the Wind

Against the Wind

EBERHARD ARNOLD AND THE BRUDERHOF

Markus Baum
Foreword by Jim Wallis

THE PLOUGH PUBLISHING HOUSE

Original Title: *Stein des Anstosses: Eberhard Arnold 1883–1935* / Markus Baum
©1996 Brendow Verlag Moers

Translated and edited by the Bruderhof Communities
with permission of Brendow Verlag

Against the Wind: Eberhard Arnold and the Bruderhof
©1998 by The Plough Publishing House
of the Bruderhof Foundation
Farmington, PA 15437 USA
Robertsbridge, E. Sussex TN32 5DR UK

ISBN 0-87486-953-6

The photographs on pages 95, 96, and 98 have been reprinted by permission of
Archiv der deutschen Jugendbewegung, Burg Ludwigstein.

The photographs on pages 80 and 217 have been reprinted by permission of
Archive Photos, New York.

A catalog record for this book is available from the British Library.

Library of Congress Cataloging-in-Publication Data

Baum, Markus, 1963–
       [Stein des Anstosses.   English]
       Against the Wind: Eberhard Arnold and the Bruderhof / Markus Baum
   ; translated and edited by the Bruderhof.
       p.   cm.
       Includes bibliographical references (p.   ) and index.
       ISBN 0-87486-953-6
       1.   Arnold, Eberhard, 1883–1935.   2. Bruderhof Communities--Germany—
–Biography.   I. Title.
BX8129.B68A6913   1998
289.7'092--dc21
[B]   98–5665
                                                                             CIP

Printed in the USA.

Contents

Since the time of Jesus, small groups of earnest Christians have tried to live by the ethics of the Sermon on the Mount. From St. Francis to the Benedictines to the Anabaptists, living as disciples of Jesus in community has been a sought-for ideal. While many Christians have viewed these ethics as for a time yet to come, others have insisted that Jesus meant for his followers to live them in the here and now. Here is the account of one such Christian.

The aim of this book is not to exalt the man, Eberhard Arnold, or the Bruderhof movement he helped to found. Rather, it is to witness to God's faithfulness and God's intervention in human history. Yet it remains true that God can only act in human history through people. Arnold's commitment to discipleship, community, nonviolence, and his faith in the immediate reality of God's kingdom continue to inspire and challenge all who seek to follow Christ.

And it is also true that the Bruderhof movement is today a vibrant community of faith from which we at Sojourners have received great insight and strength over the years. Our 1984 visit to the Woodcrest Bruderhof in upstate New York was one of the most profound community exchanges I have ever experienced. There is a deep wisdom at the Bruderhof about how Christians can live together. A strong presence of love exists among them – not the sentimental kind that relies on excessive words, but rather a mutual respect, a readiness to serve, and a joy in one another that has been born of much faith and struggle.

Our life at Sojourners has been enriched and strengthened through sharing with the Bruderhof the joys and struggles of our attempt to faithfully live the kingdom of God in the world. Our shared belief that the gospel calls us to live in relationship with the poor continues to shape our vision and work at Sojourners.

The Bruderhof is continuing on a journey, one that in recent years has led them into the pain, injustice, and suffering of the world. A new movement of the Spirit has led them to minister in the prisons, to march for peace, and to journey to far-off places of conflict. Their involvement in the campaign against capital punishment has powerfully demonstrated the truth of the gospel.

This active involvement remains grounded in the faithful witness of the past, in the integrity and vitality of community life. It also raises a challenge for the future: is this involvement in the world putting the integral life of Christian community at risk? From our experience at Sojourners, I can testify to the inevitable tensions that arise in the efforts to maintain community while being involved with suffering humanity. I pray that the Bruderhof will continue to follow the way of Jesus in community and in the world.

And as I witness the rising involvement of the Bruderhof, I sometimes wonder what Eberhard Arnold would be thinking. I suspect he would be smiling.

Jim Wallis, Sojourners
March, 1998

Eberhard Arnold is one of the most remarkable figures of this century. A contemporary of theological giants Karl Barth and Martin Buber, he dialogued with both these men and with many other great thinkers of his day. His life's multiple interests and influences form an impressive résumé: an active commentator and publisher; an innovative educator and developer of an amazing educational method; a driving force behind the German youth movement, and its chronicler; the father of a dynamic and unique Christian community; and the rediscoverer and interpreter of a centuries-old spiritual tradition. He wrote average poetry, but his thoughts penetrate. Eberhard is, quite literally, an outstanding figure. In the Berlin of the Weimar era, he turned heads. People on the sidewalk gaped at him as they would at a prodigy. And more than one person dubbed him a "modern-day St. Francis."

Wherever something of Eberhard's personality surfaces, one immediately senses a powerful eruption of life. Strangely, though, he himself seems hidden behind all his writings: articles, books, and thousands of letters. His image and influence is diffused throughout a movement that still recognizes his authority today. But Eberhard Arnold the man remains in the background, out of the limelight, sheltered in the shadows of the truth he represented. He staked his life on an overwhelming reality. It completely consumed him.

Eberhard's life story reads like a novel. It is gripping drama. But this biography can also be viewed as a slice of history – contemporary, church, and cultural – and hardly a boring one, considering Eberhard's era. Hence the notes and index, which readers with specific interests will find useful.

Who was Eberhard Arnold? Undoubtedly he was a man, not a polished monolith. How did he become the man he was? What was he like? What brought him happiness or torment? What challenged him? What were his weaknesses? When were his decisive moments? What was the sum total of his life, and why is it relevant today? These questions prompted this book. Some of their answers, however, must be found by probing between the lines.

Markus Baum

Chapter One

"To hear and read
the words of Jesus
is dangerous."

Eberhard Arnold, 1929[1]

The future lay open – at least for one young man in his early twenties. Eberhard Arnold was twenty-two when he registered at the Royal Martin Luther University in Halle an der Saale, on November 11, 1905. For the moment, his was just another face in the crowd of nearly two thousand first-year theology students. A young man with principles and self-control. Tall, earnest-faced, brown eyes behind pince-nez, dark hair parted to the right, and a mustache. To look at him, it would have been hard to guess that Eberhard was registering to study theology against his own inner conviction and in submission to his father. In actual fact, however, in the fall of 1905 Eberhard was not at all clear what direction his future should take, and he felt somewhat unsure of himself. And though he, like other young men of his day, sought honor and credibility, he felt simultaneously tormented by emotions of ambition and pride. These emotions would be recurring themes in the introspective poetry of his early student years.

Nevertheless, in spite of his personal doubts, Eberhard was certain of his faith – an almost childlike relationship to Jesus Christ. And he was waiting for a clear call from him.[2] The call eventually came, though not overnight, and not in a blinding vision. It came step by step.

Origins

Eberhard was born on July 26, 1883, in the farming country near Königsberg. His full name was Eberhard Arthur Julius Arnold.[3] He was the third child born to Elisabeth Arnold née Voigt.[4] His mother came from a family of scholars. Her father was a professor of church history and dogmatic theology at the Königsberg University. Her grandfather and great-uncle on her mother's side were also theology professors and influential men in the Prussian Union of the Evangelical Church.

The family tree of Eberhard's father is equally interesting. Carl Franklin Arnold was a doctor of theology and philosophy.[5] At the time of Eberhard's birth he was teaching at a high school in Königsberg. The son of American and German missionaries, Carl Franklin Arnold had grown up in Bremen in the care of an aristocratic family named Gildemeister. Eberhard's paternal grandfather, Franklin Luther Arnold, had been pastor of a reformed Protestant church in the United States. He met his wife, Maria Arnold née Ramsauer, while he was serving as a missionary in Africa. Her family, of Swiss origin, claimed several generations of educators, lawyers, and theologians; Eberhard's great-grandfather, Johannes Ramsauer, had worked closely with the famous Swiss educator Heinrich Pestalozzi. In short, Eberhard Arnold was born into an upper middle-class family, proud of its heritage and intellectually gifted. His brother, Hermann, was three years his senior. So Eberhard felt closer to his older sister, Clara, since they were only seventeen months apart. Two more children followed Eberhard: Elisabeth ("Betty"), born in 1885, and Hannah, born three years later.

In 1888 Carl Franklin Arnold was appointed professor of church history at Breslau University. As a result, Eberhard's world shifted from East Prussia to Silesia. He was a happy child ("sunny and harmonious," his sister Clara described him),[6] somewhat dreamy and inattentive in school. But already as a boy he showed a pronounced sense of justice and a sensitivity to the atmosphere emanating from other people. From the briefest encounter, he seemed able to discern the essence of a person's nature. However, he preferred to share such observations with his sisters rather than his classmates.

Four-year-old Eberhard
with his brother,
Hermann, in 1887.

Parental Influence

It is hard to decide which of Eberhard's parents most influenced him since the two relationships differed considerably. His father devoted himself first and foremost to his own studies. During Eberhard's boyhood years Carl Franklin Arnold was chiefly occupied with the history of the Gallic Church under Caesar the Arelate II. Later he studied the Salzburg Protestants and their expulsion by Archbishop Firmian in the eighteenth century. He habitually withdrew to his study, only emerging at mealtimes. When he invited company it was almost always other university professors or senior students, with whom he would have heated discussions.

Each morning the family gathered and Carl Franklin Arnold read from the Moravian Brethren's daily texts.[7] In the evening he treated his children, some of whom had not even reached school age, to "The Sorcerer's Apprentice" and other poetic works of Goethe, whom he greatly admired. Neither the daily texts nor Goethe's poetry seem to have made any lasting impression on the children; presumably for the little ones it all simply passed over their heads. But as they grew older, their father expected them to participate in intellectual discussions on topics ranging from the cultural history of the eighteenth century and the German idealism of Fichte, Schelling, and Schleiermacher to the intellectual prowess of Carlyle and Macaulay. Carl Franklin Arnold's enthusiasm for the German philosophers was summed up in his harsh censure of those closing years of the nineteenth century: "Our era is extremely boring as far as any higher thought is concerned. Since Bismarck's day our policies have been thoroughly stupid, if not fundamentally flawed."[8]

Eberhard's father rarely relaxed or enjoyed himself. He could be cheerful, even happy, but for the most part reserved these emotions for family celebrations. Surprisingly, he raised no objections to the children's absorption in the wildly fanciful adventure stories of Karl May. Eberhard crafted the fine art of smuggling these books – full of Arabian mystique or Native-American suspense – into the Sunday church service. But his father had little understanding for children's nonsense. "You are intellectually dead," he once informed his offspring when he caught them in trivial conversation.

Eberhard's mother had a more practical nature. She highly respected her husband's erudition, but from time to time questioned the point of his endless research, or would have liked to see more of him – "You should have been a monk," she would say. A hospitable woman who enjoyed company, Elisabeth Arnold was always full of bustling activity, a trait she passed on to her son. Her husband permitted her – although not entirely voluntarily – the unrestricted control of her household. This required considerable organization, since it totaled nine members: the parents, five children, and two maids. Elisabeth Arnold insisted that her children be careful and thorough. It was usually late evening before she allowed herself to relax and to read newspapers and magazines. Her manner towards others was very direct and could even appear unfeeling, though in fact she was warmhearted and quite approachable.[9] Unlike her husband, she possessed a vein of ironic humor. She was tall, blonde, and blue-eyed. Eberhard wrote about his mother's unusually penetrating gaze, apparently without any idea that many people saw the same from his eyes.[10]

In spite of her strictness, Elisabeth Arnold always maintained a good relationship with her children and never let a rift develop between them.[11] Carl Franklin Arnold, on the other hand, in his eagerness to foster intellectual discussion, was ready to push things to extremes, even when the children were quite young. All in all, Eberhard and his siblings went through a strenuous but markedly successful course of character building.

One question, however, was not up for discussion in the Arnold household: the matter of class differences. Until he was twelve, Eberhard had very little contact with the "common people." At school he interacted almost exclusively with middle-class boys, who were all well aware of their social standing. So it startled him to discover that many people lived a life far simpler and less complicated than his, and yet could still be happy, warm-hearted, and genuine. Then, Eberhard met a homeless man and brought him into his parents' elegant home. A short time later, while on a trip to the mountains, he exchanged his hat for the filthy cap of an elderly destitute man, and was rewarded with not only a scolding from his parents but head lice as well. Why, Eberhard began to wonder, should someone who was poor automatically be labeled wicked and criminal? His parents could not always satisfy him with their evasive answers, and at times he contradicted them. Eberhard knew well enough from his experiences at the Johannes High School in Breslau that wealth and a highly respected family were no guarantee of good behavior or an exemplary life. A factory owner's son was a thief; the sons of army officers and government officials were rude and malicious. As Eberhard became a teenager, his youthful view of the world began to waver.

The Arnolds in 1902. *Standing, from left:* Clara, Carl Franklin, Betty; *sitting, from left:* Hermann, Elisabeth, Hannah, Eberhard.

Teenage Antics

Though it amounted to hardly more than a fling, during his eighth grade year Eberhard joined a secret school gang known as "Suevia." To prove their bravery the boys fought fencing matches, using sticks as foils, imitating the duels fought in university fraternities. There was talk of chivalry and knighthood, and beer drinking, but Eberhard's enthusiasm for these things was short-lived. When his father caught him drunk, the shame Eberhard felt and the drastic punishment levied by his school brought him up short. Together with a friend, Eberhard resolved to break completely with such pastimes.

A Disappointing Confirmation

Eberhard and his sister Clara had high hopes when they first joined church confirmation classes, so their disappointment was all the greater when the instruction proved to be just as boring and laboriously pious as the religion classes in high school. The confirmation itself brought no kind of revelation either. Carl Franklin Arnold had arranged a relatively simple celebration for the occasion.[12] A godmother from Berlin came to visit them, and as a special treat they rode the short way home from the church in a carriage. In the afternoon a few friends of Clara and Eberhard joined them. There were harmless games in the drawing room and folk songs sung in harmony.

When it was all over, Eberhard must have sought out his father again. He had a question to ask: could confirmation – the affirmation of faith – become a personal experience, and if so, how? But Carl Franklin Arnold was unable to provide a satisfactory answer. As a child in the Gildemeister household in Bremen, Eberhard's father had undoubtedly encountered a heartfelt, cheerful piety. His foster parents and their relatives had followed the traditions of the bible scholar Samuel Collenbusch[13] and the Bremen minister Gottfried Menken.[14] Carl Franklin Arnold had adopted his foster parents' respect for these role models – he subjected his wife and children to endless readings from old sermons by Menken. But the Gildemeister's natural and carefree faith remained foreign to Eberhard's father. He always had a deep reverence for God and his commandments, and felt obliged to strive in all earnestness for personal holiness and moral improvement. Carl Franklin Arnold could spend hours meditating over a text from the Psalms or wrestling with God in prayer over the most profound concerns of humanity. At such times he would shut himself into his study. When he left it hours later, the children often saw that their father was crushed and depressed. Carl Franklin Arnold obviously found neither strength nor joy in prayer. He could tell his son nothing different: he won certainty of forgiveness, even of eternal salvation, only in this hard and painful manner – through continuous wrestling in prayer.

Through his confirmation Eberhard became more keenly aware than ever before of the social abyss between the educated, prosperous elite and the simple working-class people. The manner in which his family dressed sparked this awareness. Only the upper crust could attend church as they did – for confirmation, Eberhard wore a new black suit and Clara a white dress. Poorer children did not have special clothes for special occasions. Eberhard found this unjust and decided that he would not recognize class distinctions. At first the only practical consequence of his decision was his attitude toward the family's maids. He now treated them more considerately and occasionally lent them a helping hand.

Diversions

At school, Eberhard still did not apply himself. He thought everything would fall into his lap, the same way as it did with material things. Sports were his only interest: soccer, gymnastics, rowing, and swimming in the Oder River. In his free time he liked to stroll down the Schweidnitzer Strasse, through the heart of the fashionable shopping district of this provincial capital of Lower Silesia. In addition, he held a season ticket to the horse races. Although the races themselves would be left behind, throughout his life he maintained this enthusiasm for swift, thoroughbred horses.

Decisive Weeks

Meanwhile Eberhard's brother, Hermann, had begun his university studies. Clara was now seventeen, and Eberhard's sixteenth birthday was approaching. Summer vacations for the whole family were no longer feasible, since Eberhard and his sister would return to school on August 7, around the same time that university lectures ended for their older brother. Consequently, their mother arranged for the two of them to spend their vacation with her cousin Lisbeth and her husband, Ernst (they were simply "aunt" and "uncle" to the Arnold children).

Ernst Ferdinand Klein was a pastor in Lichtenrade, near Berlin. He had formerly been a pastor in a Silesian weavers' village. There he had stood up for the interests of these cottage-industry workers far more strongly than was customary, and he had publicly denounced their exploitation by the textile mill owners. As a result, the Silesian Lutheran Church Counsel had transferred him to another district.[15] The sixteen-year-old Eberhard naturally admired the militant pastor.

In the summer of 1899, Ernst Ferdinand Klein's uncompromising love of truth had once again made him enemies. As pastor, he had insisted that the choirmaster be dismissed for indecent behavior with several school girls. Though the man was removed, a large number of villagers now boycotted the church services. So when Eberhard and Clara arrived, they found the parsonage resembling a barricaded fortress. From time to time window panes were shattered and threatening messages thrown through the holes.

These circumstances raised Eberhard's estimation of his uncle still higher. Here was a man like none other; the young man had never felt so well understood by an adult. And there was something else about his uncle that impressed Eberhard: he wrote later that in Uncle Ernst he found a courageous, joyful Christianity and a love of Jesus and the poor such as he had never before encountered.

One occasion in particular left Eberhard speechless. A "soldier" from the Salvation Army was invited to a meal, and Ernst Ferdinand Klein welcomed him warmly, calling him "brother" and listening attentively to his account of "work to save souls" in the dark corners of Berlin.[16] As Eberhard would later relate, even though he was deeply impressed by his uncle's respect for the simple man from the Salvation Army, he was still more impressed by the dedication and self-denial that he sensed in this guest.[17]

During the four weeks at his aunt and uncle's home, Eberhard discovered the New Testament, and the Gospels in particular. He was embarrassed when relatives suddenly came in and surprised him at his bible reading. He neither wanted nor felt able to speak – even to his uncle – about the questions it raised for him. Only when it came time to leave did Eberhard disclose his anxiety that he had no one at his home who could help him to a clearer understanding of Jesus. Ernst Ferdinand Klein tried to dispel his worries.

Back in Breslau at the beginning of August, Eberhard and Clara each stayed with different family friends while their parents vacationed on the North Sea coast with the two youngest daughters, Betty and Hannah. Eberhard stayed with an elderly professor and his family. This man was also a professing Christian, but he was very sober and rigid – hardly a confidant. Fortunately, Eberhard discovered in his room a copy of Thomas à Kempis's *The Imitation of Christ*, a work already five centuries old. Eberhard Arnold had found a key to the Gospels and a guide for following in Jesus' footsteps: "'He who follows me, does not walk in darkness,' says the Lord. In these words Christ urges us to imitate his life and actions if we want to find true enlightenment and be freed from all blindness of heart. Therefore it must be our first concern to immerse ourselves in the life of Jesus Christ."[18]

Dedication

In the ensuing weeks Eberhard must have used almost every free moment to read and think things over. He would say later that the image of Jesus had come to him in blinding clarity. To follow Jesus became the most urgent demand on his life; it was an inner vocation that called him above everything else. His parents, who returned home in early September, did not realize at first the drama taking place in their son's heart. He withdrew into himself. The only noticeable sign of this spiritual change was that he began attending youth meetings held by a young pastor.[19]

On the surface Eberhard's behavior hardly altered – at least not until October 2, 1899. While walking downtown that day he suddenly came to a decision, turned off the main street, and made his way to the young pastor's house. Apparently the pastor was not particularly surprised to see him, and he listened to Eberhard's flood of questions and reproaches, among them, "Why do I hear so little about the Holy Spirit from you? I long for the working of Jesus' spirit."[20] To this the pastor calmly responded that it was simply and solely the working of the Holy Spirit that had brought his "young friend" to him. After imparting some careful advice, he sent Eberhard home. Once there, Eberhard shut himself in the drawing room, leafed through his pocket Bible to the third chapter of John's Gospel, and read it aloud. Then and there, on October 2, 1899, Eberhard Arnold spelled out for himself the meaning of "born again" (John 3:3); confessed his belief in Jesus, the Son of God (John 3:16); and in reading the words of John 3:21, resolved to break with all sinful behavior and, in the future, "to act according to the truth." What is more, he weighed in detail the change in lifestyle and the costs that this step would demand of him.

This was undoubtedly a far-reaching decision for a sixteen-year-old, but it brought its reward. More than thirty years later Eberhard described this experience as a stream of God's love flooding his heart with inexpressible joy. When he finally left the drawing room, shaken to the core, he found the family gathered for dinner in the dining room. He turned to his parents and told them, in a voice bursting with emotion, what had taken place and what it meant for him. His father said nothing and remained doubtful and cautious; his mother uttered some soothing remark but did not quite know what to make of her son's words. His siblings sat silent. After a pause – embarrassing for all at the table except Eberhard – the talk returned to everyday matters.

Initial Consequences

As a first step Eberhard gave up any last trace that marked him as an upper-class gentleman. Horse races and idle promenading were now a thing of the past. His fashionable ivory walking stick now seemed merely silly. He withdrew from the teenage boasting of his peers. Eberhard bid a formal farewell to the curvaceous sculptures of Venus in the town museum that had on occasion inflamed the student's imagination. With greater difficulty he denied himself all the little tricks and schemes he had previously employed to wriggle through his school days. In the last weeks of fall he visited each of his teachers, one after the other, to tell them of his inner change of direction and to ask forgiveness for his past arrogance and sometimes disrespectful behavior. Most listened skeptically (one thought he was showing off and sent him home). But in the following months, their appreciation grew as this once mediocre student improved his performance with unexpected diligence. As for Eberhard's classmates, some were indifferent to his testimony, while some were annoyed at losing the instigator of so many jokes and adventures. Even the top students were not very welcoming when for a short time he joined their ranks. He did not share their interest in excelling merely for the sake of excelling. Eberhard cared little for recognition.

A Widening Rift

Eberhard began avoiding the usual parties and social events. He refused invitations from professors' families in the Arnolds' circle of friends – all at once these affairs seemed empty and pointless. This led to serious differences with his parents, especially with his father, who labeled his son's behavior the "impudence of an immature boy."

In his intense enthusiasm, the sixteen-year-old set stipulations: he agreed to attend the gatherings on the condition that he could speak openly to the guests and point out the errors of their ways.

Even on New Year's Eve, when the family and a few students sat together over a bowl of punch to welcome in the year 1900, Eberhard related his encounter with Jesus and challenged the relatives and guests to seize the hour and seek such experiences. His father attempted to play down the guests' embarrassment by reading Psalm 103, as he did every year, and then starting their traditional chorale, "Now let us enter with singing and prayer before the Lord who has given us strength to live until this time."

The rift between father and son increased when Eberhard questioned the large reception his parents held twice a year. He criticized the tremendous expense – "two hundred marks for food and drink" – and pointed out that all the invited guests were wealthy and well-fed. He reminded his father of the working-class families in the eastern section of Breslau and of Jesus' words: "When you give a party…go out into the streets and invite the very poorest who can never invite you in return" (Luke 14:12). To Carl Franklin Arnold, this behavior was nothing short of insolent, and he ordered his son to stay in his room. Misunderstandings between father and son continued. Both suffered as a result.

Missionary Zeal

Through the young pastor who had helped him take his first decisive steps, Eberhard found contacts with other young Christians. This pastor arranged a bible study group for older high school students. At first the only members other than Eberhard were two boys from another high school. Together they studied Mark's Gospel. With the pastor's encouragement, they invited their classmates to join them. Eberhard succeeded in interesting two friends from his "Suevia" days. In time, more than ten of his fellow students were infected by his glowing enthusiasm for Jesus. They gathered for discussions at recess under the walnut trees on the school grounds. Alone or in small groups, they visited Eberhard at his house and listened as he spoke about the joy of unconditional discipleship of Jesus and the happiness and strength that Jesus can give. Clara Arnold describes how she and her siblings sometimes discovered Eberhard in the drawing room engaged in deep, earnest conversation with one or more of his friends.[21] Apparently he had helped some of them find the same breakthrough that he had experienced.

In the meantime the bible study group grew to fifty members. When the young pastor was transferred, leadership fell to Eberhard. His missionary zeal and his strong sense of responsibility for his friends as fellow seekers cost him much time and energy. Small wonder that his achievement level at high school sank once again.

The Salvation Army

Eberhard had felt drawn to the Salvation Army ever since meeting one of its members in his uncle's Lichtenrade home. Their "soldiers," as these committed men and women were called, cared for both body and soul – "soup, soap, and salvation" – and went undaunted into the worst housing projects and seediest dives.[22] This struck a chord with Eberhard's social conscience and with his enthusiasm for Jesus. Besides attending the bible study group, he went time and again to the local Salvation Army meeting place, a room in the cellar of a dilapidated house in the Stockgasse district – not exactly the most distinguished address in Breslau.

Most of the soldiers were themselves poor and were usually malnourished and pale, but they shared an amazing repertoire of spirited Salvation Army marching songs. Eberhard felt right at home in their company. At the age of eighteen he began on occasion to preach in the Stockgasse district. At twenty, he could be found with the Salvation Army's newspaper, *The War Cry*, in hand, addressing strangers on sidewalks and in department stores. Without much ceremony, he would challenge them to surrender their lives to Jesus.[23]

Thanks to a Breslau Salvation Army captain, he learned an important lesson. Eberhard had witnessed the captain in conversation with a down-and-out man. Later Eberhard let slip the remark, "What a terrible face!" The captain retorted sharply, "What would you look like if you had gone through all the sufferings of this unfortunate man?" This episode reminded Eberhard that through no merit or choice of his own he belonged to a privileged class, and that misery is not necessarily the consequence of personal guilt. As a result, his judgments of people became more cautious. He tried to be unprejudiced when he met poor or burdened people and to show them more love. And sometimes he succeeded.

Once he helped break up a fist fight outside a tavern and accompanied one of the drunks home. Horrified by the misery he saw there, he appealed to the man's conscience and asked if he believed that Jesus could help him. The man snapped back that the "young gentleman" should help him first. So Eberhard rose an hour earlier than usual every morning to walk the man to work – past the many tempting taverns. At evening, he walked the man home again. This routine continued until the man stood up during a Salvation Army meeting and testified to his discipleship of Jesus. He had regained a solid foundation for his life.

During Eberhard's last two years at high school he identified so fully with the aims and work of the Salvation Army that he seriously considered forgoing further education and donning the uniform himself. His parents, dubious about his commitment, were able to prevent him from pursuing this idea. Yet they neither kept him from attending the Salvation Army meetings nor hindered his work with the bible study group. Naturally, however, they interfered when they read placards on advertising kiosks announcing that "Missionary Eberhard Arnold" would be addressing a large meeting at the request of the Salvation Army. It was neither customary nor permitted for a student to address a public meeting. Carl Franklin Arnold was so horrified at first that he thought he would have to resign from his teaching post on account of his misguided son.

Introduction to the Anabaptists

During 1901 the Breslau bible study group was captivated by a young aristocrat from East Prussia. In an account of his youth, Eberhard refers to this man as "von Gürten."[24] He was set on uncompromising and clear discipleship of Jesus, but forced himself and others into a straitjacket of rules and regulations. Though passionately enthusiastic in manner, von Gürten was also overbearing and domineering. He never had a good word for other Christians. At first the study group members admired him almost unreservedly with only a vague feeling that his attitude threatened to restrict their newly won faith and freedom. As time went on, however, they backed off from his influence. Yet in spite of the divisions he caused, he was an important inspiration to many. And it was von Gürten who first kindled Eberhard's interest in early church history, which then led him to ask his father about the sixteenth-century Anabaptist movement.[25]

Eberhard had finally found a topic his father could support, though it troubled Carl Franklin Arnold a little that his son was interested in – of all things – what seemed to him an unsuccessful offshoot of the Reformation. Nonetheless, he put his research library of scholarly books at his son's disposal and entertained long conversations about the Anabaptist movement, comparing its path to the course of Martin Luther's church.

Through his father, Eberhard became aware of a famous Austrian history professor, Johann Loserth, who had researched the history of Jakob Hutter's Moravian Anabaptist movement. Eberhard had discovered the two volumes of Loserth's *Anabaptism in Tirol* [26] in his father's library, and he later wrote of a discussion with his father about Loserth's acknowledgment that the Moravian Anabaptists were "good, faithful people with a pure way of life and love of Jesus."[27] The knowledge and impressions Eberhard gained through these conversations and readings continued to work in him, resurfacing with decisive effects at intervals of as long as six or seven years.[28] Three decades later he would cultivate a scholarly exchange with Professor Loserth.[29] But for the moment his discovery of Anabaptist history only served to awaken doubts about the Prussian state church – the same church that meant so infinitely much to his father. This illustrates the paradox in the relationship between son and father: they shared a burning interest in Christianity's history, but at the same time grew noticeably further and further apart in their personal evaluation of it.

Time Out

One thing was clear: Eberhard's missionary zeal, his ministry to the souls of his schoolmates and others his own age, his talent for speaking, and his involvement with the Salvation Army and the bible group – all these came at the cost of his schoolwork. Clara Arnold writes that her brother was indifferent about school, even that he had a "passive resistance" to it. By a simple calculation from established dates, it is evident that Eberhard had been lagging behind in his studies during the years following his sixteenth birthday. His parents ultimately convinced him to concentrate on his high school final examination, but he always maintained the worth of his missionary activities: "I can never regret having worked for Jesus in caring for souls, and I must state clearly that it was his call and his spirit that urged me to do it."[30] Since Breslau contained too many distractions from his studies, Eberhard's parents sent him to a boarding school in the Silesian town of Jauer.[31] There he passed his final examination at the royal high school during the first weeks of 1905.[32] He was twenty-one years old.

Chapter Two

For souls, for each brother,
I trust and believe;
Each one in faith holding,
Them ne'er can I leave.

I love all the brothers;
For them I shall fight
And steadfast will seek them
In truth and in light.

Ich glaube für Seelen,
Ich lasse sie nie,
Ich will es erwählen
Zu glauben für sie.

Ich liebe die Brüder,
Ich lasse sie nicht.
Ich will immer wieder
Sie suchen im Licht.

ca. 1905

Without Conviction

Had he followed his own wishes, Eberhard would have studied medicine. He dreamed of a selfless vocation in compassionate service where physical and pastoral care would go hand in hand. Over several years, Eberhard nurtured these secret plans, but he never disclosed them to his parents. They, meanwhile, formed their own ideas about his future – ideas along totally different lines.

On the evening following his high school graduation, the rug was pulled out from under him when his father, the theology professor, announced to the entire family that he expected to see his own son among his lecture audience.[1] Eberhard struggled for arguments against this pronouncement: he felt no vocation for theology. He already knew he could not become a pastor; however, he could picture himself working diligently as a doctor.

But Carl Franklin Arnold swept aside his son's doubts and wishes. He made it plain that he would see at least one of his sons study theology. (Hermann, his first-born, had already become a lawyer.)

Eberhard's father pointed to the wide sphere of influence assured by a career in the pulpit and to the long line of theologians and pastors among his forebears. His final, crushing argument: studying medicine demanded a great deal of time and money; his son had already procrastinated his studies long enough. "You will study theology!" Carl Franklin Arnold ordered. Case closed.

The Student Christian Movement

So it was that in the summer term of 1905, Eberhard found himself at Breslau University as a theology student. Although he met a fair number of his fellow students who shared his love of Jesus and his thirst for uncompromising discipleship, he still was not happy. The meeting place for young professing Christians at the university was the Breslau chapter of the Student Christian Movement (SCM).[2] There, students met several times a week to study the Bible, talk about their daily experiences, and share their ups and downs. Eberhard felt at home in this circle. But he did not approach it with the same fiery dedication that he had brought to his first bible study group or to the Salvation Army. He felt inwardly empty, dissatisfied with himself, irritated by unimportant discussions and trivialities, and almost desperate in his impatience to go minister to the poor and destitute.

A letter from the founder of the Salvation Army, General William Booth, seemed to confirm Eberhard's feelings.[3] Between June 1902 and November 1904, Booth made five evangelistic missions ("campaigns" in Salvation Army language) to various German towns. It is no longer possible to establish who first called his attention to the young enthusiast with missionary and pastoral gifts, nor when and where this occurred. Be that as it may, in the letter in question Booth invited Eberhard to serve in the Salvation Army.[4]

This letter played a part in a talk Eberhard had with his parents, but it did not make the same impression on Carl Franklin and Elisabeth Arnold as it had on their son. His parents showed understanding for his inner turmoil and self-doubt, and they urged him not to rush to a decision. They encouraged him first to attend an upcoming SCM conference where he could discuss his situation with friends.

The fifteenth general conference of Christian students was held at the beginning of August 1905 in Wernigerode (about seventy miles northwest of Halle). Eberhard attended with his sister Clara. Consequently she was present for the founding of the women's branch of the SCM – four years after the first German universities had opened their doors to women. SCM conferences were always small, intimate gatherings, drawing between 180 and 250 people from every region of Germany.[5]

At the Wernigerode conference Eberhard and Clara were surrounded by an open and warm-hearted atmosphere. Clara would write later of "enthusiastic love of Jesus" and "deep unity in their way of thinking." It was here in Wernigerode that Eberhard first crossed paths with Karl Heim, who gave a memorable lecture titled "Are Unsolved Questions a Hindrance to Faith?"

A guest from overseas, the evangelist Dr. Torrey of Chicago, provided still more topics for discussion.[6] He spoke enthusiastically about "the personal experience of the Holy Spirit's power" and of the experience of "baptism by the Spirit," sprinkling his lecture with impressive anecdotes from the life of Dwight L. Moody. Clara did not make any specific written reference to Torrey, but did allude to him, affirming that "the presence of the Holy Spirit could be clearly sensed" in many of the people at the conference. Years later Eberhard would still value and recommend Torrey's little volume *How to Obtain Fullness of Power*. He would write that "Torrey is actually very good."[7]

All these impressions and the encouragement of both older and younger SCM members put an end to the past months of colorless existence and helped Eberhard to overcome his dissatisfaction. Following the conference, a few weeks on the North Sea island of Langeoog completed the cure. With his parents' consent he took a break from the family to spend time alone in nature, to think and to be with God. Afterwards, he was still not convinced that he was really called to study theology, but he was at least ready to fall in step with his parents' wishes and to push on resolutely with his theological studies.

Halle

At this point in Eberhard's life, November of 1905, the curtain rises on Halle an der Saale: a proud, prosperous city, fully conscious of its history. Three and a half decades of peace have spawned rapid economic development and expansion, particularly to the north. Marked by late-nineteenth century architecture and design, the city boasts wide streets, shady avenues, spacious town houses, clean-cut façades, ornamental cornices, and enormous window fronts. High-class shops along the Grosse Ulrichstrasse and advertisements in Halle's daily paper testify to the city's flourishing business and commerce...

Culturally, too, Halle had much to offer. A dozen student associations vied for the attention of the city's two thousand students. These associations ran the gamut from "Christian" student fraternities and Protestant and Catholic societies for young people (the YMCA and Youth for Christ, for example) to various athletic and cultural clubs, as well as political and patriotic societies. Naturally, this spectrum included a chapter of the SCM, located in the neighborhood of the Royal University of Halle-Wittenberg. Eberhard's name first appeared on the roster there in November 1905.

That fall semester marked his first as a student in this imposing city on the Saale River. In the university's attendance register, Eberhard's address appears in his own hand: Albrechtstrasse 13. Three floors up in that apartment building was the home of Heinrich Voigt, Elisabeth Arnold's younger brother. Eberhard's uncle was a quintessential scholar right out of a picture book: doctor of theology, guest member of the scientific academy in Prague, and an associate professor of church history in Halle since 1894. He was also an eccentric, unsociable bachelor, who was sensitive to noise and had weak nerves. But he possessed a deep faith – and golden fingers.

Playing the piano and organ compositions of Gluck, Mendelssohn, and Schubert, as well as chorales from the Reformation and hymns from the English revival movement, helped him overcome his loneliness. And now he had his nephew to keep him company.

For Eberhard this was in all respects a favorable place to live. At the YMCA just around the corner in the Geiststrasse was the meeting room used by the SCM every Thursday evening at 8:30. Fifteen minutes on foot along the Friedrichstrasse took him to the university. The Rosenthal Mission House, located on a side street behind the theater, was only a ten-minute walk. But his uncle's home lacked the hospitality of his parents' house in Breslau. Heinrich Voigt had been granted a sabbatical during the winter term 1905–1906 in order to write his book *The Oldest Accounts of the Resurrection of Jesus Christ: A Critical-Historical Examination.*[8] Hosting visitors was out of the question. However, the professor was quite content to have his nephew available in the evenings for conversation or a game of chess. On those occasions, for better or for worse, Eberhard had to cancel his own plans and let his fellow students go out without him.

As far as Eberhard's studies were concerned, his uncle's proximity and advice were worth gold, particularly with regard to questions concerning his theology major. Eberhard registered for lectures in philosophy as well as in theological subjects. Later this would prove crucial to the continuation of his university studies. He took courses in logic, the history of philosophy, and psychology. Under the influential professors Kähler and Lütgert he studied dogmatic and systematic theology. Nor can it be overlooked that Eberhard confronted traces of his scholarly father at every turn. (To this day the name of Carl Franklin Arnold gleams from the spines of half a dozen books in the theology department's library.) For his student son this was both a

Eberhard's father, Dr. Carl Franklin Arnold, Professor of Protestant Theology at Breslau, ca. 1910.

challenge and a burden; whether consciously or not, Eberhard's professors always compared him to his father.

Of the more than three hundred theology majors, Eberhard's SCM friends were undoubtedly the closest to him. Among these are names like Hermann Schafft and Friedrich Siegmund-Schultze, whom Eberhard Arnold had known since his schooldays in Breslau – men who would play a role in his future. His acquaintance with other students was not limited to those with a marked revivalist background, however. For example, Eberhard attended a semester's worth of theology lectures with a student named Paul Tillich. Though their ways parted, their paths crossed again many years later.[9]

The Silesian Seminary

At the beginning of the 1906 summer term, Eberhard's cloistered life in his uncle's house ended. His parents understood from the few visits their son made to Breslau that he craved younger and more lively company. Eberhard found it in the seminary of the Lutheran Church of Silesia, Wilhelmstrasse 10. The massive edifice still greets visitors and passersby with a quotation from Psalm 27:11 chiseled in its stone: "Teach me thy way, O Lord; and lead me on a level path." Several theology students from Silesia roomed in the seminary, including a few from the SCM ranks. Some of them felt cramped by the rules of the institution and by what they considered to be a bourgeois ambience. For Eberhard, however, life in the Silesian seminary brought a measure of freedom. Moreover, the housefather was Dr. Karl Heim.

Karl Heim, hardly ten years older than the students, was regarded by many of them as a quasi-father figure. This was especially true of SCM members, who found in him a spiritual kinship and common language. Until 1898 Dr. Heim had served on the executive committee of the SCM chapter in Halle, and from 1899 until 1902 he had made the circuit as full-time traveling secretary for the movement. His spiritual authority was unquestionable.

The seminary offered ample opportunities for the exchange of ideas. Here, Eberhard and Karl Heim laid the foundation for a lasting (if not particularly close) friendship. In the years to come, the two would hold many discussions. They would argue over the consequences stemming from their shared spiritual recognitions. They would draw entirely different conclusions and move in completely different directions. Yet, right until the end of Eberhard's life, Karl Heim always took an interest in him.

Growing Responsibility in the SCM

On April 26, 1906, as the summer term opened, Eberhard was elected chairman of the SCM chapter in Halle. "Honor to Jesus, to our King, is what we want to represent in the student world," he announced in his inaugural address:

> He alone is the firm rock of salvation for the anchorless wrecks that are tossed here and there in the opinions and tendencies of the present day…We want to put him in the center of a world that mocks him and says he is outdated…We do not want to be or become an isolated sect, but rather a missionizing power for all groups in our universities. We do not want to set up a party or direction within Christianity, but rather to unite Christians of every hue under the banner of Jesus…Only Jesus! That is the motto of our movement. We know we do not belong to ourselves any longer, but that he has redeemed us to God by his blood.[10]

The local SCM chapter had grown steadily in strength ever since Eberhard had joined during the previous fall. "When I came to Halle," Eberhard later wrote, "the confusion in the SCM was beyond description. God granted the grace to bring the spirit of Jesus to rulership and to drive out what was alien and unclear. We have had wonderful, glorious experiences. It was not my work, nor anyone else's, but only the work of the Lord and his spirit."[11]

Eberhard's maturity and his activity in the local SCM soon gained wider recognition. Before long he was asked to participate as a "student member" on the SCM's national executive committee. Within the circle of intellectual and influential men in which Eberhard now found himself was a face not altogether unfamiliar to him – he already knew Ludwig von Gerdtell from the itinerant Baptist lecturer's early days as SCM secretary.

Back in 1902, a week of lectures by von Gerdtell in Breslau had inspired a small revival among the local secondary students.[12] Von

Gerdtell, eleven years Eberhard's senior, was a brilliant and powerful speaker. Originally, aside from his law practice, he had also traveled around the country giving popular religious lectures for the general public. He rejected infant baptism, lashed out at the state church, and did not shrink from taking the offensive in discussions on modern science. He attached importance to cultivated manners, but could be deliberately rude and hurtful. He enjoyed making jokes at other

people's expense. This had assured him of an attentive audience over many years. Karl Heim, who admired von Gerdtell, wrote of him in 1906: "The truth of Jesus' sayings is proved with a lawyer's logic and is interspersed with strikingly powerful testimonies."[13]

Von Gerdtell's relentless manner of speech coupled with his uncompromising lifestyle could not fail to impress a young man of similarly keen intellect. So it is not surprising that Eberhard initially associated closely with him during this early time in the SCM. Frequently, Eberhard supported von Gerdtell's direction in the SCM executive committee meetings, and he adopted much of his manner of speech and argumentative method. At times he even called von Gerdtell his "best friend."[14]

Eberhard's relationship with Karl Heim may well have influenced his assessment of von Gerdtell since, in spite of their undeniable

Conference of SCM leaders in Halle, 1907. Eberhard, who chaired the conference, is standing in the back row, fifth from left.

friendship, Eberhard found Heim "too compliant and, as a Christian, too ready to yield."[15] Perhaps von Gerdtell's resolve and unbending pursuit of truth attracted Eberhard the most. All the same, others felt this to be truthfulness without love, firmness to the point of opinionatedness. Did all this pass unnoticed by only this one particular student who possessed an acute mind and a delicate appreciation for what was genuine and what was not? Some things in the one-sided relationship remain enigmatic.

Von Gerdtell's vocation was "work among educated people"[16] – bringing the gospel to the elite, rich, influential upper class. Eberhard found out firsthand the success of this strategy. Ludwig von Gerdtell gave two sensational lecture courses in Halle, one before Christmas 1906 and one at the beginning of 1907.[17] Eberhard and Karl Heim played a leading part in their preparation. Themes for von Gerdtell's lectures included "Christ's Atoning Sacrifice" and "Can Modern Man Still Believe in the Resurrection of Jesus?" This stirred up an outright revival among educated middle-class people. True, the Halle daily newspaper gave it only a brief nod and quickly reverted to its usual bill of fare of current events: turmoil in Russia, the South African Boer War, the Kaiser's birthday, and what might be expected from the Social Democrats. But for many people the lectures provided topics of conversation for months to come. Printed copies were passed on from hand to hand, and prayer and bible study groups formed in the private homes of prominent Halle citizens.

Bernhard Kühn and the *Evangelical Alliance Magazine*

The focal point of this revival in Halle became the fellowship on the Alte Promenade, which met in the reconstructed studio of the painter Sallwürk. It is possible that Eberhard founded this fellowship himself, or was at least a co-founder.[18] There is proof that he worked in a responsible capacity in it for a number of years.

A frequent guest in this group was Bernhard Kühn, secretary for the Evangelical Alliance House in Bad Blankenburg.[19] Kühn was a simple man, small and physically deformed. He was anything but an intellectual, yet he possessed immense charisma. He edited the

Evangelical Alliance Magazine, the mouthpiece for the Evangelical Alliance center. The magazine did not have a wide circulation – about four thousand in 1907. But Kühn's Free Brethren background quickly became a bone of contention because he lacked any understanding or sympathy for the state church, and he forcefully pronounced his criticisms right and left.[20] In spite of this, or perhaps even because of it, the *Evangelical Alliance Magazine* served as a first-rate pulpit and was attentively read.

Whether Eberhard offered his services (which is rather unlikely) or someone else recommended him is of little importance. Bernhard Kühn took him on as a writer for the magazine and can be credited with having promoted Eberhard's fruitful and many-sided talent for writing.[21]

At First Sight

On Monday, March 4, 1907, Eberhard led a bible study meeting in the home of an energetic, bustling Christian, Else Baehr, the wife of Major Baehr, a medical officer. What did he anticipate there? Perhaps he was already in a farewell mood – his time at Halle was almost over. In a week he planned to leave the university and return to Breslau, where he would resume his studies the following semester. Obviously he would need to give up his leadership of the local SCM. The SCM planned a further conference to be held in April to discuss the work of the regional leaders with students. He was to chair this executive committee. After that he would pull out.

On this particular evening at the Baehrs' home, Eberhard spoke on a passage from Hebrews 10. About twenty-five people – Karl Heim among them – heard the young theology student give a penetrating, very personal talk on the Bible. "He spoke with such burning power, such fire and conviction, that at the end everyone crowded around him, asking if he intended to become a missionary…I had never heard or experienced anything like it in my life," wrote an eye- and ear-witness, a nurse who worked in a deaconess hospital in Salzwedel and happened to be spending her vacation with her parents in Halle.[22] Eberhard had noticed her as soon as he entered the drawing room and found himself thinking, the girl I marry should be like that. The young woman's name was Emmy von Hollander. Eberhard only discovered this a few days later.

Emmy von Hollander, Eberhard Arnold's fiancée, in 1907.

With her self-assured manner, her natural, blond curls (which seemed reluctant to be put up in the fashionable style), and her direct gaze from conspicuously blue eyes, Emmy Monika Else von Hollander made an attractive first impression. Born on December 25, 1884, in the Latvian capital of Riga, she had grown up first in Jena and then, following 1897, in Halle. Spiritual matters had fascinated her ever since a friend had introduced her to the family of Pastor Meinhof, a minister in Halle. As a teenager she had taken great interest in the history of the Moravian Brethren and their founder, Zinzendorf. She became absorbed in studying old and new hymns and spiritual songs, and read with enthusiasm Thomas à Kempis's *Imitation of Christ.* A parallel experience?

At seventeen Emmy enrolled as a student nurse at the deaconesses' institute in Halle. At nineteen she worked for a time as a nanny for Pastor Freybe and his family, friends in Stappenbeck near Salzwedel (about seventy miles southeast of Hamburg). She spent 1905 working as an intern at the deaconesses' center, but gave it up by the end of the year because of poor health and emotional burnout. Pastor Freybe arranged for her to begin work in February of 1906 at the hospital of the Order of St. John in Salzwedel. Emmy worked gladly and dedicatedly as a nurse, but the suffering and death that so often confronted her – both in the hospital and, from an early age, within her own family – made her think about the sometimes mysterious will of

God, about his compassion, and about the brevity of life. "What troubled me was that I felt something divided me from God," she later said about this period. "I could not understand how God, who is pure and holy, had chosen such unholy people for his own, and I found no real answer to this question…"

In this inner state and lured by a certain curiosity, Emmy von Hollander made her way to Frau Baehr's drawing room. Upon arrival in

Halle for a month's holiday with her parents, she had found her siblings full of enthusiasm over Ludwig von Gerdtell's lectures. At afternoon coffee and other social occasions she had heard people openly discussing "whether the atonement of Christ still has power and significance today." The whole city seemed to breathe a different spirit. "How I longed that I, too, would be gripped by this spirit."

After the evening at Frau Baehr's, Emmy did not see Eberhard for a while. He had gone to the Harz Mountains for a few days to become clear about his own feelings toward this young woman and about God's will concerning her. Still deeply stirred by his talk, Emmy went several days later, on March 15, to visit Frau Baehr and find out from her the way to "peace in God and in Christ." And she continued to attend the meetings.

Harmony from the Outset

On Palm Sunday, March 24, Bernhard Kühn began a series of meetings. Emmy did not miss either the afternoon or the evening sessions. Eberhard was also there that first evening. They exchanged only a few words. Then, on Monday evening, they spoke again. On Tuesday he accompanied her home. Love was yet to be mentioned. Instead, the two discussed what had been said at the meetings. They talked of their earlier years, of what they hoped for in a life with Jesus, and of the future. They understood one another immediately – there was no difference in their views.

On Wednesday evening Eberhard escorted Emmy to the meeting, where, to his joy, she publicly declared that in the past few days she had decided for a life with Jesus. On the way home he expressed his certainty that God had led them together and told Emmy that he wanted to visit her parents on Good Friday.

At that time the von Hollanders lived in a newly built town house,

Dessauer Strasse 8A, on the eastern edge of Halle, only a few steps away from the water tower – an imposing structure even today. The family was not exactly prosperous or, better said, they were no longer prosperous. Emmy's father, Johann Heinrich von Hollander, was the son of the last German Mayor of Riga, a major city in northern East Prussia. Her mother, Monika, was the daughter of Piers Otto, who had been pastor of the German Lutheran Church of St. Gertrude's in Riga. The von Hollander-Otto family tree had roots extending all the way back into the 1700s and was replete with councilors, patricians, and knights of the German Order. However, all this would only have had significance until the first Russian Revolution, 1904–1905, at the very latest.

Emmy's father, a lawyer, had moved his family to Germany in 1890 to avoid the russification policy of Tsar Alexander III and to provide a German education for his children. Repeating his bar examinations had cost Johann Heinrich von Hollander the greater part of the family's resources. He had hoped to qualify as a university lecturer in Jena but could not make any headway in his profession there. A suitable opening did not appear until 1896 at the university in Halle. The family's first home in Halle was in Giebichenstein; later, they moved to the suburb of Ammendorf. When Eberhard met Emmy, the von Hollanders lived on Dessauer Strasse. There were seven in the family; the two youngest of Emmy's six siblings had died early. Still living with their parents were her older sister, Olga; Else, who was only eleven months younger than Emmy; her brother, Heinrich ("Heinz"); and the youngest, Monika ("Mimi").[23]

Courtship and Engagement

Eberhard Arnold called on the von Hollander family on the morning of Good Friday, March 29, 1907. Decked out in a black suit and top hat, he formally introduced himself to the parents of the woman of his choice. They were quite impressed. Still, they did not like the idea of an immediate engagement; they would, however, give their agreement to the relationship if Eberhard's parents consented to an engagement. All the same, Emmy's mother accepted a bouquet of white roses. The engagement was not to be announced until Eberhard could provide proof of his ability to support a wife. The prospective son-in-law was tactfully left alone with their daughter for a short time. He told Emmy again of his conviction that God had led them together and added, "I fell in love with you the very first moment I saw you." Pale with excitement, she replied, "It was just the same for me." They exchanged their first kiss. Then – together – they read Psalm 34: "I will praise the Lord continually…Those who look to him will be radiant with joy…" In prayer, they gave their lives into God's hands, "to serve and to witness for him."[24] Then the family came back in. Emmy's brother and sisters accepted their future brother-in-law at once. The couple spent the following day and a half partly alone with each other and partly with the rest of the family. On Saturday Eberhard left by train for Breslau. By Easter morning his fiancée already had his first letter in her hands. At the top was written: "Always Phil. 4:4! Eph. 1:14! My Emmy…"

"May God give both of us truth in its fullness and love in its entirety. Absolute weakness and fullness of power. Deep earnestness and unceasing joy. Firm decision and tactful gentleness."

From Eberhard to Emmy, July 20, 1908.

Love Letters

Little is so well documented as Eberhard and Emmy's engagement. The couple wrote to each other daily, sometimes more than once. To the credit of the Prussian postal service it must be said that the letters never took more than a day to arrive. Of course the letters were always preoccupied with the joys and sorrows of two young people very much in love. But at the same time, and sometimes preponderantly, the letters focused upon Jesus and the couple's relationship to him. Emmy's mother remarked that she had never read such odd love letters. They were full of nothing but "Jesus alone – Amen – Hallelujah."

If ever two people were of one heart and one soul, they were Eberhard Arnold and Emmy von Hollander: He writes poems to her, and pleads with her to send him one of her blond curls. And requests photos, again and again. He sends her books – parcels of them – by authors like Finney, Torrey, Catherine Booth, Count Korff, and many others. Emmy wants to hear about his work, the articles he's writing – everything. He suggests they read books from the Bible concurrently and tell each other everything that strikes them. She is enthusiastic and picks Matthew's Gospel as a starting point. Within half a year they have worked through the New Testament. Eberhard tells her she is beautiful, and that he is enchanted by her blue eyes. She can hardly believe her

A rare meeting in 1908, during Eberhard and Emmy's year-long engagement.

happiness. He writes about his bike tours to the Oder River, and about his course load at the university. She advises him not to overdo it. He advises her to get more rest and sleep. She confesses to him that she gossiped. After a few months he becomes aware, to his horror, that two other girls had apparently pinned their hopes on him. Emmy then begs him to avoid compromising situations, and to let others do spiritual counseling with young girls. And the matter is closed. He reflects on events from his earlier days, she relates incidents from hers. He keeps her up to date with all that is happening in Breslau. She tells him in great detail what is going on in the family, among people in the Alte Promenade Fellowship, and in Christian circles in Halle. And there are always many and often complex events to recount.

The Issue of Baptism

External events forced the issue of baptism on Eberhard and his fiancée. Influenced by members of the fellowship, in May 1907 Emmy's sister Else announced her wish to be baptized. The von Hollander parents stood strictly opposed to the idea and wrote to Eberhard via Emmy, urging their future son-in-law to apply his theological knowledge to dissuade Else from her plans. Their request impelled Eberhard to search out the biblical arguments for and against both infant and adult baptism. Until this moment it had never been an issue for him. Once the question arose, however, it took Eberhard nearly five months to draw a final conclusion. Emmy, through their regular exchange of ideas and by pursuing her own line of thought, arrived at the same conclusion. This process of recognition unfolds step by step through the pages of their correspondence. Their letters clearly illustrate how Eberhard thought, what his faith meant to him, and how consistently he followed it. Quite clear as well is the fact that Emmy played an important role in the process and is by no means a minor character in this drama. For these reasons this development of the topic of baptism is recounted below in detail:

May 11, 1907: Referring to Romans 3:1–39, Eberhard holds that "infant baptism is not invalid, but is the will of Jesus and God; if any person longs to possess its saving power he must undergo circumcision of the heart (conversion) and experience the baptism of the Spirit."

May 31: He writes to the von Hollander parents: "We owe a great amount to the church and must regard as unproven the frequently asserted contradiction between its baptismal practice and the Scriptures."

June 16: Then, to Emmy he writes: "These days I am having serious doubts about my baptism theory and am leaning strongly toward believer's baptism! My doubts arise from a difficult question: if baptism should be widely practiced in the sense I have held, how would it be conceivable to have the strictly separated fellowship of believers, as required and carried into effect by Jesus and the apostles? This shakes my position – almost takes it by storm…It is all still unclear and perhaps quite wrong."

June 25: Emmy records the stage she has reached in her considerations: "I still haven't come to any really clear conclusion about baptism. I know only one thing: I, personally, received nothing at all from my baptism as an infant. I came to God through my conversion, not through baptism."

June 29: Eberhard warns Emmy that to receive believer's baptism "without an inviolably firm, deeply grounded conviction would be a sin, a sin with serious consequences! Rom. 14:23!"

On the same day a letter from Emmy to him reports about the first baptism service in the fellowship. Some of the candidates were "rather excited," she felt. "If one day we come to baptism, let's ask especially for a holy quietness, a holy peace beforehand."

June 30: Eberhard drafts what amounts to a list of personal principles:

> Under all circumstances I shall do the clearly recognized will of God. I shall do nothing except that of which I am convinced after examining it from all sides.

> I shall embark on nothing that I cannot clearly verify as biblical.

> As far as my present experiences go, I will search through the New Testament and history quite objectively in connection with the question of baptism. If I find confirmation for my present impression that only believer's baptism is biblical, I will have myself baptized as soon as I know for sure that it accords with the Bible and history…But as a practical conclusion, I cannot be baptized yet without committing a sin.

In the same letter he worries over how his parents would view such a step.

July 2: Eberhard writes, "Baptism with water is neither baptism by the Spirit nor death and resurrection. This causes disappointments or disillusionment."

July 30: Emmy says there is danger of a split among believers within the revival movement in Halle over this very issue: "The baptism issue is pushed to center stage instead of the cross, and people's consciences are disquieted." Emmy cannot approve unreservedly of everything the supporters of believer's baptism are doing: "Not everything was true – there was so much secrecy – I can't go along with it."

August 6: Eberhard responds to this news with a quotation from Ludwig von Gerdtell: "It is terrible that, as so often happens, baptism propaganda is also in this instance the death of the revival."

August 10: Emmy has had to listen to a sister in the fellowship tell her that she, Emmy, is still a corpse, because she has died with Jesus, but, being unbaptized, is still unburied and has not come to resurrection.

August 11: "Do you think I am a corpse? What deplorable nonsense!" she writes to Eberhard. Meanwhile his search for final certainty continues.

September 3: "I cannot get over Galatians 3:26–27," he reports. "I feel that I am facing enormous decisions, and I will simply and surely obey God as soon as I am certain. Follow the Lamb, wherever he leads!"

September 4: Eberhard announces his verdict: "This time of prayer and dedication has brought me to a serious decision, which will have grave consequences and will give our life a clearly defined direction, full of suffering. You, my courageous and faithful bride-to-be, are naturally the first person to whom I am telling this: today I have been convinced by God, in quietness and sober biblical certainty, that only the baptism of believers is justified."

How had he come to this recognition, and where would it lead? "Starting with Galatians 3:26–27, thinking it over continually with Jesus, in simple, sincere prayer," Eberhard explained, "I became clear that Scripture recognizes only one baptism – the baptism of those who have become believers…I therefore regard myself as unbaptized, and hereby declare war on the existing church systems." He would, of course, wait for Emmy's decision on the subject and then tell both

"My glorious bride!..."
A letter from Eberhard Arnold to Emmy von Hollander, September 4, 1907.

sets of parents. But he indicated that he wanted to be baptized and to leave the state church as soon as possible. He promised that before the winter term began he would investigate whether he could still take his first exam in theology under these circumstances. If not, he would immediately switch to a philosophy major. With this, Eberhard had sketched out the events that were to follow. He had no idea they would be drawn out over twelve tense months.

For the time being he asked Emmy to promise not to mention these intentions. Only briefly did he entertain the notion that she might, unexpectedly, come to a different decision – "but of course I don't need to say that our relationship will not in any way be affected by this." What would have actually happened in such a case cannot be imagined. Was Eberhard's remark unrealistic, or is it fresh evidence of an absolute trust in God, a trust that sometimes appears naïve? But as for Emmy, she declared a few days later that she could not "look on infant baptism as the biblically valid baptism," and so must let herself be baptized.

Eberhard endeavored to find a theological basis for his decision in an intensely thorough manner. Already on July 13 he had written, "I, of all people, must prove that it is a steady and deeply-founded conviction of the will of Jesus and the apostles. Otherwise it will immedi-

ately be said, 'First the Salvation Army! Now the Baptists![1] Always
going to extremes! That's part of his temperament!' No, what I do I
am going to do with my whole being."

To his surprise the result of his research was unmistakable: five of
his theology professors were themselves of the opinion that infant
baptism could not be validated from the Bible. Independently of this
he concluded, "It is not the books and articles of theologians in and
outside of the church that are crucial for me, but the words of the
Spirit in the Scriptures."[2]

Breaking with the State Church

As early as July 17 of 1907 Eberhard recognized distinctly that reject-
ing infant baptism would mean breaking with the state church. This
made his decision doubly hard: "The church has meant a great deal to
me." Now he applied the same, careful step-by-step process he had
used regarding baptism to work through his relationship to the state
church. On July 28 he wrote, "It is really a marvelous opportunity to
speak in such a church and even more so to do it every Sunday. A very
thorough work can be done here."

Two months later, in September, he reflected, "The baptism of babies, who have no faith, does not seem to me to be derived from the
Holy Spirit." Later in the month he concluded, "Jesus never wanted
to have unconverted masses baptized and made into Christians as a
formality. The historical rise of the church of the masses confirms the
fact that its origin was not from the Holy Spirit, who dwells only in
the reborn."

Finally, he recognized the "system of lies" that comprised the state
church as the "most perilous enemy of apostolic Christianity."[3] It
should be noted that Eberhard's mistrust applied to the institution –
the structure erected by human beings – and not to the representatives and members of the church in general: "Of course I do not fail
to recognize the integrity of many people of the church or that they
are blessed children of God." As he expressed on September 13, "I
would gladly avoid leaving the church…But as often as I consult my
conscience and the Bible, I find no other solution." For a moment he
toyed with the idea of joining the Baptist Church, "since their beliefs,

more so than their way of life, correspond so closely with my ideal."[4] But a few days later he put aside this thought "forever," after Emmy pointed out to him that in the Baptist Church, baptism was a categorical demand for every member. In Eberhard's eyes, this made them a sect. His view: "We want to emphasize only one thing in time and in eternity: Jesus Christ! Jesus only! Jesus as God and Lord, whatever it may cost. Baptism belongs to this, but only for the individual who comes to this free-willing recognition."

Exasperated Parents

On September 16 Eberhard wrote to the von Hollander parents to break the news of his decisive conclusion:

> The question of baptism has become crucial for me...Contrary to my earlier opinion and as a result of my studies I have reached the objective conviction that early Christianity and the New Testament only knew the baptism of believers. In light of this, the systematic untruthfulness of our large state churches...has come so forcefully to my attention that I must leave the Lutheran state church. I believe in the ideal of gathering all true Christians with the one purpose of obeying Jesus in faith. Therefore I am not joining any denomination and I still feel very close to the many upright and truly Christian people in the Lutheran church as well as in all the free churches.[5]

In his letter Eberhard pleaded "for forbearance toward Emmy and me; it is really with heavy hearts that we break away from our tradition, but we do so because we must." Emmy wrote home to her parents in a similar vein, though more simply and briefly.

Their answer proved "very loving, but curt and categorical." Although Johann Heinrich von Hollander acknowledged at heart that the decision was a matter of conscience for both Emmy and Eberhard, he set conditions for this concession. As he had done with Else, he insisted on a year's time of consideration before Emmy's baptism. Harder still, he demanded that she reach her decision quite independently of Eberhard and forbade them to meet during this year. Each would only be permitted to write two letters a week. Further, he stipulated that Eberhard must pass his first theology examination before the engagement could be made public.

As for Eberhard's parents, Elisabeth Arnold did not take her son's announcement very seriously at first. Carl Franklin Arnold would not speak of the matter until several days later, and was then, as Eberhard put it, "more loving and patient than I had ever expected." His father's reservations were mainly connected with Eberhard's university studies; he believed it would be out of the question for his son to obtain permission to sit for the examinations if he were an "Anabaptist."

Eberhard was confident that he could give his word to the von Hollanders regarding his examinations. He took his father's objections to mean that he could not be prevented from taking his first theology examination as long as he had not yet left the state church or received believer's baptism. He did not mind postponing baptism and separation from the church until after his exams. Emmy would not make any promises about the date of her baptism. Both of them agreed to curb their letter writing at least for the moment. They expressly avoided submitting to the yearlong ban on visits, but did not want to oppose it directly. "Unless God plainly shows us something else" was their constant reservation.

Separation

"All appearances to the contrary, the way of complete obedience in faith must be the best gift we can give our own families, too. Truth always has a redeeming and healing effect – on the upright. All the more we want to pray for our loved ones and be more loving than ever."[6] Eberhard had written these words to Emmy before the conflict and tension erupted. Soon, each of them would learn how difficult it would be to maintain that love for their unsympathetic parents.

Emmy spent the second half of 1907 in a parson's household in Brumby. She had a good relationship with those in the parsonage, but it was not nearly as warm-hearted as it could have been. She was allowed – and she permitted herself – hardly a moment's rest. The parson's wife sometimes found it embarrassing when Emmy, in keeping with her nature, bubbled over in free expression of her love for Jesus. Consequently Emmy felt she had to pretend to be different than she really was. Occasionally, though, an exasperated phrase or two escaped her as she puzzled over her parents' – particularly her father's – attitude. Eberhard soon realized that his otherwise happy "little blackbird" could no longer sing.

In reality, he was not faring much better. His longing to see his Emmy grew to the point of becoming unbearable. Several times in his letters he had to confess that he had been about to board the next train. More than once he let his mind run over places and times for a rendezvous, only immediately to forbid either of them from entertaining any such thoughts. "I have the most joyful hopes of seeing you again – would it be impossible for you to get to Charlottenburg on the 17th or 24th? I am not persuading you. In my opinion you should wait a year…But please don't let my opinion count too much in such a question of conscience."[7]

Eberhard had aggravated his inner anxiety by keeping the decrees of his future parents-in-law secret from his own family. As a result, even when his mother or sisters teased him quite mildly, he lost his temper. "I have a terribly dark look when I am angry," he confessed to Emmy. "I was glad when Jesus and all of them forgave me."[8] In short, both Eberhard and Emmy experienced their separation as an almost unbearable and pointless torture.

The von Hollander parents were not altogether heartless, however, and they suffered from the separation too. By mid-November, at the latest, Emmy and Eberhard had reason to look forward to seeing each other at Christmas. But the intervening time still seemed an eternity. In all events, on the afternoon of December 22, 1907, the Breslau central railway station beheld two infinitely happy people – with a great deal to say to each other. After that reunion, the forced separation was rescinded. Due to the miles between them, Eberhard and Emmy met seldom enough. But when they could meet, they met with a clear conscience. Looking back at that time, they would regard the "hurts, injuries, tactlessness, and hostility" as "specks of dust in the sunshine…No one can shut out our light, because it comes from above."[9]

Fundamental Disagreements among SCM Leaders

Eberhard and Emmy's forced separation wasn't the only shadow cast on the second half of 1907. Within the leadership circles of the SCM trouble was brewing. Eberhard had to contend with "strong opposition" primarily targeted at him and Ludwig von Gerdtell. In brief, many of the leaders found Eberhard and von Gerdtell's decisiveness too challenging. As a result, deep-rooted animosities developed. Matters came to a head when some within the leadership raised questions concerning the authenticity of the Second Letter of Peter and its place in the New Testament. In a statement unmistakably drafted by his hand, Eberhard protested that "the absolute authority of the scriptures has been called into question by some members of the executive committee." He asserted: "If what we find between the two covers of the Bible is no longer the scriptures, if we consider the Second Letter of Peter the writing of a swindler, or if we set no definite limits to criticism, then our purely formal adherence to this scriptural basis will lead to dishonesty and hypocrisy, which is bound to drive God's spirit from our work."[10]

Ludwig von Gerdtell wanted all committee members to sign a statement affirming the entire holy scriptures – no ifs, ands, or buts – and proposed a referendum. It failed by one vote.

Since compromise was out of the question for either of the two, this marked the end of both von Gerdtell's and Eberhard's days on the SCM executive committee. Von Gerdtell left with much thunder and little applause, cutting all brotherly relationships with SCM members. Eberhard, on the other hand, though grieved by "the inconsistency that leads to hypocrisy," still regarded all committee members "as brothers." Despite his withdrawal from this particular committee, he remained in close touch with the movement.

The Pentecostal Movement Begins

Apart from the SCM struggles and the weighty questions of church and baptism, an ever-recurring concern in Eberhard and Emmy's engagement letters was the duration and future of the revival evident in Halle and in many other places at the time. Eberhard believed that he could detect "an increasingly pure return to primitive Christianity" in progress: "Our revival bears the marks of the Last Days, the glorious expectation of His coming…There is still much to do: a great lack of freedom, and much confusion to overcome, to fight until the Word in the Spirit is the only authority and sin is put away as a dead thing."[11] It is not surprising that he had his ear to the ground for news about particularly striking events in Christian circles. In one of his first letters to Emmy, on April 4, 1907, he summarized an account of the unusual happenings during a revival in Frederiksand near Oslo, Norway, "in which many came to a complete surrender to Jesus, and the Spirit descended with a power like that at Pentecost in the story in Acts, so that people are speaking in tongues there even today." Eberhard was overjoyed at "how quietly, unassumingly, and yet wonderfully the spirit of God is working in our days."

Three months later Emmy reported about "four brothers and sisters from Norway" who, according to their own account, were sent to Halle by the Holy Spirit and arrived without previous arrangement to stay with a sister in the fellowship for "perhaps a week, perhaps a year, according to what the Spirit shows them."[12] She was surprised at their unstructured and incomprehensible manner of prayer, but was ready to explore the matter thoroughly. After meeting them a second time she wrote: "Their focus is not the cross...Rather, it is being filled with the Spirit, and (it seems to me) they try to force this to happen." Eberhard's dry response to this: "Preaching in the Spirit without proclaiming Christ is very dangerous fanaticism. The Spirit is there only to glorify Christ and to testify to him and his words." After a third meeting with the Norwegians, Emmy thought that the movement might nonetheless be from God. Later, this issue provided a popular discussion theme at the conference of the Blankenburg Evangelical Alliance and on all other possible occasions.[13] Without further commentary Eberhard forwarded to Emmy for her opinion the positive report from "an extremely level-headed colleague in the SCM" on the Pentecostal movement.[14] Eberhard placed great value on Emmy's assessment, which for the moment was cautiously positive.

When it became clear that the Pentecostal movement was causing even more disturbance and conflict in the Evangelical Alliance movement than the baptism issue had done, Eberhard supported the leaders of the Blankenburg Evangelical Alliance. In a statement in the *Evangelical Alliance Magazine* on December 19, 1907, they called for a halt to eliminate the confusion: speaking in tongues, prophesying, and other New Testament gifts of the Spirit should not be practiced at the Blankenburg conference – for the sake of unity.[15]

Eberhard is not known to have had close contact with Pentecostal church groups or fellowships at any later time. But there is also no reason to believe that he sweepingly condemned the Pentecostal movement or purposely avoided it. How could he have gone against the obvious impression made on him by Torrey and Finney? And as the years went on, his life revealed the working of a number of charismatic gifts: power of judgment, breadth of prophetic vision, and active love.

YMCA and YWCA

During the first months of 1908 Eberhard and Emmy lived fairly harmoniously with their families, he in Breslau, she in Halle. If Eberhard had any time left over from studying church history and philosophy, he devoted little of it – and that only reluctantly – to the SCM. He committed equally little time, but greater inner participation, to the Breslau Salvation Army. On Sunday afternoons he ministered nearby to a group of about thirty young men, a task the Breslau YMCA had given him. Some of these young people decided to follow Jesus. In May, when Eberhard handed over the group to other workers, he was pleased about what had developed there. Personally, though, he felt unable to become a permanent member of the YMCA, "because there are a few points in their constitution and in their use of speakers that I cannot square with my conscience."[16]

Meanwhile Emmy actively participated in the Halle city mission's organization for young women, an association linked with the YWCA. This was not without its difficulties. Some of the proponents of adult baptism from the Alte Promenade Fellowship, the very same fellowship with which Eberhard and Emmy had for so long been involved, now publicly voiced their doubts about the degree of "conviction" of the city mission people. They feared that Emmy would recruit young women from one organization to the other. In the city mission group, these same fears were mirrored in reverse, and Emmy soon came under criticism because she would not deny her conviction about baptism. Emmy's involvement with the YWCA and Eberhard's affiliation with the YMCA each remained merely an episode, although both of them preserved close and friendly contacts with the respective movements throughout the years.

Plans

Amid all these complex events, problems, and obligations, it is easy to lose sight of the fact that Eberhard was still a student. With his newly won conviction about baptism he felt that it was all the more urgent to forge full steam ahead with his studies. He was not the only person to wonder what vocation he should follow after the examinations were over, or what position he should seek. But Eberhard remained open-minded, convinced that God would lead him.

For a while he entertained the idea of missionary work in China "as long as no distinct leading from God holds me back." At the same time he was courted by many closer to home. Among these was Ludwig von Gerdtell, who urged him to join the Baptist mission committee, but Eberhard already had his reservations about joining the Baptists. A Christian millionaire, Baron von Tiele-Winckler, offered him a post as a private tutor – "including work for Jesus, free accommodations, a 1200-mark annual stipend, and free time for thesis work" – but time restraints forced Eberhard to decline. At one point he contemplated taking on follow-up work for von Gerdtell's lectures, calling it "a good way to start because of my youth," while understanding that he would "gradually become more and more independent in my work and evangelizing." But it was von Gerdtell who raised "objective reservations" to this idea. "I am afraid 'non-Baptist' is the decisive factor," was Eberhard's comment. In early July 1908 the Halle SCM seriously considered appointing him to chapter secretary – not exactly a livelihood, but it seemed a viable option. Even his parents wished "not to stand in the way" if their son "chose a vocation as a fellowship or student worker." Their only concern was to prevent his baptism.

All these ideas and schemes were shoved into the background by a turn of events that, up to this point, neither Eberhard nor Emmy had seriously considered.

Examination Denied

Right up until the beginning of August 1908 everyone accepted as a matter of course that Eberhard would sit for his first theology exam that fall – and he was the most firmly convinced of them all. In March of 1908 he had applied to sit for the examination and, when

the affirmative response arrived on April 6, he received the news ec-
statically and enthused over his allotted examination theme: "The
subject is simply splendid, one of the most suitable I could have been
given…And the sermon, too, has a wonderful text for someone like
me who wants to live as a sower of seed for God's kingdom."[17] Eberhard convinced his parents that the countryside would be the only
place where he could find the undisturbed concentration he needed
for studying. At the end of May he went to stay in Bebra at the family
home of an SCM friend. The environment did him good: "I am as if
renewed in this atmosphere pervaded by the spirit of God." In addition, Emmy had just returned to live with her parents in Halle, and so
"had moved much, much nearer" to Eberhard. He had finished writing his thesis by mid-July and had handed it in to the theological faculty of Breslau University.

45

Suddenly, complications came from an unexpected source. During
a visit to the Arnolds in early August by Dr. Genrich, the head official
of the Breslau church council, Clara Arnold casually referred to her
brother's intentions about baptism. Carl Franklin stated his conviction that his son's baptism would never, under any circumstances,
take place. Dr. Genrich then intimated that, although it was against
his official duty, he would make no use of this information, since a
candidate was granted permission to sit for the examination on the
assumption that he was willing to serve within the state church. How
Eberhard, miles away in Bebra, learned of this discussion is not
known, but it remains a fact that he caught wind of the incident.
Consequently, on August 8 he reported to his fiancée that "for the
sake of honesty I had to include in my application…that after the examination I was going to leave the church and receive believer's baptism." Two weeks later, he wrote again on the same topic: "Honesty
demanded that I add my additional statement about baptism…It
would have been hypocrisy and cowardly deceit if…I had kept silence
in this situation. I cannot thank the Lord enough for having preserved me from such crooked action."

Eberhard was still uncertain of the consequences that would flow
from this step. "The most correct official action would be my rejection," he wrote on August 21. He went to Breslau to clear the matter
up by speaking directly to the council. By September 12 he was as

good as certain of their decision. On September 22 the General Superintendent of the Silesian state church confirmed it to him by word of mouth, and on October 2 it became official: the Silesian state church would not permit Eberhard Arnold to take the theology examination.

Was Eberhard "misguided, wrong, on the way to ruin?" Had he, as his parents declared in their first outrage, recklessly and unnecessarily "made it impossible to take the examination and obtain a sensible means of earning a livelihood?" Yet how could he have gone on preaching absolute trust in God and uncompromising honesty if he had adopted underhanded means or resorted to clever tactics? "I hate compliance and every kind of diplomacy" was one of his own declared principles.[18]

Emmy, recuperating on the North Sea island of Langeoog during these tumultuous weeks, had always firmly supported his attitude, even at the cost of a breach with her parents. Several hundred miles apart and in the middle of all the turmoil, the two celebrated the one-and-a-half-year anniversary of their engagement on September 29. Eberhard expressed their shared sentiments:

"Perfect happiness!
Perfect sincerity!
Perfect love!
Perfect trust!"

"The first step in Christian life is the egotism of complete self-absorption in order to have one's own personality redeemed and transformed by Jesus. But once a person stands firmly on both feet, once a person becomes whole, then he or she can and must love."

From Eberhard's doctoral thesis on Nietzsche.

Changing Course

Eberhard did not wait in Breslau to receive the official refusal from the church council but left on October 2, 1908, for a two-week stay in Lichtenrade with his uncle Ernst Ferdinand Klein. His real destination, however, was the SCM in Halle. There, his plans for baptism created only momentary ripples, and the SCM stood by their job offer. The part-time position in the SCM allowed him to regain perspective, at least for the moment, and it enabled him to continue his studies without his parents' financial support. On September 23 it had been necessary for him to tell his fiancée, "My parents refuse to pay my expenses for a new course of study." For a moment he even considered choosing a completely different field: "Should I study medicine?" he mused in the same letter. But he did not mention this again and returned to the most obvious solution: philosophy.

On October 16 he arrived in Halle and placed an ad in the *Generalanzeiger* (the classified ads) for a room. For the time being he would board at the home of Sievert, the mine director. By now Emmy had returned from her restful getaway, and Eberhard wasted no time.

He arranged to meet her that very afternoon to celebrate their re-union and to discuss the many things they had been waiting to tell each other. Above all, they wanted to prepare themselves in prayer for the urgently necessary talk with Emmy's parents.

Most likely they met with the von Hollander parents that same evening. None of them could have anticipated a harmonious conver-sation; too many spoken and unspoken reproaches stood between them. Else von Hollander, Emmy's sister, had been baptized in Halle on August 2. This had especially angered her mother who, after the fact, concocted her own theory that Emmy and Eberhard had per-suaded Else to be baptized.[1] When, on September 23, Eberhard had written openly to his future father-in-law about the problems with his theology examination – "My only comfort is that I am sure no one can prevent me from receiving my doctorate" – the immediate re-sponse was "loving in manner, but harsh in its demands." Simply put, Johann Heinrich von Hollander wanted the engagement canceled and the couple separated again until his prospective son-in-law had proved his scholastic abilities through a formal examination. Now, ever since Emmy's return, her parents had carefully avoided the sub-jects of engagement and examination.

Predictably, the talk that evening ended badly. An objective discus-sion was hardly possible. Johann Heinrich von Hollander wound himself into a rage. Among other things he accused Eberhard of a "breach of trust, a licentiousness on a level with Münzer and the Münsterites, and a complete lack of chivalry," called him "unreliable and morally dubious," and added a whole list of other slanders and insults.[2] Eberhard insisted that these expressions and reproaches be taken back and his honor cleared in the eyes of his bride-to-be, other-wise no further direct and private conversation would be possible. Then Eberhard left the house. Emmy declared that if her parents for-bade contact with Eberhard she would not obey them, because she had already been engaged to him for a year and a half. In that case, declared her parents, she could not remain under their roof.

The family quarrel affected Emmy's health immediately. Only three weeks after her North Sea recuperation, her doctor diagnosed a return of incipient pneumonia and prescribed a time for recovery in the Harz Mountains. Her parents brushed the proposal aside – it is an open question whether this was due to their principles or to their lack of means, a lack quite evident at the time. Through Eberhard's efforts and through "wonderful guidance" she eventually found a place in Pastor Köhler's household in Berlin. Pastor Köhler was a leader of the Blücher Fellowship in Hohenstaufenstrasse and of the Evangelical Alliance Bible School of the Blankenburg branch of the Evangelical Alliance movement.[3]

A strange, uneasy relationship developed between Eberhard and the von Hollander parents. While his postcards mention many happy encounters with Emmy's siblings, he consistently avoided the von Hollander home, even though it was only a few blocks from his own residence. Nothing more plainly demonstrates the serious break in his personal relationship with his future parents-in-law than the letters by which he kept in contact with them: loving and friendly, but briefly stated and always repeating the offer to return to the old closeness and warmth of heart if the exaggerated reproaches were withdrawn.

Baptism

Once the prospect of taking the theology examination evaporated, Eberhard saw no reason to postpone his baptism. In the spring he had made friends with a Leipzig physician, Dr. Gotthelf Müller, and asked to be baptized by him. For months, Eberhard had been thinking of a suitable place for his baptism, and there are several indications that he found it in the Halle suburb of Ammendorf, on the White Elster, a Saale tributary. The baptism took place there, probably on the 25th, but in all events not before the 20th, of October 1908.[4]

It is characteristic of Eberhard that he later took his baptism as a matter of course and very rarely brought up the subject himself. Believer's baptism was never a theme in his public lectures or articles except in surveys of church history.[5] In fact, the only time baptism had been an issue for him was during those months of intense seeking back in the summer of 1907. Others had far more problems with it and either created or predicted difficulties for him.

Eberhard's parents took the news of his baptism bitterly. And it was equally hard for him when, as a result, they banned him from the family home. On December 2, Elisabeth Arnold wrote a scathing letter to her son, speaking of "perversity," of a "fatal step," accusing him of "foolish, short-sighted views," and of "loveless inconsideration." She even cast him as a victim of "sectarianism with all its deceptions," and finally, regretfully, predicted for him "a very difficult life, full of disappointments." Carl Franklin Arnold declared, and not for the first time, that he could not teach students when his own son was doing the opposite of what he taught, and that therefore he would have to resign his professorship immediately (which, however, he did not do).

On Their Own Feet

The bottom line by the end of October was that both Emmy and Eberhard were deprived of parental support and sympathy – she through loyalty to him, he through baptism. In spite of this, their letters during the following year ring with the same carefree tone as those exchanged during the very first weeks of their engagement. The conflict with their parents had crystallized their situation in more ways than one: They could at last appear in public as an engaged couple, without scruples and without breaking any promises. Furthermore, unencumbered by parental expectations, Eberhard could freely follow his inner call, arrange his doctoral studies, and resume spiritual responsibilities. Neither Eberhard nor Emmy were financially dependent on their parents any longer.

As time passed this proved harder on Eberhard than on Emmy because she had never been spoiled by generous financial help from her parents. As backing, Eberhard had a small inheritance from a great-aunt in Bremen, just enough to provide a simple standard of living for another year. Eberhard certainly did not possess sufficient funds for a wedding or for setting up a household, nor even enough to cover the extra costs of a new doctoral thesis. Emmy could expect a modest sum to furnish their home from various family endowments and legacies, but for the most part, she would have to earn her own livelihood. The step to financial independence from their parents would have been rash for both Eberhard and Emmy if they had not shared a trust in God and the certainty that he would provide for all their needs.

Even before the breach with their parents, Eberhard and Emmy's first financial need had been met by a "tangible result of faith." Albert

Still, who knew of Eberhard's plans for Halle, had already sent a sum of one hundred marks at the end of September. Eberhard's work for the Halle SCM brought in a small paycheck. And it was not long before the group associated with Ludwig von Gerdtell asked Eberhard to assume the follow-up for a series of von Gerdtell talks.

So each Monday evening from the beginning of December, Eberhard gave a talk in the Erfurt Gallery about the "deeper understanding of the Christian view of the world and of life. Free admission for ladies and gentlemen. Reserved seats: fifty pfennig." Between eighty and one hundred people regularly attended these meetings for religious instruction, most of them strangers to the church, including former atheists, humanists, and theosophists.[6]

Eberhard packed his schedule to the limit during his first few weeks in Halle. Aside from attending the usual SCM meetings and occasional YMCA gatherings, he held bible study groups or other meetings almost every day with either the Southern Fellowship, the Salvation Army, the Alte Promenade Fellowship, or the Baptists. This tight schedule soon had to be cut back to allow for his studies. The von Hollander parents, who were kept well-informed by Emmy's brother and sister, viewed Eberhard's slate of commitments as a further justification for their outrage, and they repeatedly stated that this was no way to pass an examination.

Meanwhile, Emmy's days in Berlin were equally eventful. Although her mornings were free, allowing time for a little much-needed rest, her afternoons bustled with activity. She cared for the Köhler children and, in the Blücher Fellowship, held meetings for girls and led a women's bible study. In November she experienced a Salvation Army evangelization campaign. She reported enthusiastically about the sermons that Salvation Army General William Booth gave to audiences of as large as four thousand people at the Busch Circus. On some evenings as many as a hundred people flocked to the "mercy seat," publicly set their lives in order, and committed themselves to Christ.

Eberhard came to Berlin for Emmy's baptism, which took place on the evening of December 22, 1908, in the Hohenstaufenstrasse Fellowship. She was baptized by Pastor Köhler. The engaged couple spent Christmas and welcomed in the new year of 1909 among their friends in Berlin.

Erlangen University

Eberhard completed the final phase of his studies at the University of Erlangen. This was partly a result of Ludwig von Gerdtell's influence. Von Gerdtell had received his doctorate there in the spring of 1908. While Eberhard had been studying in Bebra, he visited von Gerdtell and must have heard a great deal about the university, the philosophy department, and the professors. Most likely von Gerdtell also advised him regarding his choice of both a dissertation theme and an advisor.[7]

March 31, 1909, found "candidate Arnold" in Erlangen, Villa Pfaff, Burgberg 9. Free from the inner responsibility and the numerous obligations he had carried in Halle, Eberhard was soon accomplishing an almost unbelievable amount of academic work: "Every day 45–50 pages of Kant; 17–20 pages of the history of Greek philosophy; about 15 pages of transcendental philosophy, (which compared with Kant is child's play); and occasionally literature on Nietzsche as well." By the end of April he was also attending two to three hours of lectures per day. He worked through Kant's *Prolegomena* and *Critique of Pure Reason* two or three times in preparation for his oral examination. In June he moved on to "the great atheist" Feuerbach, and blazed through dozens of volumes of secondary literature. During this period he disciplined himself drastically – even to the point of curtailing his letters to Emmy. On weekends he relaxed by taking extended bicycle tours through the Franconian Alps, but always with a textbook stuck in his rucksack.

As the topic for his doctoral thesis he chose "Nietzsche's Religious Development and Christianity." Professor Falckenberg accepted the outline in mid-May. At this time, only nine years after Nietzsche's death, a great part of his philosophical works were still not public or in print. Eberhard traveled repeatedly to Weimar to spend a day or more in the Nietzsche archives, where Elisabeth Förster-Nietzsche, the philosopher's sister and posthumous publisher, gave him access to original manuscripts.[8] By the end of July, after submitting his major final paper, on Immanuel Kant, Eberhard turned his full concentration toward his dissertation and imminent examination.

Summa Cum Laude

The tone of Eberhard's letters to Emmy grew more confident even as each passing day brought the moment of his examination nearer. Back in March he had declined an offer from the Evangelical Alliance Bible School in Berlin, which would gladly have appointed him as a teacher after his examination. On June 13 he wrote to Emmy of his belief that, "with the Lord's guidance," a committee of his friends and acquaintances in leadership circles would provide him with "a position this winter with an apartment in Jena, combined with ministry in the neighboring towns of Leipzig, Halle, and Erfurt." This came very close to describing what would actually happen. The next day, June 14, he wrote to Emmy again: "I am absolutely certain we can marry at Christmas." On June 27 he cheerfully announced, "From August on I have no prospects whatsoever" – meaning plainly and simply that he was virtually broke – "but the Lord will do wonderful things." His faithful hope did not deceive him.

Eberhard handed in his application for a doctorate on November 3 to Professor Fuchs, Dean of Philosophy at Erlangen University. In it he confirmed payment of 240 marks (the examination fee), and that he had sent 250 copies of his 79-page dissertation to the university syndicate. The dissertation's third chapter, on Nietzsche's *The Antichrist*, had to be cut for lack of space. The full text of Eberhard's uncut work first appeared in print in 1910 in the book *Early Christian and Anti-Christian Elements in the Development of Friedrich Nietzsche.*[9]

Eberhard's thesis greatly impressed Professor Falckenberg, as his report clearly shows: "Profound and exact knowledge of the subject… absolutely independent and critical evaluation of previous treatments of the question…much that is new and original, thorough use of sources…judgments always maturely considered…broad outlook, and spiritual maturity." And finally, "Performance by a young master, for which I must recommend the grade 1" – the highest possible mark.[10] Now only Eberhard's examination remained. Topics: history of philosophy, and systematic philosophy and pedagogy. Date: Tuesday, November 30. Time: six o'clock P.M.

Eberhard Arnold's doctoral diploma from Erlangen University, which he received July 1, 1910.

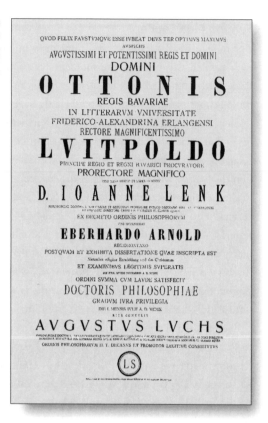

QVOD FELIX FAVSTVMQVE ESSE IVBEAT DEVS TER OPTIMVS MAXIMVS
AVSPICIIS
AVGVSTISSIMI ET POTENTISSIMI REGIS ET DOMINI
DOMINI
OTTONIS
REGIS BAVARIAE
IN LITTERARVM VNIVERSITATE
FRIDERICO-ALEXANDRINA ERLANGENSI
RECTORE MAGNIFICENTISSIMO
LVITPOLDO
PRINCIPE REGIO ET REGNI BAVARICI PROCVRATORE
PRORECTORE MAGNIFICO
VIRO ILLVSTRISSIMO ET LIBERO BARONE
D. IOANNE LENK
PHILOSOPHIAE DOCTORE E NATVRALIVM ET OECONOMICARVM FACVLTATE ORDINARIO HON. ET INTERRVMP
ET PHYSICAE DIRECTORE ORDIN. ET NATVRALIS H. CLASSIS ADSESS
EX DECRETO ORDINIS PHILOSOPHORVM
VIRO HONESTISSIMO
EBERHARDO ARNOLD
REGIOMONTANO
POSTQVAM ET EXHIBITA DISSERTATIONE QVAE INSCRIPTA EST
Nietsches religiöse Entwicklung und das Christentum
ET EXAMINIBVS LEGITIMIS SVPERATIS
EX XXX. MENSIS NOVEMBRIS A. R. MCMX
ORDINI SVMMA CVM LAVDE SATISFECIT
DOCTORIS PHILOSOPHIAE
GRADVM IVRA PRIVILEGIA
DIE I. MENSIS IVLII A. D. MCMX
RITE CONTVLIT
AVGVSTVS LVCHS
PHILOSOPHIAE DOCTOR I. THEOLOGIAE GRATVITO ET LATIGABO LVCVBRATIONE PROFESSOR ORDINARIVS FACVLTAS SEMINARII E R. SEI DEXIC DIRECTOR
ACADEMIAE ADS ACT SEX, LITTERARA REGNA ET LITT. REPHV RATVM ET A OLESALMI INTEST. SODALE E SODALIBVS T. CLANSS REPVR
ORDINIS PHILOSOPHORVM H. T. DECANVS ET PROMOTOR LEGITIME CONSTITVTVS

(LS)

To the horror of Emmy's parents, on the very eve of his examination Eberhard stopped halfway between Weimer and Erlangen to deliver a lecture. He was then taken by sleigh to the train and traveled through the entire night. The following evening professors Falckenberg, Römer, and Hensel conducted Eberhard's oral examination. Very soon afterwards Emmy received a telegram: "Summa cum laude. Arrive tomorrow morning in Halle."

Taken at Their Word

Before noon on December 1, 1909, Eberhard set foot in the von Hollander home, Dessauer Strasse 8A, for the first time in more than a year. Emmy's parents received him very kindly, just as if nothing had ever come between them. Eberhard came right to the point. He had passed his examination. Now he requested that Johann Heinrich von Hollander give him Emmy's papers and honor his promise not to further deter their marriage. After some preliminary hesitation the lawyer opened his strongbox and gave his future son-in-law Emmy's birth certificate, her certificate of nobility, and her proof of nationality. Eberhard and Emmy lost no time and went that same morning to the registrar in north Halle. The first possible date for their wedding was December 20.

The couple had already rented a small apartment in Leipzig a few days before Eberhard's examination. ("Irresponsible!" was what Emmy's parents had called the step.) Else and a former housekeeper of the von Hollanders now busied themselves setting up the new household, but Emmy's mother was conspicuous by her absence.

Eberhard's parents came to the wedding from Breslau, apparently reconciled with their son and proud of him and his bride. His sisters Clara, Hannah, and Betty were there, as were a few relatives from both sides – a company of some twenty people in all. Both fathers wished to sign as witnesses to the wedding and went to the registrar with the couple, driving in a dapper blue carriage. Of course, in keeping with the wedding couple's convictions, there was no church ceremony. But there was at least a wedding sermon. Otto Mau, from Erfurt, spoke on Mark 6:7: "Jesus sent out his disciples two by two." Then Carl Franklin Arnold took over. "As you have rejected the church's blessing, I can do no more than give you a blessing from both your parents," he said; and he blessed his son and daughter-in-law in the name of the triune God. Pastor Ernst Ferdinand Klein, Eberhard's uncle, told of Eberhard's religious awakening in the summer of 1899, and drew attention to the deep earnestness required for a couple to found their marriage on faith without any assured income. A few hymns ended the ceremony, which was followed by a wedding meal at The Crown Prince. Emmy and Eberhard soon took leave of the wedding party and traveled by train to Leipzig-Lindenau, the city of their first home, Kanzlerstrasse 17 – an apartment with four tiny rooms, a little garden, and an arbor. The honeymoon was kept short. By New Year's Eve Eberhard was back at work.

Eberhard and Emmy Arnold in 1910 outside their first home, Kanzlerstrasse 17, Leipzig-Lindenau.

Nietzsche

At this point in the story, something must be said about Eberhard's connection with Nietzsche. Nietzsche's philosophy, language, and thinking continued to concern Eberhard even after he completed his doctorate. In the following years, traces of the great impression made on him by this eccentric and extraordinary thinker surfaced in his thought, speech, and action.

It is true that Eberhard's doctoral thesis reveals a great deal about Friedrich Nietzsche's religious thought. But it reveals equally as much about Eberhard's inner viewpoint in 1909. In his report Professor Falckenberg had recognized Eberhard's "keen but not unrestrained appreciation of Nietzsche's objections and accusations against Christianity." What was it that Eberhard appreciated in Friedrich Nietzsche's criticism? That can be summarized as follows:

Eberhard agreed with Nietzsche that "the church's foundation is built upon the very opposite of the Gospels"; that the church is "a terrible hodgepodge of Greek philosophy and Judaism, of asceticism, of hierarchical order, etc." Further, he shared Nietzsche's view that originally Christianity "tolerated no connection with politics and state policies; it cannot in any way be a religion of the masses."[11]

At times Eberhard's trenchant analysis of the established churches goes even further than Nietzsche's criticisms. In the everyday life of the churches of his day Eberhard was hard-pressed to discover any argument to weaken Nietzsche's objective criticisms of Christianity. To do this he had to go back to "early Christianity, as described in the Acts of the Apostles and in the New Testament epistles."

In other words, Eberhard could not and would not in any way defend the "Christianity" that Nietzsche had in mind when he made his sometimes accurate observations and sometimes grossly abusive attacks. Eberhard painted a picture of New Testament Christianity that exposed Nietzsche's accusations – "decadent," "life-negating," "feeble," "religion of pity," etc. – as crass and arbitrary misinterpretations. Eberhard's criticism of this philosopher so well-versed in the Bible was basically as follows: Nietzsche had made it too easy for himself; he recognized false Christians but had too quickly given up the search for true ones. Against his better judgment, Nietzsche had often asserted sheer nonsense, and had finally lost his way completely.

The point of Eberhard's dissertation is obvious: he had usurped – "pirated" – Nietzsche's language and thoughts and used them to express spiritual realities. Then, Eberhard had gone on to refute Nietzsche in Nietzsche's own idiom, using Nietzsche's own arguments.

For Eberhard, Jesus is the *"Übermensch,"* the "overman" for whom Nietzsche had sought. Jesus is "the redeeming man of great and overcoming love, the creative spirit, the noonday bell that calls for a great decision, the one who sets people's will free again, who brings the earth back to its true purpose and restores hope to humanity."[12]

Eberhard believed that a life in discipleship of Jesus Christ affirms life in a comprehensive sense – more all-encompassing and complete than Nietzsche had ever dared to consider. For Eberhard, belief in Jesus meant affirmation of life, not at all the yearning for death, as Nietzsche had asserted; affirmation of the body, not self-chastisement or contempt of sexuality; and affirmation of nature and its gifts, not false asceticism.

For Eberhard, the *Gemeinde* – the church-community of Jesus' disciples – is the "extraordinary, new aristocracy," the "higher type of humanity" that Nietzsche had invoked.[13] Eberhard identified the true Christians as Nietzsche's "future masters of the earth" because, according to Revelation 20:4–6 and 22:5, at the end of time they will live and reign with Jesus.

Confronting Nietzsche

In more ways than one, Friedrich Nietzsche and Eberhard Arnold share strikingly similar characteristics. Both were precocious in the positive sense of the word. Nietzsche was a professor at the age of twenty-four, before he had even completed his studies. Eberhard, at eighteen, was already much sought after as an evangelist and pastoral worker. Each in his own way lived decisively and constantly tried to make clear distinctions and decisions. Their linguistic styles show how close their two temperaments were. Both formulated their thoughts precisely and provocatively and drove every argument to the heart of the matter. Both made frequent use of superlatives: most decisive, totally, utterly, without reservation, superabundance, most outstanding, gigantic. When an inconvenient idea arose, both pursued it to its final consequences. (Nietzsche, however, lost all sense of proportion in doing so.) Both dug deep for the truth. But the resemblance certainly goes no further. Eberhard believed in a divine, all-embracing truth that people cannot attain on their own, a truth that is revealed by God – by the God whom Nietzsche denied and fought against to the point of insanity. Nietzsche can claim the honor of being a unique philosopher and a linguistic genius, as well as a self-proclaimed prophet. Eberhard had only one purpose: to understand and obey Jesus Christ.

By the conclusion of his university studies, Eberhard's thinking had taken on a new quality. In his dissertation he had grappled with the great thinkers of his time, whether their positions were good or evil. He set out to prove that faith in Jesus Christ brought convincing answers to the questions of modern humanity. Nietzsche had provoked such questions, as had Rudolf Steiner, Karl Marx, Leo Tolstoy, Stefan

George, Peter Kropotkin, and in later years the propagators of National Socialism. Before all was said and done, Eberhard would face each of them, one after the other.

But Nietzsche came first. For an entire decade Eberhard used slogans and illustrations from Nietzsche's works to draw to his lectures both the critics of the church and the "born-again" Christians. These themes included: "The Bankruptcy of the Religious Systems," "The New Aristocracy," "Jesus and the Fight against Moralism," "The Overman," "The Will to Power and Submission to God," "The New Humanity," "The Modern Antichrist and His Defeat," "Nietzsche in the Present-Day Struggle," and finally, in 1920, Eberhard's lecture "The Descendants of Man and the Coming Order."

However much these writings and lectures may have differed in detail, the basic theme remained the same: Jesus Christ surpasses Nietzsche in every respect. Jesus fulfills what Nietzsche could at best only long for. Nietzsche's ideas were not altogether bad, but Jesus far outclasses them. If a person desires "to set the stamp of eternity on his own life," to use Nietzsche's expression, there is no need to wait for an "eternal recurrence." The best course is to hold to Jesus. Eberhard did not shrink from presenting this message loudly and clearly, even in his doctoral thesis.

In Leipzig

Life in Leipzig was by no means quiet. In a very short time a weekly bible study meeting had begun in the Arnolds' little house. Sometimes as many as twenty people participated. Eberhard spent one day a week in Halle working for the Alte Promenade Fellowship. He would catch the night train home. He performed pastoral tasks and gave sermons and lectures to the groups associated with Dr. Gotthelf Müller, the man who had baptized him. In the spring Eberhard resumed his work in the Erfurt Gallery Fellowship, but this time he was working together with Emmy, who was anything but a spectator. She led meetings, held follow-up talks for women, and planned evenings for singing and music. As in the previous year, those who attended these gatherings were, for the most part, unfamiliar with the church. At his talks, Eberhard found himself confronted by spiritualists, *Millenniumsleute* ("millennium people"), and anthroposophists.[14]

Witnesses reported that Eberhard received the questions of negative or doubting hearers with disarming openness. He could find his way unerringly to the heart of a question and then give a simple and illuminating answer, always trying to base his reply on the Gospels. Throughout his life Eberhard regarded this ability as a special gift from God.[15]

This gift helped him in two series of lectures given in January and April of 1910 in Halle's Tulpe Auditorium. These lectures on Nietzsche attracted numerous members of the Halle Theosophical Association. Some converted to Jesus on the spot. The chairman of the association, a certain Herr Krause, was eager to win back his flock. But, in making the attempt, he was himself convinced of the "Jesus of early Christianity." The Theosophical Association disbanded for lack of members, and some of them joined the Alte Promenade Fellowship.

Estrangement of a Friend

For the most part Eberhard's relationship to Ludwig von Gerdtell remained close, though not entirely without problems. Von Gerdtell's complete break with the SCM had marked just the beginning of a whole series of conflicts with former associates, culminating in a sudden and complete break with the Baptist association in the summer of 1909. Still, von Gerdtell continued his lectures, choosing Leipzig as the next scene of his "work among the educated." This undertaking became the first endurance test for the Arnolds' new marriage.

In mid-January von Gerdtell came to the Arnolds' Kanzlerstrasse home to be their guest for the duration of his lectures. He forced the whole household to conform to his daily schedule and habits. He bathed three times a day, as was his custom, and rejected spices, sugar, and salt on grounds of health, dictating an expensive dietary plan to the maid. He ate by himself on principle (for the sake of quiet) but afterwards, quite unceremoniously, he would join the Arnolds during dinner. He rose at six o'clock in the morning. At night he demanded absolute silence at the stroke of nine.

Emmy and Eberhard were somewhat put off by the elitist approach they now began to recognize in von Gerdtell. A hall to seat nine hundred had been rented for the lectures, and a reservation fee was charged. The organizing committee, which included Eberhard, had distributed thousands of fliers. At von Gerdtell's wish conspicuous announcements were posted at the city's advertising kiosks. For the first lecture ("for men only") von Gerdtell appeared in evening dress, replete with top hat and kid gloves. All this preparation only accentuated the disappointment when the lecture hall held only a sprinkling of people. Not until the second lecture, open to both men and women, did von Gerdtell find more response. Afterwards, thoroughly in keeping with his methods, he departed and left Eberhard to finish the work. This time, however, Eberhard felt confirmed in the contradictory impression he had first gained back in Erfurt: the success of von Gerdtell's work should not be overestimated. "Only a few conversions are made by him," he wrote. "He really evangelized only once, and otherwise spent his time in answering scientific and practical objections and questions." The Leipzig mission was most probably the last project on which Eberhard and von Gerdtell collaborated.

In the following years Ludwig von Gerdtell isolated himself more and more from almost all of his earlier companions. His tone grew sharper, his polemic against the state church more corrosive, his opinion of the reformers, especially of Martin Luther, more disrespectful and contemptuous. His theology acquired bizarre elements.[16] As late as 1921 Eberhard wrote to von Gerdtell pointing out some of the far too venturesome subjects and erroneous claims in his book *The Revolutionizing of the Church*.[17] If von Gerdtell sent an answer, it was not preserved. In Eberhard's correspondence the last reference to von Gerdtell occurs at the end of 1923. After this all trace of von Gerdtell disappears from his life. In reality, this unusual friendship had already grown very shaky in the spring of 1910 and no longer had any recognizable foundation.

Called to Halle

By the summer of 1910 Eberhard's duties and obligations in Halle were so numerous that to continue commuting from Leipzig once or twice a week was no longer adequate. For the time being the Arnolds took some rooms with the Rast family a mile or so northwest of Halle.[18] The Alte Promenade Fellowship voiced their request for the Arnolds to take up permanent residence in Halle. When the couple realized that their home in Leipzig would soon be too small – Emmy was expecting – they did not find the decision difficult. They gave up their home in Leipzig-Lindenau and moved in October of 1910 to Kröllwitzer Strasse 2, on the left bank of the Saale, right next to the Giebichenstein Bridge.

"Discipleship means more than imitation; it means community of and for life. Discipleship is more than service: 'If any one serves me, he must follow me' (John 12:26). Followers of Jesus are first and foremost servants. Discipleship includes everything, and service belongs to it." *From a lecture, February 14, 1913.*

Lectures and Journeys

From the fall of 1910 until the spring of 1913 Eberhard's life essentially consisted of two major yet very different elements: increasing responsibility for his growing family on the one hand, and constant spiritual responsibility for a number of people throughout Germany on the other. Often he traveled for a week or more at a time – one trip fast on the heels of another – giving lecture series in cities like Hamburg, Leipzig, Dessau, Magdeburg, Erfurt and, time and time again, in Halle itself. Everywhere he went he was received with enormous interest, and his lectures were well attended, often by many hundreds of people at a time. In November of 1910 he spoke to an audience of more than a thousand at Halle's Wintergarten.

Of course, in Eberhard's day public lectures and gatherings were considerably more important than they are in today's era of electronic mass media and glossy magazines. Without such public meetings, a person might remain totally ignorant of the trends in society at large.

The themes that Eberhard employed to draw the public to his lectures included "Jesus and the Riddle of the Future," "Poverty and the

Enslavement of the Masses," "The Greatest Deed in History," "Jesus as He Really Was," and "Doubting God." The man who spreads a stirring message must be firm and assured in his own heart. In this respect Emmy's influence on Eberhard cannot be overestimated. From the very first months of their engagement, he had found strength in her "discerning quietness." Emmy had sharpened his appreciation of art and had "rescued him from the danger of despising people in general." During the first months of their marriage they had developed a characteristic habit: after strenuous endeavors they would sit down together, relax for a while, and talk lovingly with each other. Difficult matters and problems were excluded from such moments. These were opportunities to catch their breath during the diverse rigors of their workdays – days which would soon be further enriched by a baby's cries and laughter.

Emy-Margret

Emmy's first pregnancy was a difficult one. This was an additional reason for the couple's move to Halle, where Emmy's sisters and other close friends would be close at hand to help when needed. Else, Emmy's sister, had just finished her arts and crafts course and had found employment at a store in Halle. Else took special delight in the expected baby and spent a sizable sum from her earnings on a layette. Emmy expected to give birth around the beginning of March 1911.

On March 8, 1911, Eberhard was away from home until late at night, providing pastoral help to someone in need. The following morning brought signs that the birth was beginning. After thirty-six

Poster, 1910, advertising a lecture series in Halle by Dr. Eberhard Arnold.

hours of labor, with the help of chloroform and forceps, Emy-Marga-rethe was born – a strong, thoroughly healthy baby. The young mother, however, was so weakened by the birth that on the evening of March 14 she suffered a life-threatening heart attack. Emmy hovered between life and death. Decades later, writing of this near-death expe-rience, she would still vividly recall "how all my limbs grew cold, and it was as if a dark, shadowy form drew near to me." Eberhard stayed at her bedside and prayed for her life with all his heart. By the time the doctor arrived, the worst was already over. After several weeks of intensive care, Emmy was back on her feet again.

The baby was hardly ever called by her full name, Emy-Marga-rethe. "We want to call her Emy-Margret," wrote Eberhard, but that was not the final word on the subject. At times she was called "Püppi," ("Dolly") and later, Emy-Ma. She would not remain an only child for long.

Room for Children

At the beginning of 1912 Emmy and Eberhard were jolted by per-sonal insight into a social and human catastrophe.[1] Late one evening, after one of Eberhard's lectures in Halle, a letter arrived at Kröllwitzer Strasse 2 – an SOS. An economically distressed couple with four chil-dren announced that they were about to put an end to all their lives. They had just wanted to hear Eberhard's lectures first. Eberhard rushed to these people at once and found them in utter despair. He promised to help. As an immediate intervention the Arnolds took the youngest son into their own home. Little Karl was four years old and apparently got along quite well with Emy-Margret. A little later the oldest daughter, Luise, came to the Arnolds too.

Eberhard and Emmy's involvement with this family lasted several months, until the family moved to Chemnitz. In the summer terrible news arrived: collective suicide – the husband and eleven-year-old daughter shot dead, the wife and another son seriously wounded. The Arnolds were especially horrified at sixteen-year-old Luise's passive ac-ceptance of this news. Later, when it was clear that Emmy was expect-ing a second child, little Karl was taken in by friends of the Arnolds, but Luise remained for more than two years in the Arnold household.

Even at this early stage in their family life, the Arnolds clearly felt that their home was not just theirs alone, but that they, as followers of Christ, had a task to provide shelter for needy children. The Halle institutions of August Hermann Francke, who had dedicated his life to such children, were familiar to the Arnolds, and Eberhard took a special interest in this man's activities.[2] Eberhard found a spiritual role model in another "father of orphans," George Müller, who had established five orphanages that cared for over two thousand children in Bristol, England.[3] Eberhard was too young to have met Müller, but he was deeply impressed by this man's faith. While still a student, he had read Müller's biography and had written to Emmy in 1908 that "the reality of the prayer of faith has never come home to me so strongly as through this book."[4] Now, over three years later, Eberhard and Emmy were confronted by desperate need. Though they certainly had no intentions of founding an orphanage, they had simply taken practical steps to alleviate the social deprivation of at least one child.

**Evangelical Alliance conference in 1911 at Haus Gnadenfülle, Bad Blankenburg.
Eberhard is standing at center; Emmy is seated in front of him.
The baby is their first daughter, Emy-Margret.**

Hermann Kutter and the Social Issue

With increasing frequency the fate of destitute and neglected people forced Eberhard to seek for answers as he traveled and preached. The contrasts were too glaring: on the one hand, the upper class (titled people with spacious homes, maids, and a telephone) and the middle class (officers' families and university scholars), and on the other hand, the miserable living conditions, poor wages, and illiteracy of the working class. None of these impressions was particularly new to Eberhard; he knew of his uncle Ernst Ferdinand Klein's struggle for the Silesian weavers and had himself encountered injustice through his work with the Salvation Army. In fact, something of a social conscience had long been stirring in him, spurred on by the life of George Müller and the writings of the American visionary Charles G. Finney, whose fight against slavery particularly appealed to Eberhard. Though Eberhard still lacked the language necessary to give voice to his conscience, none of these experiences left him unchanged.

Sometime during 1910 Eberhard got his hands on the book *They Must!* by the Zürich pastor Hermann Kutter.[5] This work impressed him to an extraordinary degree. At first glance this is surprising because *They Must!* is a positive evaluation of socialism and its agenda from a Christian viewpoint. Nothing in Eberhard's background or development had yet indicated any particular affinity with the Social Democratic party or explained his attraction to such a book.

But Kutter's method of critical analysis must have aroused Eberhard's curiosity. He recognized in it his own thought processes and hypotheses. In his doctoral thesis Eberhard had proved that although Nietzsche denied the existence of God and opposed Christianity, the philosopher's greatest thoughts expressed admiration for early Christianity. In a similar way Hermann Kutter did not let himself be repulsed by the aggressive atheism of the socialists but recognized that social democracy shared the same goals as did Jesus' commandments – commandments that in Kutter's view had been watered down and misinterpreted by the churches: "They have turned the living word of God into self-righteous piety, ceremonies, and statutes." Others, Kutter concluded, now had to preach what the church ought to be preaching and had to carry out the tasks that the church should have been doing. Reading Hermann Kutter did not convert Eberhard into a religious-socialist overnight.[6] Kutter had not yet provided him with the final answer to the question of social injustice. All the same Eberhard found in Kutter an indication of where an answer might be sought. In Kutter's *They Must!* Eberhard discovered the vocabulary to express what he had long recognized. The book provided him with important catchwords for the following years:

Mammonism and *Overcoming Mammon:* Kutter accused the church of "tasting mammon's witches' brew of vanity." Mammon had intoxicated the church, which now carried out its business.

The Hidden Light: According to John 1:9, it shines in every person. Long before Eberhard delved into George Fox and the Quakers, he came across this concept in Kutter's writing. Here he found respect for the integrity of other people's motives and for every honest effort to seek – a respect that is not to be confused with uncritical tolerance in the sense of Frederick the Great's maxim "Everyone should attain happiness in his own way."

Inward or *Inner Life:* Kutter diagnosed the lack of inner life within the church. In his view, when the church pointed people to an inner life, it was no more than a diversionary tactic – a clever device of the church to draw attention away from its own paralysis. "Where there is inner life it thrives and blossoms in practical life too." Eberhard would pursue this idea further than Kutter, to the point of actually finding its positive fulfillment.

The Kingdom of God: "People long for a world where justice is a reality, where mammon is really overcome. They are beginning to find an understanding for the original meaning of the expression 'the kingdom of God' – something completely new," wrote Kutter, who rejected the common understanding of the kingdom of God as a distant promise for life in the hereafter. Kutter very likely borrowed this thinking from the mid-nineteenth century pastor Johann Christoph Blumhardt and his son Christoph Friedrich Blumhardt. Perhaps their influence on Kutter provided the initial motivation for Eberhard's thorough study of both Blumhardts.

Eberhard first began incorporating thoughts and themes from Herman Kutter into his lectures during the late fall and winter of 1910. Now he testified that personal faith in Jesus Christ gives strength for a new life, for overcoming egotism, for love – and thereby for a change in social conditions.[7] Faith demands action on behalf of social justice, and can have nothing to do with capitalism and mammonism. Bible passages such as James 5:1–5 (about the rich who withhold wages from the workers) suddenly became intensely relevant to Eberhard. Like Hermann Kutter and the Blumhardts, Eberhard spoke of the kingdom of God as a reality on earth – something that has already been here for a long time and does not first come into being in some distant future or some other world.[8]

Particularly in this regard, however, it becomes clear that Eberhard did not simply rely on other people's ideas. He did not share Kutter's admiration of the Social Democratic party, and he criticized the superficiality of socialism and its band-aid remedies for outward symptoms. Unable to ignore the atheism of the communists, Eberhard quoted Karl Liebknecht: "If there is a living God, then we are the ones who have been duped." He agreed with Schopenhauer's view that an optimistic belief in progress is a "wicked way of thinking," because it shows "bitter contempt for the nameless sufferings of mankind."[9] Eberhard took Kutter more seriously than Kutter took himself: Jesus is the pivotal point. Through Jesus, problems will be solved. Only the crucified one gives strength for a new life. Eberhard never left this standpoint, and he made no exception for "religious-socialism."

Speaking of his own spiritual development, Eberhard once coined the deft phrase "from Luther to Kutter." This could easily be misconstrued to mean that Kutter had replaced Luther in Eberhard's thinking, but the truth is that Eberhard had placed the two side by side. In the following years Eberhard studied Martin Luther and the Reformation more thoroughly than ever before. At the same time, from 1910 on, contemporary social concerns occupied more and more of Eberhard's and Emmy's thoughts and discussions.

Hardy

On August 18, 1912, Emmy's second child was born. This time the birth presented no complications. Eberhard Heinrich, unlike his sister Emy-Margret, was a delicate child. Known to the family as Hardy, he spent much of his childhood sick and developed into a quiet, thoughtful boy.

The Arnolds' first Christmas as a family of four passed harmoniously. The only one not quite able to celebrate freely and happily was Eberhard himself, who had felt unwell for several months. He complained of a sore throat, which had affected his otherwise impressive, clear, and far-reaching voice, but he did not take these symptoms very seriously at first.

Eberhard arranged a series of lectures in Halle for February 1913, on the theme "Discipleship of Jesus in Our Day." Halfway through the series, Dr. Beleite's diagnosis of Eberhard's condition crashed like a bombshell: tuberculosis of the larynx, caused by advanced tuberculosis of the lungs. For Eberhard, this amounted to debarment from his profession. The doctor ordered him to stop lecturing immediately. Eberhard, however, felt he had an obligation to the hundreds of people who regularly attended the meetings, and he insisted on finishing the lecture series. Just as he had done before the shattering diagnosis, Eberhard stood before each audience, urging discipleship of Jesus, and he actually helped a number of people to change their lives. Immediately after he completed the lecture series he underwent two operations on his larynx.

Enforced Rest

Eberhard's doctors prescribed a lengthy stay in a sanatorium for lung patients, suggesting that the whole family move to a health resort, preferably in the Alps. They considered it unlikely that Eberhard would ever recover his health. Emmy and her husband agreed that under such circumstances it was essential for the family to remain together. Carl Franklin and Elisabeth Arnold came from Breslau to discuss the situation. They considered Eberhard and Emmy's decision to move the entire family shortsighted and refused to bear any responsibility for their financial support. Eberhard's parents did not feel in a position to pay for anything more than the doctors' fees and the medication. Needless to say, this put quite a damper on the celebration of Carl Franklin's sixtieth birthday and Emy-Margret's second birthday on March 10.

A tip from a former theosophist who had been converted during Eberhard's memorable Halle lecture series at the Tulpe Auditorium called the Arnolds' attention to the Pichler cottage, standing empty on the Ritten, the mountain above the town of Bozen in the Tyrolean Alps. After a swift decision, Eberhard set off for the southern Tirol on April 2 or 3, leaving Emmy, with Luise's help, to close down the apartment in Halle. Since the Pichler cottage was unfurnished, Emmy had to pack up some of the furniture for transport and have the rest put in storage. Emmy's sister Else was recovering from surgery at that time and was unable to help. On the evening of April 26 Emmy and the children tore themselves away from the von Hollander grandparents and boarded an express train to Bozen. By the afternoon of April 27 the family was reunited.

Tirol

Situated near a little woods and surrounded by mountain meadows, the Pichler cottage was reached by a cog railroad up the Ritten. The cottage sat just below the Maria Himmelfahrt station, at an elevation of thirty-six hundred feet. From there it was a half hour's walk by uphill footpath to Oberbozen. The view to the east was breathtaking, especially in the evening when the sinking sun gilded the Dolomite peaks. The Arnolds soon reached an agreement with the owner of the cottage, a Herr Schweigkofler, and within a few days moved in with Emy-Margret, Hardy, Luise, and a mass of household goods, including a piano. In

Eberhard in 1913, during his recuperation from tuberculosis in Tirol.

June, Else von Hollander joined them, and the little house with its five tiny rooms was filled to capacity. Included in the household were a white goat and a St. Bernard named Lampo, which was soon to be joined by a mate.

The family spent as much time as possible outdoors, not only for the sake of the fresh air, but more importantly, to avoid the risk of contagion. Eberhard took his prescribed hours of rest in a little arbor. He strictly observed the daily routine ordered by the doctors: rests, walks, rests. He was helped in this by his rare ability to fully relax at will. On the other hand, when he had the strength, he was able to work with intense concentration. He did not remain inactive for long in his new home. Even after a few months had passed he still held obediently to his therapy program – lying down, resting, relaxing, and, at most, reading or taking walks. But, in his "free time," he once more began to write.

At first Emmy was hardly less exhausted than her husband. Agitation over his illness and the arrangements for the move had taken their toll. In addition, she was expecting another child. Nor must it be forgotten that Else – "Tata" as the children called her (a corruption of "*Tante,*" meaning "aunt") – still needed to recuperate from her stomach operation. In spite of all this the Arnolds managed to shake off outward worries and stress. They tried to hear clearly what God was saying to them through Eberhard's sickness, and they pledged to each other that in future they would devote their lives even more wholeheartedly to the cause of Jesus. From this point on they never doubted that Eberhard would recover.

Financial support arrived sporadically, often from unexpected quarters. They had no income of their own, and had not asked anyone for assistance. Yet friends from back home sent just enough to allow the Arnolds to cover the rent and to avoid an empty pantry or a cold stove. In later, similar situations, such experiences would give the Arnolds an ability to trust in God and the courage to make decisions.

In the Homeland of the Anabaptists

Was it mere chance that brought Eberhard and his family to the Tirol, right to the area where the Anabaptist movement began and flourished in the early sixteenth century? To this very place – the Adige, Eisack, and Puster valleys – the movement spread after 1525. Here, after 1528, the authorities took intensive measures to persecute and suppress the "damned sect." From this place, Jakob Hutter led the Tyrolean community to Moravia, where they remained until persecution broke out there as well. To this place he returned with a few brothers and sisters in the spring of 1535 and reported in his "first letter to the church" in Moravia: "The Lord protected our journey and speeded our way to the Puster and Adige valleys…Since then we have been traveling in the mountains and valleys, seeking out those who hunger and thirst for the truth…The almighty God and Father has again established his church here and multiplies his people daily."[10] It was here that Jakob Hutter was betrayed by a fellow Anabaptist named Jerome and captured in November 1535, to be publicly executed in the Innsbruck marketplace on February 25, 1536. In Brixen (thirty miles south of Innsbruck), the town archives have preserved the court records regarding Jakob Hutter and numerous other Anabaptists.

Totally different reasons had led to Eberhard's choice of this health resort. The recommendation had come from an uninvolved third party, and it had been seconded by Emmy's grandmother, who had previously taken a tuberculosis cure in Gries, near Bozen. (She had raved to her granddaughter about the landscape and the mountains' evening-glow phenomenon.) But it was not long before the Arnolds learned of the rich history of this stretch of country. They obtained writings on the Moravian and Tyrolean Anabaptists and studied epistles and articles by Balthasar Hubmaier and Hans Denck with growing enthusiasm.[11]

Though deeply impressed by the surrounding grandeur and the wealth of Anabaptist history, Eberhard nonetheless felt cut off from the intensive fellowship of recent years. More than ever, he was open and ready for direction from the New Testament. In the last months of 1913 he put together a little book, *Living Churches: The Essence of Their Life.*[12] It was published in December as a "personal testimony and greeting to all who know us back home." In the introduction to *Living Churches,* Eberhard referred to himself as someone whose "only allegiance is to the Lord himself and to all those belonging to him." The purpose of the booklet was "to bring vigorous new life to present-day religious movements and to overcome the danger of them wasting and exhausting their efforts in conflict." Newspapers and fellowship magazines brought from the valley to the Pichler cottage by the cog railroad must have given Eberhard some idea of the gradual splintering and waning of the fellowship movement.

For Eberhard, the life and vitality of a church hinged upon eight crucial characteristics: love of the Lord Jesus, the conquering power of prayer life, the vital strength of God's word, the overcoming of sin, love of the brothers and sisters, the constructive use of all powers and talents, work on behalf of the world, and the expectation of the Lord.

As the title indicates, *Living Churches: The Essence of Their Life* is a kind of litmus test for the spiritual condition of a church. A closer look reveals Hermann Kutter's influence here as well. Eberhard had been thinking over Kutter's challenging statements and had applied them to the inner life from two points of view. He recognized lovelessness, pride, and gossip within the church as the prime enemies of the inner life. The primary goal of "work on behalf of the world" should not be to change society but to give Jesus Christ the honor in everything achieved. Moreover, the "imperative of divine love" (Kutter's term) should motivate the believers:

> Just as God seeks the hearts of men through Christ, so our saving love must aim at understanding all people, sharing in their feelings and their struggles. To real love belongs the thorough exploration of people's difficulties, questions, and hindrances in order to overcome them. If we want to save people, we must show a sincere and unequivocal concern for their inner struggles and convictions.

In Eberhard's eyes the kingdom of God "has not yet been established on earth, but through Jesus it lives in the hearts of the faithful as justice, peace, and joy in the Holy Spirit." They take part "in sowing seed for the kingdom just because they know that the full growth of the mustard seed can be expected only through his – meaning Christ's – coming." Even many years later, a slightly changed edition of *Living Churches* once more found a response in many hearts.[13]

Heinrich

By the time *Living Churches* had been printed and distributed, the Arnolds had vacated the drafty Pichler cottage for the winter and had moved into the nearby Maria-Schnee house. A chapel of the same name adjoined it. In this house Johann Heinrich was born on the evening of December 23, 1913. "My little Alpen boy, my little Tyrolean boy!" was Eberhard's greeting to the new arrival. Heinrich seemed well equipped for life's struggles – a strong, happy infant. At three weeks old, however, he had a bad bout of pneumonia. He survived the illness, thanks to Else's devoted care. This had its influence on both of them, and an unusually close relationship developed between aunt and nephew, a relationship all the other family members respected.

In the spring of 1914 the Arnold family moved back into the Pichler cottage. Meanwhile Emmy and Else had decided that it was impractical for each of them to try to do everything. In the future, Emmy would concentrate her strength on looking after the children and guests. Else was to be available to help Eberhard in his publishing work. It hardly occurred to either of them that, as a result of purely practical considerations, they had formed a highly effective team – an arrangement that would last for nineteen years. Until her death in 1932, Else von Hollander continued to be Eberhard's secretary and his right hand in all publishing matters.

Though life in the mountains removed the family from the demands of their former city life, the Arnolds were in no way cut off from the rest of the world during their stay in Tirol. Letters from and

Emmy's sister Else "Tata" von Hollander, shown here in 1913, lived with the Arnold family during their year at the Pichler cottage in Tirol.

to Germany were constant. So were visitors. Clara Arnold, mother Elisabeth Arnold from Breslau, Monika ("Mimi") von Hollander, cousins from Hamburg, and a number of friends came to visit for several days or weeks at a time. The guests rented rooms at a nearby farm because the Pichler cottage was too small to accommodate them all. A visit meant even more singing than usual, which was always accompanied by Emmy on the piano. Spurred on by Mimi, Eberhard learned to take photographs and preserved a variety of family scenes on his camera plates. The St. Bernards presented the family with a litter in the spring of 1914. Eberhard would enjoy romping around with the puppies, totally carefree, after which he would sit down to work on his articles again, completely engrossed in spiritual matters. A greater contrast is hard to imagine.

Mapping Out *Inner Land*[14]

In the spring and summer of 1914 Eberhard's thoughts began turning back home to Germany. He felt sufficiently recovered and, despite the doctors' urgings that he spend a second winter in Tirol, he wondered if he could resume his preaching and ministering in the fall. But first and foremost in his thoughts was a series of articles he was writing, articles intended to summarize his spiritual insights. Two of these appeared in print in the newspaper *Auf der Warte (On Guard)*: "Sin and Pride," in May 1914, and "Soul and Spirit," in August. Eight more articles were printed in the *Evangelical Alliance Magazine*. The first of these appeared on May 3, 1914, under the title "Inner Experiences." It picked up almost word for word where *Living Churches* had left off – with the kingdom of God.[15] The other articles followed at two-week intervals: "Peace and Moods"; "The Inward Life" (once again, an example of Kutter's influence); "The Conscience: Its Origin and Activity"; "The Conscience: Its Healing in God"; "The Inner Light"; "The Living Word within Us"; and finally, "The Temple of the Spirit and Our Inner Heart."

Alongside this last article, in July of 1914, the *Evangelical Alliance Magazine* announced the publication of Eberhard's book *Inward Life*. But everything turned out differently.

On June 28, 1914, Archduke Franz Ferdinand, the heir to the Austrian throne, was assassinated in Sarajevo. Then, on July 28, two days after Eberhard's thirty-first birthday, Austria-Hungary declared war on Serbia. Russia mobilized on July 30, Germany on August 1. News of these events penetrated even to the remote Pichler cottage. During the night of August 1, 1914, Eberhard received a telegram ordering him to report immediately to a reserve unit in Halle. He left that very day – a Sunday.

Chapter Six

"When our inner hearts are governed by the realization that true strength is to be found in God's nature alone, then we will begin to put God's will into practice among people, not with new hate, but with new love."

Innenland (1918 edition).

Three Weeks at the Front

The short distance from the cog railhead in the valley to the Bozen train station tore Eberhard from his peaceful mountainside refuge and plunged him into a scene of feverish enthusiasm. It was August 2, 1914. The streets of Germany throbbed with the animated pulse of war. The city squares rocked with patriotism: speeches, cheers, tumult. Steaming through town after town on a train with hundreds of other German recruits, Eberhard finally arrived at the Halle station.

"Reservist without defects, but too weak" had exempted him from military service in 1908, but this diagnosis now qualified him for the army transport corps.[1] After a few days of training he was sent with a supply unit to Thorn, on the Weichsel River, facing the Russian front in occupied Poland. Eberhard's adventure lasted no more than three weeks. Due to his precarious health he was dismissed from military service and arrived back in Halle before Emmy, Else, and the children, who reached the city on August 24 after a wearing five-day trek by train.[2]

What would cause Eberhard to change from this military wagoner into an ardent pacifist? The transformation would be involved and a long time in coming. Some parts of it can no longer be clearly traced. Looking back, Emmy wrote that she and her husband were already wondering "even in this first period of war psychosis, how a Christian, whose mission is to proclaim life and love, could possibly kill any of his brothers." But her memory may be faulty on this point because it contradicts not only all written evidence from the first years of the war, but it also contradicts itself: in the same context she wrote that after the Battle of the Marne (September 1914) had gone against Germany, Eberhard had actually considered volunteering for service at the front, regardless of his health problem.[3] If at the outbreak of the war he had really had scruples or doubts about military service, they must have been very vague. They found expression neither in his public speeches nor in his actions – in fact, quite the opposite is true.

Blinded

Lured by the wholesome air the Arnolds moved into a house in the Halle suburb of Dölau, at the edge of the Dölau woods. Friends from fellowship groups in Halle came and went, and their home took on a semblance of prewar normalcy. Worship meetings took place in the woods, and songs rang out – hymns like "O God is love, He it is who frees me" and "Come let us sing in joyful song, God's love is great." Meanwhile Eberhard reworked his book *Inward Life.*[4] It was already prepared for press, but he completely revised it by introducing patriotic undertones. When it hit the market it carried the title *The War: A*

Young volunteers for the German army parade through Berlin in 1914.

Call to Inwardness.[5] The cover sported a billowing black, white, and red flag brandishing the iron cross. Nothing in particular distinguished it from the dozens of other books that appeared in those days in support of the "just and righteous war."[6] With Eberhard's book, as with all the others, the flag masked the truth. Nationalistic feeling drowned out any insight into historical reality. Sideswipes about "the enemy's crimes" promoted only self-justification and limited the work's significance to the immediate moment.

Inward Life was intended to lead Christians in German-speaking lands to a more conscious faith, a greater dedication, and a deeper knowledge of God. Against the mounting thunderheads of war, all of Eberhard's carefully considered statements about the inner renewal of mankind could have made a powerful impact – and this would doubtless have been the case had he left the book unaltered. In the first weeks of the war, however, with German troops almost at Paris in the west and German victories at Gumbinnen and Tannenberg in the east, it appears that he had instead constructed a theory about the war's spiritual-historical significance. He had narrowed his viewpoint to such a degree that the reader had either to agree without reservation or else reject his premise completely.

In the chapter "Soul and Spirit," for example, the original text ran:

> What would become of an empire that was in a condition of utter confusion and weakness at home if it flung its small remaining supply of strength against other lands to gain territory and treasure? In spite of any acquisitions, its failing existence would face certain end.

Here is the same passage from the "war version":

> France and Russia have shown the fate of a world power when the inner state of the country is distressed and enfeebled in the extreme. Even if such a power flings its little-remaining strength against others…

In this fashion Eberhard needlessly reduced a great number of timeless statements to fit the "short-term context of the recent outbreak of war."[7]

Der Krieg marked the first edition of a project that was the focus of Eberhard Arnold's literary energies for the rest of his life. Later retitled *Innenland,* the book appeared in expanded and revised editions in 1918, 1923, and from 1932–1935. In 1936, a year after Eberhard's death, the final version was printed.

Of course he did not consciously intend to disseminate hatred. *The War: A Call to Inwardness* is also a universal call to repentance. Yet this cannot compensate for the unrealistic ideas behind his writing: Eberhard called the war "a crucial battle for freedom of conscience," which would help "shatter petty egotism." The war, he contended, could become "a blessing for us if in the depth of our souls we turn away from our sins and turn to God…If extensive groups of people are pierced to their very hearts and lifted up to God, it would bring complete and indisputable victory over all our enemies." Again and again he invoked "the greatness of the present moment." He found no serious inner problem with the "massive loss of life that must accompany this most drastic of all wars." Only "faith in eternal life enables us to bear with joyful courage all that is now placed upon us."

Eberhard could hardly have recognized the cynicism of this statement – or did he intend to suggest that good Christians make better soldiers?! The war, he declared, "will open up great tasks for Germany of constructive work among the nations." Eberhard even argued the improbable case that the war would "bring God's will to reality in the innermost heart of many people," anticipating "the most fruitful contribution to the whole world's happiness."

Why did he think that the war would bring such results? Why was there no mention of war in the original version of the book's ten chapters? Why did biblical truth speak for itself in the original version of the work, and why was it suddenly no longer sufficient? Why did Eberhard mix his clear, biblical reasoning with the feverish emotions of the moment, with the nationalistic "honest war" philosophy of Fichte, and Ernst Moritz Arndt's theory of "hereditary enmity" between the fatherland and France?

"Nothing, not even the military mail service, has failed so miserably as the German spirit," wrote one of the very few Germans who abstained from the hysterical enthusiasm for war at that time – one of the lonely and unloved prophets who could not proclaim pleasing messages during these war days.[8] The German spirit had failed miserably. This judgment indicts Eberhard too, and it is no real comfort that it falls on a long list of other prominent theologians and leaders of the Evangelical Alliance Movement as well.

Did God Want the War?

Eberhard titled his first article after the outbreak of war "God Speaks in Serious Times."[9] In the opening paragraphs he borrowed a statement from his father: "World history is world judgment." As a nineteen-year-old Eberhard had rebelled with every sinew of his being against this viewpoint. Now, at thirty-one, he had lost his youthful edge. Had he grown more staid and middle-class? It almost seems so, judging by his explanation of the war to readers of the *Evangelical Alliance Magazine:* "God wants us to recognize that this war, the most terrible the world has ever known, is a proof of his goodness, patience, and long-suffering."

A full year into the war he still wrote that the war was "from God," contending that God was pursuing a "vein of good," which in this case was "the defense of righteousness by the more righteous of the warring governments."[10] His theological basis began to take a dubious slant. "Because unrighteousness has gained the upper hand in recent years, we must consider every war as a merciful check against the satanic and anti-Christian powers, and as directed against evil." Shortly afterwards he wrote on the same theme that "Satan and his spirits must be fought with the weapons of violence and wrath, war and the sword, fire and brimstone."[11] Through such words as these, Eberhard had fallen back on a Gnostic pattern of thought as a recourse to bolster his war theories: God will win in the final battle, but only by a hair's breadth. God bears responsibility for the fight, but the devil prescribes the weapons of battle.

This is the essence at the core of his war premise, and it is not without a certain dramatic effect. It does, however, present various drawbacks, the most obvious being that it is simply not Christian. Only drastic distortion can bring it to any biblical foundation. Furthermore, such a statement is incomplete and illogical. Wasn't it actually the war itself that had unleashed satanic and anti-Christian forces? At the end of the first year of the war, hundreds of thousands had already bled, burned, or suffocated to death in Flanders, in Champagne, in Alsace, and in Galicia. Proofs of God's goodness, patience, and long-suffering?...

Solid Ground or Bottomless Pit

There is no logical explanation for Eberhard's attitude to the war during the first year or so after 1914, which means that other factors must have molded his rationale. The fate of his nearest relatives may have been one of these factors. Eberhard's elder brother, Hermann Arnold, was severely wounded on the eastern front in the spring of 1915 and died in an army hospital at Königsberg on May 5, 1915. The two brothers had not been particularly close, and Hermann had distanced himself from his family while still a university student.[12]

Yet Eberhard always felt he had a certain spiritual responsibility for his brother and sisters. He got along very well with his sister-in-law, Käthe. Now, after only six years of marriage, Käthe Arnold was a widow. Already the mother of a four-year-old daughter, she gave birth to a son on August 31, 1915, and named him after his father. So little Hermann, Eberhard's nephew, was half-orphaned even before he was born. It can only be conjectured what emotions and subliminal thoughts his brother's death may have stirred in Eberhard.

As a further speculation, is it possible that Eberhard was subconsciously resisting his foreign ancestry? In his writings during the first years of war his harsh, anti-English criticisms are especially disconcerting. He saw "inward powers collapsed and buried in England and America" – not so, of course, in Germany.[13] He discovered "greed and envy" in England – and only there.[14] For him it was "a fact that service of Mammon was the outstanding characteristic of the English mindset – life aimed at advantage and advancement, pleasure and enjoyment."[15] In a book review he wrote, "The incapacity to rise above pragmatism is typical of the English." He tore Bacon, Hobbes, and Locke to bits.[16] Finally, he rejoiced that the war had at last made possible "a complete release from the superficiality of English hymns." This was said in reference to favorite revivalist hymns in German translation, hymns such as "What joy it is to be redeemed" and "I know a river whose glorious waters." He and Emmy had been happy to sing these songs in earlier days, but now Eberhard claimed that they "took away from the clear and certain proclamation of the Lord."[17] Reading this today it seems almost too farfetched to be taken seriously – and seems all the more ludicrous in light of Eberhard's English heritage on his father's side, and his American grandfather.

How much of his true self must he have disowned before reaching this contempt for what was supposed to be typically English in the English people? How much warping of heart and mind had he already undergone, perhaps while studying philosophy, that he could so euphorically acclaim what was alleged to be German in the Germans? "The German spirit…wants to dedicate life to a higher life, a sacrificial life devoted to the loftiest tasks. Here are the generous virtues of obedience and loyalty, of courage and readiness for sacrifice, of truthfulness, and creative energy of character." With views so far removed from reality, it took a long time – at least two and a half years – before his feet were once more planted on firm ground.

Die Furche and the Furche Publishing House

In the late summer of 1915 a telegram arrived in Dölau for the Arnolds from Undersecretary of State Georg Michaelis, who at that time was head of the SCM:[18] Eberhard was to serve the SCM as literary advisor and media relations manager, and to oversee both the editing of Die Furche (The Furrow) magazine and the development of the Furche Publishing House.[19] The offer came at just the right time, and Eberhard essentially accepted it, seeing it as the logical continuation of his previous direction and as "God's call."[20] In preliminary discussions it was agreed that as advisor he would oversee "charitable gifts," a service to soldiers at the front that supplied them with books and magazines. He would also act as assistant editor for *Die Furche*. For the time being Dr. Gerhard Niedermeyer, the SCM's general secretary, would retain the magazine's editorship. Under the agreement Eberhard was to be free to work with student groups in Berlin. The SCM rented a house for the Arnold family in the Berlin suburb of Wilmersdorf: Landauerstrasse 14, a newly built, modern house with six rooms and a view over a beautiful park.

Life in Dölau had been peaceful and idyllic. Wartime Berlin was all rush, commotion, and excitement. At first nothing in the office of *Die Furche* ran according to plan. The Arnold parents in Breslau had to lend the money for the move. During October and November Eberhard was buried under piles of office work that was not even included in his job description. When he was finally given a secretary, she was entirely unable to cope. Not until the formal founding of the Furche Publishing House several months later was Eberhard able to regain Else von Hollander's well-proven assistance.[21] To make matters

The Arnold family in Halle, summer 1915. *From left:* Emmy, Emy-Margret, Heinrich, Eberhard, Hardy.

worse Dr. Niedermeyer, the editor of *Die Furche,* suddenly insisted that he knew nothing of Eberhard's joint editorial responsibilities, and it took multiple emphatic references to the terms of the agreement before Eberhard could get one of his articles printed or could work on others. His first piece ran in the January 1916 issue.

The unfriendly, all-business attitude of his SCM colleagues shocked Eberhard. In December, after more than one urgent request to discuss the matter, he had a talk with Niedermeyer and Michaelis to clear things up. Eberhard complained bitterly about the lack of trust and Niedermeyer's repeated and unjustified public reprimands. Even after they had clarified roles and mapped out work areas, Eberhard's relationship with Niedermeyer remained distant. On the other hand, his relationship with "His Excellency Michaelis" soon improved. After a time Michaelis's home became the venue for a weekly evening discussion with other old SCM friends.

War Work of the SCM

By the middle of the war the SCM was not at all as it had been in 1910. In those days full oversight of the fellowship of Christian students had still been possible. But during the very first months of the war about three thousand SCM members were already active in military service. It was considered a duty of love to provide them with regular issues of *Die Furche* and with the *Small Wartime Newsletter for Academics.*[22] At the end of 1914 the SCM central office began printing booklets on specific subjects, sending them as "gifts of love from German students" to "brothers on active duty." Tens of thousands of poetry collections, sets of art prints, and scholarly sermons for soldiers were prepared. As the war continued hundreds of thousands of books and other printed matter went to the front and to prisoner-of-war camps all over Europe. Book wagons were mobilized and sent to individual units of the army.

This is an indication of the level of responsibility that Eberhard was intended to assume, although he certainly had to fight for it first. His work objectives for the first three months were as follows: assemble a portfolio of Ludwig Richter's artwork; familiarize himself with, and write a foreword to, *Der Heliand (The Savior),* an epic Saxon poem on Christ from the early middle ages; edit between thirty and forty manuscripts; and compile collections of quotations and aphorisms from Luther and from Bismarck. Then there were the archives of *Die Furche* to be set in order (no one had filed anything for years); letters to write to about fifty contributing authors, and letters to reviewers and university rectors; and plans to be made for the next issues of *Die Furche* – various book reviews to write; and so on and so forth. It is not surprising that Eberhard wrote of his "fragmenting spiritual, intellectual, and physical strength" and of his "deteriorating health."[23]

Hans-Hermann

Matters did not improve in the following months. During the winter of 1915–1916, the people of the Central Powers began to feel the full effects of the Allied blockade. The menu grew monotonous: skim milk, turnips, potatoes, stale bread, and everything else measured out in minute quantities in exchange for food stamps. Under these conditions on December 10, 1915, Emmy brought her fourth child into the world. He was named Hans-Hermann after Eberhard's brother. "Hansemann," as the other children found it easiest to call him, was a giant among dwarfs. At birth he weighed ten pounds – astonishing under the circumstances, and a strain for his mother. A nanny now had to be employed in addition to the hired help for cooking and housework. Hans-Hermann developed slowly and learned to walk late. In spite of extra rations for mothers and babies the nourishing food he needed was simply not available.

The Arnolds resorted to self-help methods. They rented a garden plot with a shed about a quarter of an hour's walk from Landauerstrasse and managed to acquire two milk goats. Eberhard tried his hand at gardening, planting radishes, carrots, potatoes, and even tomatoes, which at that time were regarded as exotic fruit. The plot was big enough to provide a small paradise for the children. Hardy and Emy-Margret, at four and five years old, could already help. The weekends and long summer evenings provided free time for the family, but at other times Eberhard and Else had to spend more hours than they wished at the publishing house.

Even had anyone in the SCM wished to escape from the prevalent atmosphere of war fever, it would hardly have been possible. In his September 1915 report on the annual student conference at

Wernigerode Eberhard wrote: "It is certain that in the future, even after the war, the SCM conference will place more emphasis on the German element in its name and character and so form a strong and lasting counterweight to the English type of Christian activity."

During the summer of 1916 he addressed "a few words to fellow students" in the name of the SCM executive committee: "The great war, which we have now lived through for four semesters, is a German war for freedom." In this sense he demanded "freedom and lordship of the Spirit."

The main speech at the 1916 Wernigerode conference was delivered by a Professor Schaeder from Kiel. The ranks of the conference members were far thinner than in previous years; nearly all those born between 1880 and 1899 were at the front. Professor Schaeder's theme boiled down to one point: for a Christian, patriotic duty represented "service to God and service to Christ."

In the *Small Wartime Newsletter for Academics* Eberhard summed up this speech:

> It revealed with ruthless clarity the terrible burden of conscience that the war means for all of us; it stated plainly the whole difficulty of the problem of how to reconcile participation in the war with the spirit of the Sermon on the Mount. Clear and convincing proof was given that in the world we live in today, organic life can, in all instances, achieve its development only through mutual strife and the expulsion of competitors.

To put it plainly the body of Christian scholars did not look to Jesus for a standard by which to judge the war – they looked to Darwin. The strong devour the weak. And in this case there was every confidence that, in the final analysis, Germany would be the stronger side. That was in August 1916. Then, the bloodbath of Verdun swallowed one division after another. And on the eastern front the forces of the Central Powers retreated with heavy losses from the Russian offensive at Brussilow.

Change

For a long time Eberhard swam with the broad current of popular sentiment. And yet, though hard to pinpoint, there is a trace of uneasiness in many of his reports. On his visits to various universities he observed that the war was weakening the student groups and that bible study and prayer groups were dying out. He complained that relationships within the groups were growing looser and less committed.[24]

But it was Emmy who pointed out to him that some of the "gifts of love" and other writings from the Furche Publishing House proclaimed a bit too German of a gospel. In *Die Furche,* some authors were beginning to adopt an ugly, anti-Semitic tone. They slandered the Jews even as Jews and Christians fought side by side in the trenches for emperor, nation, and fatherland. In the publishing house Eberhard had to listen to Dr. Niedermeyer's declaration: "Dr. Arnold, there's no time for inwardness now. It is war, war, and again war, Dr. Arnold!" On Eberhard's regular visits to military hospitals in Berlin he listened as wounded soldiers confessed their agonizing feelings of guilt and distress of conscience. The superficial solutions recommended by various articles in *Die Furche* and by speeches at the SCM conferences were cast into quite a different light: they seemed suddenly cynical and unrealistic.

A 1916 song sheet provides some insight. This martial "Hymn of hate against England," scored for men and illustrated with bayonet-wielding German soldiers, bristles with hate – exactly as the title indicates.[25] Underlined in the margin is a one-word note in Eberhard's handwriting, in bold, large strokes: "Love?"

He now made more time to study the Bible and Christian authors, especially the mystics.[26] He read Jakob Böhme, Meister Eckhart, and others. Was this the *result of* or was it a *reason for* the change that took place in him?

After the spate of pompous pronouncements on the meaning and course of the war, after all the self-confident commentaries, it is all the more noticeable that by the end of 1916 this sententious tone began to fade from Eberhard's style and finally ceased altogether. Of course he diligently continued to write articles, but he cut his words to the minimum and was cautious in his assessment of the war. All at once the sense of patriotic mission seems to have vanished. In *Die Furche* Eberhard featured biographical and literary articles and a series on significant people in the history of thought, including Rudolf Steiner and Martin Buber. [27] No more glorification of the "German spirit." No more sideswipes against the English, French, and Russians – at least not from Eberhard's pen.

At the beginning of March 1917 Eberhard held a series of revival meetings in the Rannischer Platz Fellowship. His theme for the final evening is noteworthy: "Love and Unity within a Divided Mankind." For the first time in years, he referred to the suffering of all humanity – no more talk of the mission of the German people. Unfortunately, extensive notes of this meeting no longer exist.

In the weeks that followed Eberhard and Emmy paused for rest and reflection at Braunlage in the Harz Mountains. It was one of those increasingly rare occasions when the two could spend time completely alone. Here they could find perspective at a sufficient distance from the publishing house, the SCM, and all the old imperial saber-rattling, as well as from Berlin's emaciated people and discontented mutterings. Eberhard and Emmy used the time to take stock of the past few years and to gain clarity about the road ahead. While skiing in the mountains Eberhard injured his left eye, detaching the retina. Back in Berlin, care and quiet healed Eberhard's eye and extended the opportunity to pause and reflect.

Meanwhile the political situation had changed dramatically. There was no prospect of a military breakthrough for either side. People were war-weary. Hunger protests arose in Berlin and in other major German cities. In April the munitions workers went on strike. In the Reichstag, members of both the left-wing and bourgeois parties called for a peace agreement without victors or vanquished. On July 14 the unfortunate imperial chancellor Bethman Hollweg was dismissed and Georg Michaelis was appointed his successor. For four months Michaelis struggled in vain to mediate between the Reichstag, which was ready to make peace, and the army's high command. Then, freed from this difficult task, he once more had time for the SCM. [28] Even before Michaelis had become chancellor, however, the staff of the main SCM office and the associated Furche Publishing House would have been fully informed about the opinions of those closest to the centers of power.

All this and many unknown factors as well may have contributed to the inner change in Eberhard. In a fellowship meeting on Repentance Day 1917 he gave a talk titled "Repentance as Revolution," which showed the full extent of his transformation.[29] Here is a short extract:

> Due to the war, the European culture in which we live is undergoing a tremendous upheaval that has brought what was at the bottom to the top, and what was on top to the very bottom. An upheaval that is a judgment on what people believed they had so securely in hand. An upheaval that has toppled the European from his illusory heights reared by pride. We sense that in the economic field vast upheavals are going on and that the hoped-for peace will only strengthen and deepen such upheavals. Furthermore, we see how a new wave of social upheaval is beginning in Russia, and we cannot predict the consequences of such events.

Here Eberhard alludes to the very recent October Revolution,[30] and for the first time he speaks of the collapse of spiritual values due to the war: "The message that the Social Democrats, anarchists, and related movements have always inscribed on their banners is gaining more recognition. Mankind needs a revolution." The illusion that war and mass killing can produce something good has been completely conquered. Eberhard talks of Europeans, of all humanity – not of Germans. He has returned to what he learned from Hermann Kutter. He treats other spiritual movements, including the Social Democrats and the anarchists, with respect and looks for the core of truth in them. He refers to socioeconomic revolution and apparently is not afraid of the prospect: "And so we people of today need an upheaval, the complete reversal and reevaluation of all conditions and standards."

Everything now is obviously judged and assessed quite differently from only a year before. Now Eberhard speaks of "the deceiver of mankind, the father of lies, the murderer from the beginning, who is the original instigator of this war, this dreadful experience of increased sin and increased death." He has seen his error, and he no longer calls a thing white when it is black. The war cannot be evidence of God's goodness and patience because God does not want any person to die, but wants rather that each should find repentance and live. "This is the upheaval worked by repentance: this conversion from the spirit of darkness to the spirit of Light, this redemption from all delusions and blindness." This includes the delusion of nationalism too. It is almost as if Eberhard were preaching to himself: "In cultural and political life as well, this upheaval must find expression as peace, justice, and love."

In this manner the course was set for the journey ahead.[31]

Monika-Elisabeth

Emmy's mother, Monika von Hollander, died in September 1917 while Emmy was pregnant once again. Her only brother, Heinz, died in January 1918 of tuberculosis, contracted while serving as a soldier at the front. Then in February of 1918 Emmy gave birth to a little girl and named her Monika-Elisabeth, after both grandmothers. She, too, was a typical wartime baby, slow to develop and always hungry. Yet in spite of all the hardships the Arnolds were still doing relatively well. Other families, particularly of the working class, lived in considerably worse circumstances. Cramped, stuffy, damp, and unhealthy living quarters and low incomes were the norm. Most men were still at the front, and the women and children were going hungry. One day when a working-class man came to the Arnolds' house and was received and ushered into the sitting room by a maid, he said to Eberhard, "Oh, I see you really aren't in need of a thing, Dr. Arnold." He had brought some money tied up in his handkerchief and had intended to give it to the family, but now he changed his mind and took it away with him. Eberhard felt deeply ashamed.[32] Such incidents did not fail to affect him.

Inner Land II

Before the end of 1917, under the hopeless weight of the war situation and the growing social distress, Eberhard began a revision of *War: A Call to Inwardness,* making use of his newly won insights and renewed spirituality. As a start he expunged from the manuscript all the patriotic, nationalistic insertions. But Eberhard did not wish merely to reconstruct the original, prewar version of *Inward Life,* and he expanded the work considerably. He restructured it as a journey into the "inner land of the unseen, to God and the Spirit" and as a "guide into the soul of the Bible."[33] In addition Eberhard now pursued a clearly conceived purpose with *Inner Land.* To recognize this the reader must open to the last page of the book. The purpose of *Inner Land* was to promote peace and reconciliation. It was to help establish true human nature and fellowship in the time after the war (which, of course, must first be concluded). *Inner Land* was published five months before the war's end, in July 1918, by the Furche Publishing House in Berlin.[34]

"We must extend our field of activity, but the more we widen our circle of contacts, the more firmly must the compass point be fixed at the center."

Spoken at the SCM conference in Eisenach, 1918.

Youth on the Move

The years of war sapped Eberhard's energy, attention, and spiritual strength. But when at last Eberhard shook free of the shackles of war, his entire perception of reality suddenly changed. Social deprivation and similar real-life issues concerned him. Once again he pondered humanity's primordial vocation to live in interdependent community. Though he had already mulled over this theme in earlier times, Eberhard felt compelled to take it up again, primarily in response to the youth movement phenomenon.[1]

Back in October of 1913 about two thousand young people from the *Wandervogel* movement had met on the Hohe Meissner mountain and, setting aside their individual perspectives and social standings, had drafted a statement of their common aims and shared beliefs.[2] "The members of the Free German Youth want to determine the shape of their lives for themselves, on their own responsibility, and with integrity. They band together to represent this inner freedom under all circumstances," declared these so-called Meissner principles.

A year later these same young people – all the men at least – marched off to war with enthusiastic cheers. What became of these ideals at the front? Self-determination? Officers drove the young men forward, wherever forward might be. Personal responsibility? It was not required in the army. And as for integrity, it was welcomed only so long as it made a soldier compliant and ready to sacrifice himself. In such cases it was taken advantage of; otherwise, it was suppressed.

"The members of the Free German Youth want to determine the shape of their lives for themselves..." Conference on the Hohe Meissner, October 1913.

At the time of Eberhard's reevaluation of the war this deceived generation was still at the front. The next was growing up, however, and was discovering that the Meissner ideals had survived the war and still held good. War was disaster. War was death. The principles of the Free German Youth proclaimed the exact opposite: joy in life, courage to venture out and discover life in all its diversity, to be open to all its promises, and to face every situation in life.

Eberhard, seriously ill in Tirol in 1913, had heard almost nothing of the "Festival of German Youth." Even had he caught wind of the gathering, he would most likely not have paid it much attention. By its own admission the youth movement was anti-middle-class, despised the "cheap patriotism" common under Kaiser Wilhelm II, and had an international outlook – altogether too broad-hearted and open-minded for Eberhard at that time. But now, four years later, a completely different world had suddenly opened up to him – right on his own doorstep.[3] On excursions into the woods and countryside it was impossible to avoid these colorfully clad young people – the men in knee britches, the women with bright hair ribbons – who carried on boisterously, as though oblivious to the ongoing meager war rations. Circle games and folk dances. Sentimental songs, funny songs, political songs, hiking songs. Shining eyes. Excited discussions around the campfire and on every other possible occasion. This was the norm. Traces of the movement could be found in literature as well. Authors Stefan George and Franz Werfel were by far the most convincing writers on the feeling for life and the ideals of the "Free German."[4]

What Eberhard saw and read must have come to him like a revelation. Here was a movement that set itself "against the gross overvaluation of outward and material things," a movement that wanted to discover and share "a religiously oriented attitude to the world, a religious sensitivity of outlook on the world, an experience completely opposed to the godforsakenness and hostility to God of our materialistic age." In the youth movement he found a fresh and natural longing for inwardness. These young people, though undirected, naïve, brash, and all too open for every available life philosophy and the fantastic ideas of any shaman or freethinker, were nonetheless completely genuine. They were really seeking, eager for answers, and ready for noble goals. Once they had recognized an inner call they were prepared to follow it. Eberhard quickly recognized these positive characteristics, but he did not overlook the negative aspect: such idealistic young people would run unhesitatingly after every pied piper, provided he piped the right tune. To Eberhard it was absolutely clear that one Leader alone merited their devotion.

In April of 1918 Eberhard wrote in *Die Furche* about "the concept of an ideal leader in the contemporary youth movement."[5] Not surprisingly, the one he named as the fulfillment and paragon for their longings was Jesus Christ. In August he participated in a *Weltanschauungswoche* (literally, a "world outlook week") held in Tübingen by the Free German Youth, and later he reported of those meetings that "a generation of youth is arising that from its innermost heart wants to discover the highest and noblest calling of humanity, to make itself independent of all outside pressure, and to persist in the face of everything base and hateful."

Among the leading men of the Free German Youth, however, he discovered only unclear, lukewarm religious ideas, and a nebulous, emotional feeling about the world. Eberhard raised important criticisms. The movement overestimated the good in people and either played down the evil or argued away its existence. The Meissner principles were deceptive and lacked compassion: "Refusal to allow any place for authority drives the individual into so boundless an isolation that the slogan of 'Friendship and Community' is not sufficient to keep the inner life awake or to enrich it."[6]

A few days later at the general conference of the SCM in Eisenach, Eberhard delivered the keynote address, titled "The Religiosity of Today's Youth." To confront his old friends and fellow SCM comrades, he picked the youth movement as his theme – a decidedly challenging topic for these seeking, religiously motivated young people. Eberhard quoted a representative of the Free Germans: "We need a new Christ. We have had enough of people like Marx. Institutions are easier to change than souls." Statements such as these were like outstretched hands that simply had to be grasped. Many of his listeners understood this; others grew uneasy. One conference member wrote in the *Small Wartime Newsletter for Academics,* "It was a keen wind that blew at Eisenach, perhaps too keen, but many things became clear all the same."

Later a smaller group decided to hike up to the Wartburg. On the summit they held what would become known as the "Wartburg discussion on religion." It proved to be the highlight of the conference. The discussion probed deeply, and Eberhard's message found acceptance. One of those present declared, "We must become one with our

Members of the German youth movement enjoyed free-spirited companionship and out-of-doors recreation. Folk dancing was a customary expression of their shared goals.

comrades whom we want to win for Christ. We must speak their language, just as Jesus became man and spoke our language." That was just the beginning. The subject of the youth movement would keep the SCM in a stir for years.

Revolution

Despite the many warning signs, Germany's collapse caught most of her people by surprise. On October 29, 1918, German sailors mutinied in Wilhelmshaven. Soldiers' and workers' councils formed in the towns. On November 7 revolution broke out in Munich, on November 9 in Berlin. "The Kaiser has abdicated!" newspaper special editions announced. "No shots fired!" The Social Democrat Philip Scheidemann declared the country a republic. Still acting in his official capacity, Chancellor Max von Baden handed over the government to the Social Democratic party's leader, Friedrich Ebert. Eberhard and Emmy were among the thousands of Berliners present at the election of the new government in the Busch Circus, the largest hall in Berlin. They had been as shocked and downcast as most other Germans by the terms of the armistice, which had destroyed any hope of an honorable peace agreement.

During the communists' Spartacus revolt of January 1919 and the consequent clash with the army, the sound of gunfire became accustomed background noise in Landauerstrasse. While Emy-Margret and Hardy walked to school in the mornings, the rattle of machine guns ceased for a time – a touch of humanity amid the civil war. At some places in the city center the streetcars ran directly between the fighters' barricades. The survival rules were simple: keep your head in, lie flat. Such matter-of-fact methods helped the Arnolds and most other Berliners through these dangerous times.

There was no revolution in the Furche Publishing House, but the general agitation could be sensed in the letters to the editor printed in *Die Furche*. Criticisms such as "catering to an artistic taste," "affectation," and "forced style" may be dismissed as a matter of bias. More serious was the accusation of "the misguided urge to 'discover' a search for God and partial comrades wherever any religious material appears in print." This was aimed directly at Eberhard. Was it misunderstanding, or malice? Clearly not all readers could comprehend the change in him, and many preferred the former Dr. Arnold.

Within the ranks of the SCM executive committee it was no different. In a meeting at the beginning of April 1919 the opinion was voiced: "We are not a youth movement any more than we are a senior citizens' movement."[7] Judging from the circumstances this appears to be the dictum of Paul Humburg, who chaired the SCM at the time. In point of fact, he was correct. Yet he had fundamentally misunderstood Eberhard by thinking that Eberhard wanted to remodel the SCM on a Free German pattern. A serious problem of mutual misunderstanding developed between the two men, though at heart both wanted exactly the same thing: to go the whole way with Jesus. Verification of this shared objective came only a few days later when, at the end of one of his lecture series, Eberhard dealt with the theme of "World Revolution and World Redemption." He spoke of "personal salvation, which brings us closer to Jesus. Only someone who has known this experience of faith can believe in world redemption as happiness for the individual, as rebirth for humanity and for the entire earth."[8]

Defeat and revolution had aroused profound questions in even the calmest people. Visitors came one after another to the Arnolds' home (first in Wilmersdorf, and after Easter of 1919 in Steglitz, at Lutherstrasse 14 – "another big house, but simpler").[9] Sometimes people stayed overnight, sleeping on the living room sofa or on the dining room floor. Some had to keep out of sight because of their political views. On one occasion two diametrically opposed extremists were put in different rooms; they knew nothing of each other's presence and, like sodium and water, were not to meet under any circumstances. A Thursday evening discussion group (which would later meet several times a week) gathered at the Arnolds' house and attracted SCM members, officers, journalists, anarchists, artists, pietists, and English Quakers, as well as people from the revival movement and representatives of every aspect of the youth movement.[10] Soon as many as fifty to seventy people were regularly participating in the group, and on occasion as many as one hundred people attended.

These discussions could easily have become dead-end dialogs, fruitlessly rehashing the problems of humanity – had it not been for the Sermon on the Mount. Emmy would later write that the meaning of these passages from the Gospel of Matthew, chapters 5–8, was revealed to them in a wonderful way: "The Beatitudes, the words about love of enemies, the 'Our Father,' giving in charity, seeking the kingdom of God and his righteousness – all these struck us like a bolt of lightning. After the injustice of the war and the years leading up to it, Jesus' words burst on us with the force of a thunderclap. We felt we could not go on living as we had. Faith must lead to action, and we must set out on new ways."[11]

Pentecost in Marburg

"We had planned a bible study to speak about the Sermon on the Mount. And – lo and behold! – something very rare happened: the Bible spoke directly to us!" reported an enthusiastic member of the gathering that assembled one sunny morning on the lawns around the Frauenberg ruins, a castle in Marburg. It was June 13, 1919, and the Pentecost conference for Christian scholars was in progress. On this memorable day Eberhard described the change that occurs when a person is seized by the reality of the Beatitudes. According to the report printed in the SCM newsletter:

> Speaking with a simplicity that can come only from humble discipleship of Jesus, and in a wonderful way that can derive only from the holy assurance of the message of revelation in Christ, Eberhard described this new type of person…The meetings for general discussion were nearly all occupied with questions concerning the practical application of this type of life which now burst upon us as the way for a Christian to live out the Sermon on the Mount consistently.[12]

In the words of another SCM member:

> What was it that took hold of us? It was the spirit of the Sermon on the Mount, the spirit of Jesus himself. The Sermon on the Mount spelled out for us the consequences of Jesus' words: "repent and believe in the gospel." And what are the consequences? What is new about them? The Beatitudes became very important for us; they showed us the character of the citizens of the kingdom. Citizens of the kingdom are people with unconquerably joyful hearts, happy people. They are charged with the explosive power of the

life that flows from God. That is what they should manifest to the world. They are to possess the earth; they are called to serve the earth…We felt in Arnold's words that Jesus was seeking for our souls, seeking for us to belong to him completely, for us to love in earnest – and we strove for this with all our might.[13]

Is any further explanation necessary? In Marburg at Pentecost 1919 a miracle not unlike the first Pentecost took place: these young men and women heard in their own twentieth-century language the age-old, yet timeless, words of Jesus – and understood them as never before. Eberhard himself was filled with wonder: "I felt so caught up by Jesus' spirit of absolute truth and absolute love, that I had to speak and testify from my very heart with a directness that has seldom come to me in my life."[14] Unfortunately only a short summary of Eberhard's bible study on the Sermon on the Mount has been preserved, but even these few lines are telling:

> The true and natural objective of the Sermon on the Mount is human nature in its fullest sense of representing the image of God: to be human means to love, again to love – and only to love. Therefore citizens of the kingdom surrender all legal rights. They do not resist evil by force. They reach out in love to everyone. Such a life takes place in secret and shuns all desire for recognition by the masses…The prayer of a citizen of the kingdom is characterized by clearness and few words…People who base their lives on communion with God in this manner know only a holy either-or. They reject all wealth and possessions. They declare unrelenting war on mammon and oppose the whole mammonistic world order. They have only one purpose: to set their hearts on God.[15]

All previous spiritual threads in Eberhard's life now seem inextricably interwoven: the dedication and obedience of faith in the revival period; Hermann Kutter's social conscience and the war against the spirit of mammon; the community of love among the early Christians. And for the first time there are echoes of the Moravian Anabaptists' refusal to bear arms, their rejection of all use of courts of law, and their renunciation of private property. These particular tenets of faith had not hit home during his study of Anabaptist history in 1913. But now, for Eberhard as for so many others, the Sermon on the Mount had become a key – the Word affirmed history, and history affirmed the Word.

For some the conference would remain unforgettable. Still it cannot be ignored that other participants left the Marburg Pentecost conference of 1919 with quite a different impression. For many old associates of the SCM the whole event was ruined by a lack of organization, very casual behavior, and (in reference to the folk dances of the youth movement members) the "frolicking around like spring lambs."

When all was said and done, the question still remained: at what point in the Arnolds' life would they put this renunciation of private property into effect? They were still firmly ensconced in their middle-class lifestyle – not exactly extravagant, but far from poverty-stricken. As a starting point they made attempts to break down class distinctions, at least within their own home. Eberhard made a practice of cleaning the shoes for everyone in the household without exception. The servant girls were moved into a spacious room. When guests came to visit, Eberhard and Emmy vacated their bedroom and shifted to the servants' quarters. Despite their best intentions the Arnolds' steps were of a rather clumsy and symbolic nature. The servants absorbed only half of the message, and this resulted in unrealistic demands and considerable head shaking.

After one particular Free German Youth conference in Tübingen, Eberhard returned home to Berlin sporting a new look.[16] He had left home dressed in his typical, conventional dark business suit, stiff collar, necktie, hat, and coat. Now he cheerfully presented himself to his family in knee britches and a loose tunic with a Byron collar open at the neck – the costume adopted by the youth movement as a sign of their determined and irreversible departure from the bourgeoisie. At first Emmy did not know whether to laugh or to cry, and so she did both.[17] After her initial astonishment she agreed with the change, and she would later recount that the family never wore conventional styles again. But even this change of wardrobe could not disguise the fact that the Arnolds still had not arrived at a practical life of faith. They had not yet found the new way they were seeking.

Can a Christian Be a Police Officer?

Marburg served as the prelude to a series of conferences during the summer and fall of 1919. That year the usual SCM general conference was divided into two regional conferences, one of which was held in Bad Oeynhausen (about thirty miles west of Hannover) from August 4–7, 1919. It was the first "annual" conference since the war's end and the revolution, and it took place under the slogan "Constructive Powers of our Faith in a Time of Collapse." Eberhard, as the second speaker on this theme, sparked a discussion that five months later had not yet reached a satisfactory conclusion: "Our new position in the world is that of ambassadors who must proclaim the will of their King in its entirety."[18] By calling them ambassadors Eberhard meant that Christians are no longer subject to the laws of the world.

In the next day's discussion he put it even more plainly: whenever the gospel was to be preached, the moral values of Jesus were to be taught with it. True, Jesus had acknowledged the authority of the state, but he had described the kingdom of God as something completely different. A Christian represented a constant corrective to the state – a spur to conscience, a reinforcement of the will for justice, a leaven, an alien element. Whenever the state employed violence, a Christian must refuse to cooperate. Therefore a Christian could not be a soldier, an executioner, or a police officer.[19]

Hermann Schafft, one of Eberhard's fellow students from his first semester in Halle, took up the gauntlet: no, Christians are not completely separate and perfect; they are bound and limited by the sins of all humankind. To this Eberhard replied, "We continue sharing in the collective sins of humanity only because on earth, due to our weakness, we never become completely spiritual people." He refused to agree that a Christian was compelled to participate consciously in the sins of humanity.

Schafft, on the contrary, maintained that a life in full harmony with the purity of Christ's spirit is impossible. Even though economic life is dominated by egoism, he reasoned, everyone must take part in it in order to survive.

The central question of the conference (though no one ever stated it so transparently) became whether it was possible to live in accordance with the demands of the Sermon on the Mount. Is it true that

Christians are redeemed from the compulsion to do evil? If they are, then they must really avoid any tasks that involve force and violence. If they are not, then they may not and must not shy away from their responsibility to the state, the use of violence, and coercive methods.

Hermann Schafft's answer amounted to a no. Christians, like others, constantly find themselves confronted by situations where a choice must be made between two equally evil, sinful alternatives. Therefore Christians are also compelled to do evil. Why shouldn't they be police officers, soldiers, or executioners?

But that would not be the final word on the subject. A week later at the second SCM conference the debate resumed. Eberhard reiterated his position: "Government authority does not fulfill the law; we fulfill it when we act in accordance with God's kingdom…It is our duty to witness in word and deed that Jesus' words must not be distorted! The unconditional demand to obey God rather than people is always there. We believe that we are in the world as a corrective to the accepted norm."[20]

Eberhard had stepped out on a limb. But he was by no means alone. Karl Heim, now a professor in Münster, basically seconded him with a lecture titled "Tolstoy and Jesus" that attracted much attention.[21] "The church…went to sleep on the pillow of grace." How did that happen? "Because the Sermon on the Mount had been robbed of its power." Heim censured the "negotiated peace between the Sermon on the Mount and capitalism, between the Sermon on the Mount and power politics…[which is] just as much a fault of Lutheranism as of pietism. As if it were possible to have peace of heart without following God's commandments and working to transform the world. Every compromise between the Sermon on the Mount and the power politics of this world is like a water ditch dug by human firefighters – it limits the movement of divine life, dampens the spirit, and prevents the holy fire from spreading."

Eberhard gave his closing lecture on Heim's heels, with only a slight shift in emphasis.[22] His talk made it particularly obvious that he was not exaggerating the role of a Christian in a fanatical way. "Even our living in the spirit of Jesus will not turn the world into the kingdom of God. But the demands of the Sermon on the Mount remain if we understand and live them out according to Romans 8."[23]

Speechless at Barth's Message

Germany, unlike neighboring Switzerland, still had no organized religious-socialist movement. In the post-revolution era, however, hundreds of theologians identified themselves as religious-socialists for
as many different reasons. Pastor Otto Herpel of Lissberg made an
attempt in the late summer of 1919 to gather together all these self-
styled religious-socialists, inviting about five hundred pastors, minis-

ters, and socially active Christians from Germany and Switzerland to a
September conference at Tambach on the theme of "The Christian in
Church, State, and Society." About one hundred actually took part,
sixty of them theologians. Zurich pastor Leonhard Ragaz, a leading
representative of the religious-socialist movement in Switzerland, was
solicited for the keynote address, but he was not particularly enthusiastic and declined, citing poor health. In his place came the Swiss pastor
Karl Barth. Apparently Barth, who was still completely unknown in
Germany, had certain preconceived notions for the coming conference.[24] Even beforehand he had written to a friend, "What is to be done
in this atmosphere where one can still hear undertones of 'with God for
emperor and fatherland' echoing through the cheers for religious socialism? How can any kind of hearing be won for a reminder of the *totaliter
aliter* of the kingdom of heaven?" *Totaliter aliter* – totally other – was
the attractive common denominator of Barth's theology. The German
conference participants, many of them young theologians with the
greater part of their careers still before them, would receive their first
dose of Barth's theology at these meetings.

At first everything proceeded in an orderly pattern: a lecture from a
Swiss and then from a German, followed by a discussion. It was soon
clear that the Swiss participants were not too keen on the Germans'
revolutionary fire or their radical criticism of the church.

Then, on September 25, Karl Barth launched into his theme: "The
Christian in Society." What his listeners expected to hear is not clear.
What they did hear is. Barth's argumentation soared to the highest
heights, where the air was so thin that few could follow him. But everyone understood that something incredible was happening. He began by
asserting that the traditional, church-oriented religion "is the only religion conceivable and possible within society." He declared that Søren
Kierkegaard and Leo Tolstoy were lovable utopians and dreamers –

nothing more. So were Fyodor Dostoevsky, Hermann Kutter, the Christian mystics, the Anabaptists, and a formidable list of others. The kind of people that were counted blessed in the Sermon on the Mount simply did not exist. For Christ's "truly, I say to you…" commands, there was no imaginable application, neither in today's society nor in any other. "Thus," Barth asserted, "we must now safeguard ourselves from the error of trying to satisfy the conditions of the kingdom of God by criticizing, protesting, reforming, organizing, or by introducing democracy, socialism, or revolution." His methods were obvious: First of all he shattered everything that had been important and holy to his dear colleagues moments before. Then came the formula, *totaliter aliter* – God is totally different. In a nutshell: man is insignificant. God spans the entire horizon, end to end, top to bottom. Man can do nothing. God must do everything.

Barth summed up his pronouncement in his closing words: "What should we do, then?…There is but one thing we can do. And even that one thing is not really done by us. For what can a Christian do in society other than pay attention to what God is doing?"[25]

What a scene! In point of fact, however, Barth's lecture was merely a dry run for what would later become known as "dialectic theology." And it is impossible to avoid the impression that Barth had his fun in taking the wind right out of the sails of this learned assembly. Undoubtedly it was a brilliant lecture, a rhetorical stroke of genius. But at what a cost! He had snubbed the conference organizers and had split the meeting. In the end he was left surrounded by a speechless, admiring group of followers, while a helpless, bewildered group remained sidelined. Many left the conference early. Others puzzled through to the end of the conference, wondering what had just happened – a thunderstorm, a revelation?

Barth's talk provoked such a strong reaction that it nearly blotted out awareness of anything else at the conference. At times scholars have even disputed whether Eberhard ever gave the scheduled second lecture on the same theme. But he most certainly did – contemporary documents prove it beyond all doubt.[26] In doing so, Eberhard showed courage. From the very outset Barth had denied all meaning and validity to anything that had been said before him or that could be said after him. It did not matter what arguments were now put forward.

God remained totally other and was quite likely laughing up his sleeve at these laborious efforts to build up his kingdom or even to understand the tiniest part of it. *Totaliter aliter:* for some, this concept meant the death of the religious-socialist movement in Germany even before it was born.[27]

Eberhard took the affair calmly. It is possible that he alone among the German representatives at the conference had known about Barth's ideas beforehand. He had written a letter to Barth on September 13, explaining that he, Eberhard, was to lecture on the same theme, and he had asked Barth to send him the main ideas of his speech in advance.[28] Eberhard immediately acknowledged Barth's outstanding theological intellect, and he would later make repeated efforts to get him to provide articles and other material for publication.[29] Barth could not deflect Eberhard – not from his literal interpretation of the Sermon on the Mount and still less from his inner relationship to God, which, according to Barth – *totaliter aliter* – had no right to exist.[30] But that inner relationship obviously existed nonetheless.

Struggling for Direction in the SCM

Circumstances within the SCM changed more than once during the closing months of 1919. Virtually nonexistent at the war's outset, the Furche Publishing House had grown to a respectable size as a result of its wartime activities. With the return of peacetime, however, work had dwindled and programs needed to be cut. The publishing house could no longer justify two business managers. Knowing one of them would have to resign, and unhappy with his in-house career prospects, Eberhard submitted his resignation from the position of business manager at the SCM executive committee meeting on October 28. He then accepted the position of full-time SCM secretary with a special task "for those estranged from the gospel." He remained the editor and co-publisher of *Die Furche* and the literary adviser to the publishing house.

In December of 1919 Georg Michaelis reported in the SCM newsletter that "from now on Dr. Arnold is working full time as SCM secretary...Although some of the content and manner of his message seems somewhat questionable to us, so that we cannot always reject as unfounded the complaints leveled against him on these counts, we nevertheless hope that in the future he will join in the happy cooperation and harmonious spirit of our other secretaries." This put the facts plainly enough and expressed the reservations within the SCM leadership.

Eberhard viewed the situation soberly: "It is not right to see the guilt only in other people. There must be something in my way of speaking and behaving that leads to these continual misunderstandings and that therefore must be overcome. And so I beseech God to give me unmistakable clarity of expression, definite and resolute words, a comprehensive testimony to the whole gospel."[31]

In November, barely four weeks after Eberhard's appointment as secretary, the conflict came out into the open at a student conference. Eberhard spoke on the first day of the gathering, titling his lecture "World Revolution and Spiritual Revolution." That same afternoon a professor lectured on the problems of war and violence, using the opportunity to complain to the meeting about exaggerated and fanatical ideas – without naming anyone in particular, of course. Both the students and the old associates of the SCM did not fail to sense the charged atmosphere. "Were there not deep divisions that must lead to a split in the SCM?" was the question raised in a report by one conference member. "Were not two of our leaders, Pastor Humburg and Dr. Arnold, so completely at odds that any further partnership in their work could not last for long?"

Eberhard's second lecture, titled "The Search for God by Young People Today," was the cue that prompted a student's question to the SCM leadership in the discussion that followed the lecture: how far were they ready to go, and how much energy would they expend, in getting to know and cooperating with other religious movements among young people? This was to be the decisive question of the day for the SCM.

Paul Humburg, General Secretary since April, felt forced to give an answer. "On the one hand Dr. Arnold is being portrayed as the only religious leader of the SCM; on the other hand, probably the majority of voices strongly demand that the movement not deviate to the slightest degree from its old aims and purposes." However necessary big-heartedness might be, the SCM must maintain its old basis in questions of faith – in his capacity as General Secretary, Paul

Humburg clung loyally to this view.[32] Finally, the suspicion was voiced that Eberhard had somehow shifted away from the heart of the gospel – the cross and resurrection – and had fallen into ideas of self-redemption. The censure could not have been further from the truth. On November 19 Eberhard wrote to Otto Herpel, "My certainty of the pacifist and socialist ethic of Jesus means a more profound witness to the crucified and risen one, to the gospel of sin and grace." Consequently he could look Paul Humburg in the eyes and assure him, "We will remain on the old basis."

What else could Eberhard say? In 1907 he, together with von Gerdtell and others, had fought staunchly for "the old basis" at a time when scriptural authenticity was at stake. Then, it had been Paul Humburg who was not decisive enough for Eberhard. The principles Eberhard had affirmed in 1907 remained wholly unchanged: to hold unconditionally to the words of Scripture, to put oneself unconditionally in the hands of Jesus, to obey unconditionally what he commands as far as one has recognized this. In the twelve intervening years, however, Eberhard had acquired a broader horizon – a much broader horizon.

Chapter Eight

"It is a special occurrence of faith when we experience the whole gathering of believers in Christ as one living being, as one body, the body of Christ. We are inseparably joined to this body – its life is our life, its lack our lack, its weakness our weakness, its strength our strength. We have a service to fulfill, an offering to contribute to this body, and we need the services and gifts of the others just as they need ours."

From a letter to Otto Herpel, November 17, 1919.

Das Neue Werk

While Eberhard struggled for his right to remain in the SCM, while he tried to come to terms with his inner motivation, and while his future in the Furche Publishing House grew increasingly uncertain, a different door was opening for him elsewhere. At first, though, it seemed only open the merest crack.

Though they had not met in person, Eberhard had first come in contact with pastor Otto Herpel back in the summer of 1917 through Herpel's book about war poetry.[1] In connection with the founding of the German Democratic party in 1918, Herpel had started a weekly newspaper, the *Christliche Demokrat (Christian Democrat),* intending it to be the party's Christian mouthpiece. However, when Herpel changed from a Liberal and a government supporter to a Christian pacifist, the *Christian Democrat* acquired quite a different character too. Writing on June 25, 1919, he introduced himself to Eberhard in such a detailed letter that Eberhard knew immediately that they both belonged to "the same stream of life and love." This was equivalent to a declaration of friendship. Eberhard agreed to write for the *Christian Democrat* from time to time, and he invited Herpel to come to Bad Oeynhausen at the beginning of August. This would provide an opportunity for them to get to know each other and to make further plans.

So it was that Eberhard's article "Present Experience of the Future Kingdom" appeared in Otto Herpel's weekly publication on September 28, 1919.[2] By then the *Christian Democrat* had changed its name to *Das Neue Werk (The New Work)*, subtitled *Der Christ im Volksstaat (The Christian in the People's State)*. It took this new name from the Neuwerk Publishing House in Schlüchtern (about forty miles northeast of Frankfurt), which was little more than an office for advertising and collecting subscriptions for the magazine. The office's only other production was a 1920 calendar entitled *Der Pflug.*[3] Otto Herpel lacked both the money for further endeavors and a capable publishing partner.

Eberhard had just committed himself to the duties of SCM secretary, but in a letter of November 19, 1919, he alerted Herpel of his interest, saying he had decided to make his continuation as editor of *Die Furche* and his future in the SCM dependent on a book he was planning, *World Revolution and World Redemption*, "which puts all my crucial concerns in black and white. If it is rejected here in the Furche Publishing House, I shall, in fact, be free – in complete brotherliness – to give up my position."

Without Anger

World Revolution and World Redemption would never be published in book form.[4] By December of 1919 this must have already been clear to Eberhard. When the SCM executive council met on January 7 and 8, 1920, he tendered his resignation as SCM secretary, giving notice effective for April 1. At the same time he announced his intention to become director of the Neuwerk Publishing House.[5] The last issue of *Die Furche* to bear his mark was the March 1920 issue, which contained a passionate article titled "Freedom and Discipleship." In this piece Eberhard said good-bye to the magazine's four thousand readers:

> Jesus will become our liberator and leader the moment his attitude and his spirit gain a place in us…A life of discipleship can be achieved only when the thoughts, feelings, and actions of Jesus well up from deep within us into our outward lives…When his spirit leads and motivates us, we feel and respond just as he does to the distress of our fellowmen. Only those who actively step in and give a needy friend whatever they have are following in the steps of Jesus. For that was the very essence of Jesus: he gave up everything he possessed.

Eberhard took leave of the SCM executive members without any hard feelings. He wrote to an acquaintance that no one should criticize Georg Michaelis or Paul Humburg. The difficulties lay in the organization and statutes of the SCM; these were what needed to be addressed. And Eberhard added, almost with relief:

> It is completely in keeping with my own nature for me to return to the same unrestricted freedom of action I had before I was called to Berlin, a freedom that is basically indispensable to me…I am now able – unhindered – to represent the free and living Christianity of personal redemption and the practical effects of God's will among people…What I have at heart is to put all my efforts into strengthening the inwardly free and living Christian youth movement in the SCM. The way things are today, that is where new vitality must come from. And it is coming. I am certain of that![6]

Even though Eberhard had resigned as secretary, in the January session he was unanimously elected as a member of the SCM executive committee for an additional four years.[7] The network of friendships and brotherly contacts, formed over a total of nineteen years, lasted to the end of his life.

Friends

The years in Berlin brought Eberhard together with a number of people for the first time and renewed his contact with others. Friedrich Siegmund-Schultze deserves first mention. He was a friend from Eberhard's youth, from the days of the bible study group in Breslau. Like Hermann Schafft, Friedrich Siegmund-Schultze had been a fellow student in Halle and an SCM member. After attending the university he had taken a pulpit, but by 1911 he had already given it up and had established the East Berlin Team for Social Work. In this fellowship, middle-class SCM members shared a communal household with young working-class people. Preaching is not enough in East Berlin, Siegmund-Schultze said. He turned instead to "social Christian action."

Both Siegmund-Schultze's work during the war and his work following the revolution strongly influenced the Arnolds. The activities in East Berlin gave Eberhard and Emmy a definite direction in their considerations of how faith could be put into practice.

Normann Körber, when the Arnolds first met him, was a young law student with Free German inclinations and a pronounced romantic vein. After leaving the university he took up gardening and supported himself from time to time by growing vegetables. He collected young down-and-outs and took care of them, occasionally giving one of them a bed in his parents' home. For awhile he regularly attended the Arnolds' "open evenings" in Steglitz, and an easygoing friendship developed.

Emy-Margret introduced a young teacher to the family circle. Suse Hungar was a cheerful, energetic Salvation Army "soldier." When Emy-Margret entered her third-grade class, she promptly invited her teacher home for an "open evening." Suse was soon drawn into the movement. She was observant enough to realize that Emmy was on the verge of exhaustion and that the household was in a state of chaos. The housemaids had taken advantage of the new circumstances and now neglected their proper tasks. Suse Hungar did not let this pass for long. Without much fanfare or any long discussion she moved in with the Arnolds, took the children's education firmly in hand, and became a part of the family. She linked her future with theirs.

In the summer of 1919 Eberhard made contact with the Berlin pastor Günther Dehn, who was occupied in social work.[8] The relationship remained somewhat one-sided. Eberhard tried to win Dehn's cooperation, but Dehn, who had felt relieved and freed by Karl Barth's rejection of everything that appeared even remotely connected with enthusiasm or fanaticism, was always a little disconcerted by Eberhard's zest and preferred to think along conventional lines.

Pastor Heinrich Schultheis was a close friend of Otto Herpel.[9] The two had studied theology together, and even in those early days Schultheis had been a convinced socialist. He was considerably more radical than Herpel. Eberhard first met Schultheis at the Tambach conference, and over a period of three years the two men grew closer intellectually and spiritually. But, abruptly and painfully, their ways would part.

Georg Flemmig was another of Otto Herpel's friends.[10] A bachelor, he lived and worked as a teacher in his beloved Schlüchtern, where he was highly respected. Energetic and full of ideas, Flemmig was motivated by a profound love of Christ and of people. Following the war he gathered a like-minded group in Schlüchtern and, beginning in the spring of 1919, the Arnolds started receiving their newsletter. With Georg Flemmig as its moving spirit, this group became the nucleus for the Neuwerk movement. In September of 1919 he signed on as coeditor of *Das Neue Werk*, publishing the magazine from Schlüchtern. He acquired a printing shop and drew on business contacts and volunteers for distributing the magazine and for all sorts of incidental tasks. In December of 1919 it was Flemmig who issued a call for people to establish an "Early Church" in different places, with spiritual unity, common aims, and responsibility for people within and without the group. The underlying concept was to form a kind of open brotherhood. Eberhard and Emmy took up the idea with enthusiasm, as did Else von Hollander. By January of 1920 they had already become members of the "Early Church."[11] To show their membership the men wore an open ring, the women an open hair band. However, despite the initial enthusiasm, the brotherhood would last barely three years.

Plans, Plans, and More Plans

By the end of 1919 the gap between Eberhard's ideals and actual reality had widened unbearably. "I can't speak or lecture anymore until I have patterned my life after Jesus' example," he told his friends.[12] The Sermon on the Mount, the Acts of the Apostles, and a particular New Testament verse – "Let Christ Jesus be your example as to what your attitude should be" (Phil. 2:5) – all urged him at long last to give the issue hands and feet. How best to do this was discussed at the "open evenings" and among close friends. Plans were fleshed out and then rejected.

For a brief moment Eberhard and Emmy entertained the very romantic idea of buying a gypsy caravan and taking to the road. They would travel through the countryside, stop at villages, speak, hold meetings for children, and help out wherever necessary. It is easy to guess what would have happened to Eberhard's publishing work under such circumstances. But how it would have worked out practically, with five children, defies imagination.

A hotly debated topic was *Urban vs. Rural*. For those from the youth movement and from working-class groups there was but one answer: get away from the big cities! Follow the slogan of the *Wander-vogel:* "We leave the old gray city and head to the woods and fields!" To them the city was unhealthy, the breeding ground for immorality and unbearable social conditions. The Arnolds could see examples of this right before their eyes in North and East Berlin. On the other hand they knew that cities were the very places with the most problems. The inner city was most in need of constructive work, as could be seen from Siegmund-Schultze's Team for Social Work.

The Arnolds' first real opportunity for a practical undertaking came in early February of 1920 through their circle of friends back in Halle. In the intervening years since the Arnolds had moved to Berlin the Halle fellowship had started a "Hebron Charitable Society" and had bought a house, intending to establish a "biblically inspired social service in love to the poor and needy" of the city. It was proposed that the Arnolds would occupy the house and begin the work. Eberhard enthusiastically agreed to the concept. On February 10 he wrote to the mayor of Halle, Dr. Rivé, a friend of Siegmund-Schultze, and explained the plan in detail. In the end, though, the project failed because the housing office would not grant permission, and the occupant of the house in question refused to move out. That decided the matter.

In the meantime Otto Herpel, Georg Flemmig, and Eberhard Arnold forged ahead rapidly with the formation of their Neuwerk publishing association. By the middle of February Eberhard had made at least one trip to Schlüchtern to discuss the publishing work, and while he was there he formed a friendship with Georg Flemmig. Through these endeavors Eberhard's idea of the "Early Church" became much clearer, and a completely new possibility took shape. On February 26 Eberhard wrote to Otto Herpel: "By making our home in the beautiful little town of Schlüchtern, living together in close friendship with Georg Flemmig and right in the same area as you, we would completely overcome the acute business disadvantage of its remoteness. Admittedly I would only feel content to live there if I could combine my own household with a home for children and young people…a house open to a constant flow of visitors." At this point he postponed any concrete decision because the Halle plans had not yet come to a conclusion. But the purchase or lease of a particular house in Schlüchtern for establishing the Neuwerk Publishing House was already under consideration.

No less important than the practical arrangements was the question of what the inner character of an early Christian communal fellowship founded on Jesus should be. Eberhard jotted down a few short phrases about this on February 22: "Poverty and love; the poor in spirit! The poor! Sell everything! Leave everything! Follow Jesus! Live for the poor. Not law, but love! John 12:24…Community of suffering, of death, of joy, of bodily strength."[13] Of course he was not so naïve as to see the past in such a glowing light that he tried merely to copy what had happened in the lives of the early Christians. "We must not be surprised that the early church lit up the new way for only one brief stretch of time," he wrote shortly afterwards for a book by Friedrich Siegmund-Schultze, "…but new children will always be born to the Spirit. It would be senseless to try to create similar life patterns artificially or by force, for this would only result in disaster. What matters is to be open to God, to the spirit of Jesus…When love includes and permeates everything, manifest life, in all its fullness, will then inevitably arise."[14]

One thing led to another in rapid succession during the first weeks of 1920. Writing on behalf of a "free youth movement of young people for Christ," Eberhard sent out invitations for a mountaintop conference on the Inselsberg on March 7. These invitations went to hundreds of addresses: to the group centered around Schlüchtern, to *Das Neue Werk* subscribers, to people from the Marburg SCM, and of course to those who attended the Arnolds' "open evenings" in Steglitz, as well as to countless other friends all over the country. In many cases Eberhard backed up the invitation with a personal letter. He begged for support for the project and promised cash-strapped students that if they came their fares would be refunded.

On March 7, 1920, the small company left Fröttstädt at the base of the mountain and sang their way up the Inselsberg. They were such a motley assortment of humanity that an outsider would have looked in vain for some common factor: tolstoyans,[15] communists, *Wandervogel,* YMCA and SCM members, Free Germans, representatives from revolutionary and working-class youth groups, to say nothing of Marie Buchhold, a woman influenced by Buddhism. In fact the only thing that brought this remarkable group together was Eberhard's unerring eye for sincere seekers, "inner" people searching "for freedom and love, inward truthfulness and vitality." He was seldom deceived.

The Inselsberg conference focused on exchanging ideas and advice about practical steps toward a communal life. Eberhard revealed a vision to this colorful audience, the vision of an effective community, working with one common spirit and purpose. His speech appeared somewhat later in *Das Neue Werk* entitled "Extended Households and Life in Settlements."[16] A short extract:

> The way to community lies in deepened spirituality and greater intensity of spiritual experience. The uniting spirit wants to gather all those who in their innermost being belong together. When people who have an inward kinship are led together in this manner, this in no way separates them from others…Growing together in communal life results rather in an increase of strength and vitality. Only living minds and souls can form a spiritual fellowship that aims at far-reaching effects…Humankind is meant to be one living entity: a body with one spirit, one head, one soul, one heart.

This makes it clear that Eberhard did not envision a conglomeration of every possible spiritual trend. Quite to the contrary – an inward affinity was not enough for him. One spirit, one head, one soul, and one heart. No misunderstanding is possible. It is pure New Testament:

> Unless the common spirit for which we yearn is the Holy Spirit of the living God, it will deteriorate into a spirit of commonness – common in the sense of mean and base. Only the Holy Spirit can stand the test as the uniting power of true community. Only God can bring about the ultimate unity of voluntary and joyful creativity, of inner independence, social justice, genuineness in each person's life, and complete love. The spirit of God is the power of truth that separates what is bad or only half good from what is entirely genuine, and the spirit of God is the power of love to make us want and do what is good…The divine spirit is the spirit that awakens to life; it is the spirit that binds together in unity. It is the spirit of the divine life…that is in Jesus."

Eberhard called his listeners to form communities in the spirit of Jesus, to start settlements, "voluntary associations of working people." Up to this point he could count on everyone's applause. But his underlying thoughts went much further, and he made concrete suggestions: farming and gardening; schools and welfare work among children; publishing work and outreach; a children's home especially for war orphans; arts and crafts.[17] Although everyone found these proposals desirable no one could see any possibility of realizing them in the near future. Nonetheless the idea of a settlement inspired by early Christianity now captured the imaginations of a much greater number than before.

By April things had developed to such a degree that the Arnolds wanted to relocate nearer to the Schlüchtern movement.[18] They had already looked at one house in Schlüchtern, but it was not suitable. On his next visit to Schlüchtern Eberhard went with the purpose of searching the surroundings for a good place to start a settlement. Otto Herpel told him about Herrnhaag near Büdingen (about twenty miles northeast of Frankfurt). It had once been a Zinzendorf settlement of the Moravian Brethren, a community of goods and of love. Prior to that Herrnhaag had been a thirteenth-century Cistercian foundation. In the seventeenth century it had served as a place of refuge for "'Anabaptists and sectarians of every kind."

Eberhard was immediately fired with enthusiasm at the thought of restoring the Lichterburg, the rather dilapidated castle at the center of Herrnhaag, and filling it once more with the spirit of brotherly life that had radiated love and promoted communal living in the period from 1767–1790. The astronomic cost of renovation (450,000 marks, to be paid off in annual 30,000-mark installments) did not frighten him at first. In his mind's eye he could picture a medieval-type guild developing there. He also wanted to lease an empty farm nearby for a farming cooperative. The income it produced would cover the rent.[19] Doubtless this was a truly fantastic plan. His friend Kurt Woermann, a Hamburg ship owner with level-headed experience in financial matters, had to intervene and cool the ardor. The money could be obtained, but what about the countless willing hands?

In spite of this, such pipe dreams were not in vain. Eberhard synthesized his own clear direction only by grappling with other community experiments – "in the Moravian Church…in the Anabaptist communities, among the Quakers, with Jean von Labadie, in Russia, and in Palestine." Some of the goals he first expressed in such plans would take shape a few short months later, others only after several years. The specifics of Eberhard's watershed talk at the Inselsberg conference were put into practice one step at a time.

Gustav Landauer

Eberhard's plans for a settlement, his ideas of spiritual and working community, his uninhibited relationship with revolutionary and working-class young people, his public discussion of communism and anarchism, and many characteristics of the community settlement that actually took shape – all these would have been unthinkable were it not for the influence of the writer and social philosopher Gustav Landauer. Certainly Eberhard knew Landauer's book *For Socialism* inside out.[20] It is probable that Eberhard had read Landauer's writings and had adopted some of his views even before Landauer was murdered by soldiers in Munich on May 1, 1919, a murder which occurred during the suppression of the Bavarian proletarian republic. It is also possible that they had met each other. Gustav Landauer had lived in Hermsdorf, near Berlin, until May 1917. He had lectured the Free Student fellowship, a youth movement element that met in a Berlin settlement house. Landauer had published numerous articles and books, most of which would have been available to Eberhard.[21] He wrote pithy short stories and wrote about Christian and Jewish mystics, the Reformation, God and socialism, and Tolstoy. He was one of the best-read and most acute thinkers of his time. Though a Jew, he nonetheless admired and respected Jesus.

Landauer had refined Peter Kropotkin's and Bakunin's ideas about "domination-free socialism," or anarchism, developing them into a breathtaking system of thought that any attentive reader of the Bible will find peculiarly familiar.[22] Eberhard must have realized at a glance that virtually all of the admirable, practical ethics of the anarchist Gustav Landauer were drawn from the New Testament and that only a small fraction of them stemmed from new socialist ideas. If one takes the lifestyle of the early Christians minus the references to Jesus, one arrives at Landauer's anarchism. Or the other way around: if one expands Landauer's thoughts by simply adding the idea of the kingdom of God, the living Jesus Christ, and the Holy Spirit, one has the early Christian community of love. Eberhard must have seen this connection.

In February of 1920 Eberhard wrote to an SCM friend, "I find it so interesting that the most radical communists turn into anarchists and the most consistent anarchists are communists. When there is absolute consistency from the very heart in all the practical realities of life, this leads to truly Christ-like living…Here is redemption from all the enslavement to which men are subjected."[23]

Probably this insight explains why Eberhard was not afraid of contact with anarchist groups, and why from time to time he even sought them out. In his lecture at the Inselsberg on "Extended Households and Life in Settlements," Eberhard drew on Landauer's ideas in *For Socialism,* concepts which were certainly familiar to most of his audience. In 1921 Eberhard tried to obtain Martin Buber's support for a collection of extracts from Landauer's works.[24] The Neuwerk Publishing House even advertised the book in advance.[25] The justification for this project: "The memory of Gustav Landauer must not fade, and it is important to express exactly what was most important about him, what God meant to him, and what God could be for him."[26]

Even in the last years of his life, though barely able to walk, Eberhard could not be prevented from standing up each May 1 to honor the memory of Gustav Landauer as an upright and honest man. As with Friedrich Nietzsche, so too with Gustav Landauer: Eberhard tested everything in true evangelical freedom – and he held on to what was good.

Putsch

One of the most curious incidents in Eberhard's life took place during the Kapp putsch, an attempt by rightist factions within the army to overthrow the government in Berlin. Though no more than an anecdote it is a well-documented and very characteristic one. During the days of the general strike and the street fighting following March 13, 1920, the telephone rang at Lutherstrasse 14 in Steglitz. Lieutenant

Helmut von Mücke, a highly decorated marine officer, announced that he was coming to visit the Arnolds. True to his word, he stopped by for a cup of coffee.[27] His purpose: to ask Eberhard to take on the new Department of Youth that would be established under the rebel government of the former director of agriculture, Kapp. The Arnolds made it very plain to him that theirs was a different calling. A letter from Eberhard describes quite soberly the role he played during the days of the attempted revolt: "My house became a kind of headquarters for influential people. As I was constantly in touch with both warring parties, I had the opportunity to use my influence to a certain degree – not strongly enough to make our spirit victorious, but not without a certain effect…We were able to come to an understanding with the communist party leaders that led to a significant reduction of the so-called black list – the list of officers to be killed."[28]

A few days after a general strike caused the putsch's collapse, Eberhard's name appeared among others on a leaflet calling all pacifists and opponents of war to strengthen their spiritual solidarity with each other:

> We do not judge those who turn to the use of force. Rather, through total dedication to the community of our nation and of all nations, among and with the working class, we want to serve the spirit of love, which will one day bring an end to all violence. We testify that we are urged forward by the living spirit of Christ toward the kingdom of love and brotherliness, and we want to work with full commitment for a transformation of society and the establishment of a brotherly bond among all peoples.

This incident provides a clear indication of the position Eberhard took up after the war. Certainly he was no communist – he was too religious and conciliatory for the left. But he was no longer middle class either – he was too radical for bourgeois society. Eberhard was, first and foremost, a mediator and interpreter of the message of Jesus Christ, and revolutionary jargon was as much at his command as the intellectual jargon of the highly educated and the religious language of the pious. He allowed no one to dictate whom he could or could not address. But Eberhard certainly had not chosen this continually changing and thankless role of the odd man out.

The Pentecost 1920 conference in Schlüchtern reunited most of the Inselsberg conference participants, and it brought together many people associated with the "Early Church" movement as well. The Arnolds, accompanied by a crowd of young people from Berlin, traveled fifteen hours – fourth class, by slow train. They arrived in Schlüchtern at eight o'clock in the evening, with a hill still to climb. But when they crested the hilltop, the Pentecost fires blazed. On Pentecost Sunday, Eberhard spoke on "The Mystery of the Early Church."[29] He witnessed to the spirit of Pentecost, which is much more than the "collective soul of world revolution." Eberhard proclaimed that only the spirit of Pentecost could pour unreserved love and fellowship into the hearts of the believers. With this he anticipated what was in fact to happen only a few weeks later and only a few miles away.

On May 26, 1920, with the conference meetings officially behind them, Eberhard and Emmy and a handful of young people walked from Schlüchtern to nearby Ahlersbach. They stopped on their way at the little village of Sannerz and entered the inn, the Gasthaus zum Stern. They had heard that a sizable house was for sale and discovered that it was a large brick villa opposite the inn. Its owner, a certain Konrad Paul, had made money in America and on his return had invested it in this house. He was friendly and forthright and proved willing to sell or rent the property, but he would not name a fixed

Konrad Paul's villa in Sannerz was the Arnold family home, their communal settlement house, and the nerve center of the Neuwerk movement from 1920 to 1926.

price. During the days of the conference the Arnolds had visited the Habertshof, a communal settlement on a meager farm near Schlüchtern. Konrad Paul's property, with its kitchen garden, orchard, cow stalls, pig sties, and chicken coop, seemed in comparison almost too elegant. But the house had fifteen rooms, and it would surely be big enough.

Before the Arnolds returned to Berlin they arranged with Lotzenius, the innkeeper of the Gasthaus zum Stern, to lodge at the inn for several weeks during the summer. Nothing else was settled. Once home, Eberhard and Else von Hollander tied up a few loose ends at the Furche Publishing House, while Emmy began to pack up the household. Many of their acquaintances only now realized that the Arnolds were in earnest about their plans. Then, all at once, everything moved ahead rapidly. Monika, the youngest child, had suffered for a long time from enteritis and had grown very thin. A doctor had advised a stay in the country with the necessary care and nursing, and the Arnolds did not want to wait any longer. In a letter of June 8 they announced to Lotzenius that they would arrive on June 18. Lotzenius replied by telegram: "summer vacation, 3 rooms, outbuildings, wardrobe, bed linen, kitchen utensils, children's beds, 3 windows – Lotzenius." Actually it was not until June 21 that Eberhard and Emmy and two-year-old Monika could move into the outbuildings of the Gasthaus zum Stern at Sannerz and could telegraph Else von Hollander in Steglitz: "well-accommodated here – thousand greetings, Eberhard."

Chapter Nine

"I have decided not to fall in love with God's fingertips, but with his heart and his heart alone." *From a lecture, March 17, 1921.*

Sonnherz

It took only a few days for the nucleus of the Christian community settlement at Sannerz to form: Eberhard and Emmy with their five children, Suse Hungar, and Else von Hollander. The initial time in Sannerz was intended to be a "retreat for quiet work," but nothing of the sort occurred.[1] Work? Yes. Quiet? No. By the end of the very first month the little household had already accommodated thirty-five visitors in Lotzenius's work shed. By mid-July the community had grown by three: Fritz Schloss, a bookseller and former officer; a young man from Berlin – penniless, long-haired, and communist to boot; and Friedel Günther, a young girl who had been placed in the Arnolds' care by a guardianship bureau shortly after the war.

Money was scarce. The Arnolds had applied to cash in their life insurance, but even this brought in very little. Kurt Woermann, owner of the Hamburg-America Line transatlantic shipping company, had promised the "Early Church" 30,000 marks for the purchase of Konrad Paul's villa. But first Konrad Paul had to decide whether he wanted to sell or to rent and, if so, on what conditions. In the meantime guests had to sleep either in the innkeeper's shed or in the barns of neighboring farmers. There were no other options. On August 14, 1920, Eberhard reported to his sister Hannah that seven people had begun work in the relocated publishing house. It had been moved from Schlüchtern to Sannerz, where three rooms in the villa were now available for its activities. Ever the optimist, Eberhard felt confident that it would be possible for the group to occupy the entire villa by late fall. Meanwhile the Arnolds gave notice at their home in

Steglitz and shipped their furniture to Sannerz. In short, they burned every bridge to their former middle-class lifestyle.

Various lists in Eberhard's handwriting show his anticipation of rapid growth for the settlement. At one time he was hoping for twenty-two members in the community, at another time thirty-two. Some of the people named in his lists announced their willingness to work with the little group, but never made an appearance. Others

dropped by for a short while but then left. The community's core group remained small, and during the first three years it never numbered more than a dozen. Most of those present were guests or novices who stayed for an indefinite period. Perhaps many of them shrank from the conditions that Eberhard had formulated for the core group in September 1920:

> We need Christians – reborn people who have accepted the life of the Sermon on the Mount.
>
> We need people who work – people who are capable and willing to work.
>
> We need people who radiate the spirit of Christ – people who witness for Christ with their entire being.
>
> We are a working community of disciples of Jesus who give up everything to live simply and solely for love and for productive work. We must testify that we are a church of Christ, a Lord's Supper fellowship.
>
> We need Christ and the kingdom of God, protest and the call to repentance, testimony and faith, a bold commitment to life and love. Witnesses are needed – not self-idolization, not the righteousness of works, not self-appointed goals, not prophets, not leaders. We need brotherliness in forgiveness and grace, because each proclaims not himself but Christ.[2]

It is no longer known who first proposed the idea of changing the village name of Sannerz to "Sonnherz" – "Sunheart." Perhaps it was a guest, a romantic such as Normann Körber, or maybe a daughter of the muses such as Else "Tata" von Hollander. At any rate Eberhard immediately grasped the symbolic impact of the image. By the fall of 1920 his letters were referring to the "Neuwerk Sonnherz," because, as he put it, "our community life needs and feels the life-giving power of the heart of God in a particularly powerful way."[3] A little later Karl Mahr, an artist friend of the Arnolds from the days of *Die Furche,* designed the blazing sunheart emblem, a symbol that literally radiated.

Books and Papers

Back in April of 1920 Eberhard, filled with fiery enthusiasm, had set to work reconfiguring and expanding the Neuwerk Publishing House. He had enrolled a large number of friends and acquaintances – businessmen, SCM friends, and even relatives – in the Neuwerk cooperative enterprise. This brought in a sizable sum of money, which he now put to good use.

At his suggestion the design of *Das Neue Werk* was revamped, the layout made tidier, the typeface more reader-friendly. Editions would now appear twice a month. (After 1921 this would be reduced to once a month.) Eberhard secured funding for *Das Neue Werk* from the Quakers, who until this time had not published a magazine of their own in Germany. He revived his acquaintance with the respected educator and author Friedrich Wilhelm Foerster and convinced him that his concerns could be well represented in *Das Neue Werk.*[4] At that time Foerster already held a post as a university lecturer in Switzerland. His good friend in Germany, Pastor Alfred Dedo Müller, declared himself willing to work for *Das Neue Werk.* He offered his services free of charge and, together with Foerster, dropped the idea of publishing their own periodical in Germany.[5] Eberhard announced this "important acquisition" to Otto Herpel with satisfaction.[6] He had less luck in obtaining a leading editor. The Christian Jew Otto Samuel had already accepted his offer but refused to move to Sannerz, and so he was soon out of the picture, at least as far as editors were concerned.

Eberhard's printing plans had always included special issues of *Das Neue Werk.* The first issue of this kind to be printed carried the title *Die Flamme (The Flame)* and appeared in September 1920. It was dedicated to working-class youth and was sponsored by a Breslau friend who was trying to bring Christ's message to these young revolutionaries. The issue was an enthusiastic, if somewhat bewildering, side-by-side compilation of Christian and socialist thought – Rosa

Luxemburg and Dostoevsky, Tolstoy and Kropotkin. Later special issues – the "Friedrich Wilhelm Foerster issue," for instance – were more unified and, not surprisingly, found wider acceptance.

Eberhard's plans for book publishing were even more ambitious than his goals for the magazine. He conceptualized three different series of books: *Innenschau (Looking Inward),* a set of titles for meditation containing testimonies of important religious and intellectually stimulating authors; a Neuwerk collection, which would showcase books offering practical solutions to real-life issues; and, finally, a set of heart-warming books on various regions of the homeland.

In a letter to Otto Herpel on August 6, 1920, Eberhard told of no less than fourteen planned books. Among these were anthologies and biographies of Landauer, Sebastian Franck, Franz Baader, and important figures from the Quaker movement. Titles for his envisioned Neuwerk collection included: *Activism of Faith, The Importance of Judaism, The Hour of Decision for Protestantism, The Insight of the Soul and the Positive Approach to Life through Action;* and for the Homeland series, *Silesian Moors and Mountains,* and *Free German Hikes through Central Germany.*

None of these books was ever written. Neither was Eberhard's own project *Jesus and the Future State.* However, a Zinzendorf volume by Otto Herpel made its appearance in 1920, as did Georg Flemmig's *Village Musings.* A little book of legends by Fritz Schloss, illustrated with scissor-cuts by Else von Hollander, came on the market at the beginning of 1921. *Village Musings* sold very well, and *Legends* proved to be a bestseller. *Young Seed,* jointly edited by Eberhard and Normann Körber, appeared in 1921 and attracted much attention for its description of the Youth Movement's vitality. The book's themes and quotations were as varied, stimulating, and kaleidoscopic as the youth movement itself.[7]

The Neuwerk books were successful from the start. The care taken in production increased their marketability. In his days in the Furche Publishing House Eberhard had learned the value of attractive graphic design. This experience stood both the publishing house and the Neuwerk community in good stead. For a long time the publishing of the magazine and books would be the only reliable source of income for the community.

Injured

The simultaneous building up of the community and the publishing house took a heavy toll on Eberhard's strength. In mid-August he caught a cold and suffered from heart palpitations brought on by the strain of his work. But these could not deter him. Then, while chopping wood a few days later, a splinter flew into his left eye – and it was the old trouble once again: retinal detachment and severe inflammation. This forced him to rest. He had to travel to Frankfurt several times a week for extremely painful saline injections into his eye. But his eye did not regain sight.

In retrospect Eberhard felt that his time of illness was "the best thing that could have happened to me." It led him to "a new experience of inner perception, of insight into what is essential: the one and only thing that can have importance for the community growing up among us, and for humankind in general, which is the spirit of light born of unconditional love that knows nothing but love and exists to serve love alone..."[8]

Sentenced to inactivity, Eberhard was unable to participate in the Neuwerk conference at Marburg in September. As it was, he had anticipated the conference with mixed feelings. His uneasiness was confirmed after the fact by reports from Else von Hollander and others who took part. Speakers like Günther Dehn and Karl Mennicke demanded greater involvement in party politics and did not hide a certain touch of arrogance toward the "Schlüchtern pietists." Consequently the Marburg conference drove a wedge of division through the Neuwerk movement, prompting Eberhard to describe it as a defeat for the Neuwerk cause.[9] He wrote: "Since the Marburg conference we are more resolute than ever to promote the gospel and nothing else in *Das Neue Werk* and in all our work...It is crucial that there be solidarity and loyalty among those who are glad to be called 'pietists' but whose eyes are open to the social responsibilities of Jesus' disciples."

Even Otto Herpel was eventually bruised by Eberhard's energetic activity in building up the Neuwerk Publishing House. Before becoming coeditor with Eberhard, Herpel had put together the *Christian Democrat* as a sideline to his pastoral work. But *Das Neue Werk* was to be run professionally or not at all – that had been Eberhard's stipulation on assuming the management. Authorization for this and that, punctual payment of royalties, recruiting members for the cooperative, soliciting advertisements, alternating with Eberhard on the final editorial check of the magazine's bimonthly issues – all this soon grew too much for Herpel. In mid-September Otto Herpel visited Eberhard on his sickbed and informed him that he was resigning as an editor for good. He was not, he admitted, the committed person needed for such work.

It is clear enough that these two men, who had been so quickly drawn to each other, had just as quickly drawn apart in spirit. Otto Herpel had already swallowed Karl Barth's sober direction – hook, line, and sinker – at the conference in Tambach in September of 1919. Now he wrote, "Arnold's articles have too much pietism in them for me."[10] But in spite of reservations and friction Otto Herpel continued as co-publisher of *Das Neue Werk,* and in the end his resignation as editor improved, rather than impaired, his friendship with Eberhard.

City on a Hill

Community of work, community of the Lord's Supper: the first aim had been accomplished, and the other soon followed. On September 26, 1920, the household at Sannerz celebrated the Lord's Supper for the first time. Guests were included in this communion only if they could unconditionally declare themselves to be disciples of Jesus.

Eberhard himself made no claim to the leadership, and Emmy was never formally appointed housemother, but each developed a natural authority that no one questioned. At least not yet. Eberhard's pastoral gift, his keen insight into people's hearts, and his calling to proclaim the gospel were recognized even by eccentric and strong personalities – and there were several of these in the various groups closely or loosely related to the community.

Otto Salomon was one such character. An actor and writer from Berlin who had converted to Christianity from Judaism, Otto Salomon had been robbed of all ideals and illusions by the war, which had left him eking out a living as a farmhand. In October of 1920 he moved to Sannerz and tried to find a lowly position in the Neuwerk

community, where he could school himself in humility. This was not so easy. As an interesting bachelor he was more or less idolized by several young women among the guests. His great musical talent created a natural affinity with Emmy, and he soon became a kind of Charles Wesley for the Neuwerk movement. Everyone sang Otto Salomon's songs with great feeling and enthusiasm. On the first Sunday of Advent 1920, when the community at last took over Konrad Paul's villa from cellar to attic, Otto Salomon's song "In holy waiting we're at home" rang out for the first time.

He soon belonged to the innermost group in the community, a group that included Eva Oehlke, Otto Herpel's former secretary, and Gertrud Cordes, who had been in Schlüchtern at Pentecost and had then and there declared her complete readiness to live in community. To the joy of Emmy and Else von Hollander their youngest sister, Monika, also joined the community after a few months.

The winter of 1920–21 naturally brought fewer guests. Eberhard, having just regained his health after a year of inactivity following his eye injury, felt free once more to accept invitations to lecture. He always saw these as an opportunity to evangelize.[11] On January 25, 1921, Eberhard spoke in the main lecture hall at Munich University on "World Revolution and World Redemption." Friedrich Berber, the lecture organizer, was quite astonished at the speaker's clothes: "In spite of the winter cold he wore only short pants that left his bare, hairy legs in full view of the scholarly assembly." Yet for all his embarrassment Berber was impressed. He described his guest as someone radiating love, a man of great personal courage.[12]

During March and April Eberhard gave several series of lectures, including a series at the Frankfurt Institute for Adult Education. In July he spoke in Göttingen, in October in Mannheim. Without exception each of these lectures was an impassioned appeal to receive Jesus Christ, to break with the old life, and to become a disciple in total earnest. Seldom before had Eberhard delivered so clear and powerful a message or been so filled with glowing zeal by and for Jesus.[13] What amazing phenomenon produced this effect? As never before, real life action now backed up Eberhard's words. The Sannerz community enfleshed the living energy he was talking about. Some were so struck by his words that, soon after their first encounter with Eberhard, they made their way to Sannerz to hear and see more. One of these was the young teacher Gertrud Dalgas, who had heard Eberhard speak in Frankfurt in April 1921. Weeks later she took part in the Pentecost conference in Schlüchtern – "I am the short, blonde woman from north Germany who held your arm on the way home." Gertrud visited at Sannerz for a few weeks and then returned to the community in October – to stay for the rest of her life.

It must be stressed, however, that when he lectured Eberhard sought to bring people to discipleship of Jesus, not to Sannerz or to life in community. His character and attitude alone were sufficient to win people for the way of life on which he had embarked. A never-ending stream of visitors flowed through Sannerz from the spring of 1921 onward. Most of the guests had to be content to sleep on camp cots and straw-filled mattresses. Entire groups of *Wandervogel* sent word they were coming, stayed a weekend or longer, and then hiked off again. In the course of the year 1921 there were over twenty-five hundred visitors: inquisitive members of bible study groups, old friends, eccentrics and misfits like the anarchist Fritz Schwalbe and the always cheerful Hans Fiehler ("Where are you from?" –"Prison. And you?" – "The madhouse").

During this time Eberhard often wrote such phrases as "we are all stretched to our limits" or "my time is completely taken up." He complained in his letters that it was hardly possible to concern himself with individuals as much as he would have liked. But only he could have viewed it in this light; in actual fact, he had hundreds of pastoral talks. Correspondence over weeks and months showed that Eberhard followed the fates of individual guests with deep concern. Between lecture tours and his responsibilities in the community household he counseled countless young people, put the brakes on fanatical enthusiasts, encouraged the irresolute, and pled with doubters to show trust. In lengthy letters he explained the nature of the communal life, cleared up misunderstandings, and diffused suspicions: "Our settlement and household community is not the means to some particular end, not even a religious end; it is the other way round. What people term as our settlement is the unavoidable result, the fruit of something germinating in our hearts."[14]

The Arnolds at Sannerz, ca. 1925.

New Leads

In the first months of 1921 a correspondence had developed between Sannerz and Tabor College in Hillsboro, Kansas. Just another among innumerable exchanges. There was no indication that this contact would have especially far-reaching consequences. A philology professor named J. G. Evert had become interested in *Das Neue Werk* and ordered a few books from the publishing house. He introduced himself as a Mennonite and drew Eberhard's attention to two Christian communities that practiced community of goods: one a "Hutterian Bruderhof" in Alexandria, South Dakota, the other an Amish settlement in Iowa. He also enclosed in his letter the 1917 petition from the Hutterian Bruderhofs to President Woodrow Wilson. In it the Hutterites appealed to the president to respect their commitment and their consciences and to exempt the Hutterian Brethren from military service. This letter was Eberhard's first awareness that there were still Hutterites living in community and that they had remained true to their forefathers' peace witness right up to the present day. He printed the petition in the May 1921 issue of *Das Neue Werk*.[15] Shortly afterwards the journal also carried a prose translation of J. G. Evert's poem "The Martyrs of Alcatraz." This was entitled "Hutterian Brethren in Military Prison in America."[16]

Eberhard did not seek immediate contact with the Hutterian communities in North America. Now, however, he had first-hand information about them. And he had names: David Hofer, Elias Walter, and Joseph Kleinsasser, the elders of the three branches of Hutterianism: Lehrerleut, Dariusleut, and Schmiedeleut.[17] For the time being other events shunted this information to the side. But it had been found and would not be lost.

A Year of Crises

The year 1922 began with unspoken accusations. During the conference of Neuwerk coworkers in Schlüchtern at the close of 1921, tangible suspicions permeated the room: Did the Sannerz community household think that they were better than the others? Were they attempting to compel heaven to come down to earth? Eberhard felt it necessary to emphasize to people like Georg Merz, Hermann Schafft,

Georg Flemmig, and even Karl Barth that Sannerz was "nothing special, only one house among millions."[18]

The next surprise came from an unexpected quarter. Otto Salomon had grown more and more discontent, both with himself and with the community. He was caught up in Goethe's idea of "elective affinities" – community members should be akin to each other in their intellectual level, background, and education. He was not pleased that "so many worthless people" were taken into the community. Coming from this angle his next step was predictable: In February of 1922 Otto Salomon went to see Georg Flemmig in Schlüchtern and together they founded a "brotherhood of the open ring," a young men's group. He left Sannerz and moved to Schlüchtern. The two events – the formation of the "brotherhood" and Otto Salomon's desertion from the core group at Sannerz – struck a terrible blow to the little community. Gertrud Dalgas, hardly more than a newcomer to Sannerz herself, called it a breach of faith. She was not far off the mark: a brotherhood of the open ring already existed – the "Early Church" – and it was still going strong. Emmy was the hardest hit by Otto Salomon's departure. For years she could not get over the fact that it was "Otto, of all people" who had given up living in the Sannerz community.

Then the publishing house ran into difficulties. The war had ruined the nation's finances. Inflation had set in, at first gradually, then at full gallop. Prices for periodicals and books had to be adjusted – meaning raised – with increasing frequency. This worked to the advantage of customers who procrastinated payment of their bills, but not for honest businesspeople who met their obligations promptly. As the reserve capital of the Neuwerk Publishing House dwindled with the depreciating currency, the shareholders grew more and more uneasy. Eberhard, as business manager, could exert little control over the course of events.

In the spring of 1922, however, it seemed as if many problems would simply evaporate in the spring sunshine. At Easter Heinrich Schultheis gave up his pastoral position in Gelnhaar and moved with his family to Sannerz.[19] Eberhard's personal relationship with the "red parson" was as close as their political views were distant. The only clouds to mar the happy weeks that followed the Schultheises' arrival were arguments at the Neuwerk Pentecost conference in Wallroth near Schlüchtern, where Wilhelm Stählin was the main speaker. In his recent book, *Delirium and Recovery in the Youth Movement,* Stählin had vowed to end the stormy, enthusiastic phase of setting out and had championed a return to middle-class conditions.[20] At the conference Stählin addressed his theme to a Neuwerk movement that

had shifted its emphasis following the Marburg conference of 1920. "Reality" was now the buzzword. It was time to say good-bye to utopia and to move back into the encrusted movements of the past, where they could act as a leaven. Or at least that was the viewpoint of people such as Otto Herpel and the Swiss pastor Emil Blum, who had recently become leader of the Habertshof community settlement.[21]

At this, Eberhard – never lacking a flare for the dramatic – declared the Neuwerk movement dead. The wedge (the movement) had not been able to split the rotten tree (the state church, traditional Christianity, middle-class materialism) and, in the process, had split itself. As for bowing to the status quo, however piously it might be disguised, Eberhard branded it as idolatry. The discussion prompted much contradiction and head shaking, and the fiery debate only raged hotter following Eberhard's article in the June issue of *Das Neue Werk,* "On the Present Situation of the Neuwerk Cause." But in the Sannerz community household itself there was unity about the direction taken – at least for the time being.

It took only a few days for the seeds sown at Wallroth to sprout in some peoples' minds. In June of 1922 the Dutch pacifist Kees Boeke put a considerable sum of money, 180,000 marks, at the community's disposal for the purchase of a larger property. Members went to view the Scheuermühle in Franconian Ruppoden, about thirteen miles from Sannerz, a place easily large enough to allow the expansion of their work with children. But the community could not reach agreement among themselves, and this was the sole reason no purchase took place. Should they simply proceed with the purchase and take in orphans, regardless of the risk? (Such leaps of faith had been their *modus operandi* until now.) Or should they first thoroughly plan the project, arrange financial backing, and secure future operating funds?

In its very essence this disagreement illustrated that some had already relapsed into the old concern for security, a concern that could not abide the confident trust required by the Sermon on the Mount: "Do not worry. See the birds in the skies – they do not sow, they do not harvest and carry grain to the barns, and yet your Heavenly Father feeds them."

There were other warning signs: In the household community, which at times numbered as many as twenty-three adults, no one took responsibility for urgent household tasks. Some people's dedication to the community had noticeably slackened. As can be verified by their letters, both Eberhard and Emmy had detected these danger signs. But the same letters are also a testimony to their inextinguishable hope that this low point would be overcome, that "the Spirit that gives life will break forth all the more powerfully."

More Accusations

The Arnold family and Else von Hollander spent July of 1922 in Bilthoven, Holland, at the invitation of Kees and Betty Boeke. It was the first family holiday of any significant duration since 1914. In their absence leadership of the community was entrusted to Heinrich and Elisabeth Schultheis. At first everything ran as harmoniously as usual. This matched Eberhard's vision to a tee: "I feel that a point must come when the common spirit among us brings out so powerfully what is deepest and most essential in us, so that although there are great, even vital, differences in the expression of our gifts, the testimony given by all these gifts still becomes one united witness."[22]

Then, in the second half of July, the Neuwerk Publishing House received notice that its bank loan had been called in. Payment was due within days.[23] Starting with Heinrich and Elisabeth Schultheis, panic spread among some of the community members. Preposterous rumors ran wild among the guests, who did not have the faintest idea about the publishing affairs of the community. Heinrich Schultheis wrote an urgent letter to Bilthoven demanding that the Arnolds return immediately. Eberhard did not reply immediately. He struggled for clarity. When he did respond he wrote that, as previously arranged, he would end his stay in Holland on August 1. He would be back in Sannerz when payment of the loan was due. Eberhard trusted that the necessary means for continuing their work would be available by then. Gertrud Dalgas gives a vivid picture of how Eberhard's answer was received in the community:

> We were sitting on the front porch at two long tables, one on each side of the main door. I was asked to read aloud Eberhard's answer. When I had finished, those sitting at my table stood up and moved over to the other table. I was left completely alone. At that moment I realized that here were the two opposite attitudes to life described in the Gospels: the one of faith, which makes the impossible possible, and the other dependent on human thinking.

Over the next few days many more letters left Sannerz for Bilthoven – letters full of reproaches from Heinrich Schultheis in the name of the community, and letters of dejection from Gertrud Dalgas and others. Even though the travelers in Holland were kept well-informed about the atmosphere of catastrophe at home, Eberhard seemed unshaken. In a letter to Monika von Hollander he wrote: "Take courage. We must no longer look at the small things. We must be so gripped and filled by what is great that it permeates the small things and alters them…Our life will not be on a narrower, but on a broader plane; not more confined but more boundless; not more structured but more flexible; not more pedantic, but more generous."

The Arnolds returned from Holland on August 2. As he was leaving Bilthoven, Eberhard was approached by Maria Mojen, daughter of an Indonesian prince. She pressed an envelope into his hands: "For the cause."[24] Inside was a substantial sum in Dutch currency – exactly the amount necessary to repay the bank loan. On arriving in Frankfurt the following morning, Eberhard went straight to the bank and paid off the loan. A new loan was granted to keep the publishing house in business. At noon the family continued on to Schlüchtern. Monika von Hollander, Suse Hungar, and Gertrud Dalgas awaited them at the station with discouraged faces. In Sannerz itself the family received a very cool reception. There was cake for the children – they could not be blamed, the faultfinders said. But for the adults, nothing but watery soup.

A meeting was set for eight o'clock in the evening. Heinrich

Schultheis had invited others – even from outside the community – to attend. Helpers and guests, some of whom had only been in Sannerz a few days, also took part. The meeting was held in the dining room with everyone seated on the floor (chairs were regarded as "bourgeois" by the community at this time). Inquisitive spectators, including SCM members from a regional conference in Schlüchtern, gathered outside the open windows. Once the spectators were in place the meeting commenced with a barrage of complaints. Irresponsibility and fraudulent business management were among the mildest of the accusations. Finally one of the outside onlookers shouted through the window that he had heard that Eberhard had run off with the money box. At this Eberhard broke into the discussion for the first time. He demanded that such untrue rumors be clearly refuted. A statement in this vein was worked out during the night. The next morning all the members of the Neuwerk community signed an apology to Eberhard and declared themselves jointly responsible for the development of the business up to that very day.[25]

Incredible as it may seem after such a trying ordeal, Eberhard still presented his long-planned talk on Colossians to the SCM conference in Schlüchtern that same evening. Obviously worn out, but fully concentrated, he maintained his composure in the face of extremely suspicious and challenging looks. Even harder to believe, Eberhard did not refer with so much as a word to the happenings in Sannerz.

The Minimum Number

Back in May of 1922 a committee of auditors had certified and confirmed Eberhard and Else von Hollander's business accounts. Obviously the accusation of fraudulent management was completely groundless, and it was soon dropped. Yet some of the accusers persisted with a bitterness and an irrational hatred.

The hatred was mainly directed against Eberhard. The few who remained loyal to him had to meet with derision and deliberate unkindness. A guest at Sannerz noted that "people are crying all day here; others are on the verge of mental breakdown – poor Sunhearts!"[26]

The formal structure of the Neuwerk cooperative was self-destructing. Heinrich Schultheis and the treasurer, Kurt Ernst Harder, were both authorized signatories. Knowing that two-thirds of the community supported them, they took the daily business transactions into their own hands. Eberhard did nothing to resist this icy takeover, silently bearing the insults and furious outbreaks of former "brothers and sisters." Gertrud Dalgas later wrote that she watched him "with trembling awe."

Eberhard intervened in the humiliating clamor only when the topic of conversation turned, without any word of protest, to a complete revision or even dissolution of the community. To Eberhard this attitude was intolerable, and he felt compelled to confront it. Together with a small remnant of the membership he agreed that the community should be maintained on its original course. The crucial question of which of the two groups should take over the house in Sannerz brought matters to a head. The continuation of the formal structure of the Neuwerk cooperative played into this because, when the house had been rented, Eberhard and Emmy had signed the contract with Konrad Paul in the legal name of the cooperative. To maintain the legal form of the cooperative, as well as the contract, would require the support of at least seven of the twenty-three eligible voting members. The count was taken: Eberhard and Emmy Arnold, Else von Hollander, Monika von Hollander, Suse Hungar, Gertrud Dalgas, and Paul Hummel – the minimum number.[27]

Chapter Ten

That peace be given –	Dass Friede werde –
Earth shall be God's kingdom,	Gottes Reich die Erde
His possession –	Ganz besitze,
That hearts be moved,	Dass alle Herzen
Free from hate to others,	Frei von Hasses Schmerzen
Men become brothers:	Brüder werden:
We pledge this union,	Den Bund beschwöre,
Friend or foe now harken	Freund wie Gegner höre
To this watchword.	Diese Losung.
In Jesus' purity	In Christus Reinheit –
Is bond and friendship,	Das ist unserer Einheit,
Is our unity.	Bund und Freundschaft.

Sannerz, 1922.

A New Beginning

Six unbearable weeks of depressing quiet dragged by after the future of the Sannerz Neuwerk cooperative had been settled. In October of 1922 Heinrich Schultheis's group moved to a former girls' school in Gelnhaar. Others tried to return to their previous middle-class lives. The Habertshof settlement took over most of the book titles from the publishing house as well as the magazine, *Das Neue Werk*. The Sannerz household had been stripped virtually bare, the farm buildings emptied; two presumptuous young guests had even sold off the cattle to a livestock dealer at well below their real value. A small but resolute group was all that remained of the Sannerz community.[1]

Eberhard and Else wasted no time in picking up the pieces and continued the publishing work under the name Community Publishing House Eberhard Arnold.[2] (After May 1924 the name would become the Eberhard Arnold Publishing House, Sannerz and Leipzig.)[3] The publishing work was crucial to the group's survival, and its continuation was only possible because Kees Boeke wanted the money still available from his foundation to be used specifically for furthering the community and its publishing work in a pacifist and early Christian direction. Of what had once been a very attractive selection of Neuwerk books, only six titles remained with Eberhard's publishing house: Max Bürck's *From State Churches to a Religion for Humanity;* Julius Goldstein's *Race and Politics,* a book on the roots and background of anti-Semitism, which attracted much attention; Eugen Jäckh's *Blumhardt Anthology;* the *Legends* collection by Fritz Schloss; Eberhard's pamphlet *Love and the Life of Love;* and lastly, Otto Herpel's book *Zinzendorf: On Faith and Life,* to which he gave the Sannerz community the publishing rights.[4] At the beginning of 1923 a sad-looking Otto Herpel arrived at Sannerz to deliver his monograph on Hans Denck and said, "Eberhard, the dead are being disinterred and the living buried." Herpel remained a friend of the Arnolds until his unexpected death in 1925.

Motives

Was Eberhard's attitude during the crisis of August 1922 entirely out of touch with the world? Was it irresponsible? Or even dishonest and fraudulent, as his accusers declared? Looking back across the decades, is his attitude any more comprehensible? Or does it remain inexplicable, the eccentricity of an obstinate visionary, regretfully discarded by the majority?

If the expression "out of touch with the world" is taken literally, one could conclude from Eberhard's own words that he undoubtedly had taken his standards from another world: "For us, the living experience of Christ is identical with the living expectation of his future coming, so that what has already been accomplished or achieved – however it may be termed – pales before what is here and now and what is to come."[5]

"Our inner fire, our enthusiasm, our emotions, and even eros – all must be merged with the one great light, with the heart of God, and must gain new life with Jesus Christ and be newly born in him…Everything to do with desire, possessions, the will for power, or selfish demands is consumed by this blazing sun. The old world disappears…the new one, a new creation, is born with its sacrificial, all-embracing, generous love of God and joy in God."[6] Such an attitude is certainly alien to this world. In the moment of greatest tension at Sannerz, when the majority feared for their economic future, Eberhard's message was: "Work for the joy of it. Trust, and base your livelihood on trust."[7]

Max Wolf, owner of a Schlüchtern factory, had hit the nail on the head in the general meeting of the Neuwerk Publishing House on August 4, 1922, when he had stated that "what divides Eberhard from the other members is his conviction that faith must determine all earthly conditions, even economic ones." Four years later, the head administrator *(Landrat)* of the Fulda District would be curious to know what had happened during the crisis. Eberhard would explain that "those people" – by far the majority of the household community – "were unwilling to recognize that miracles, too, are a basis for economic existence."[8] Eberhard never made economic existence dependent on miracles, but neither did he exclude them – and he certainly experienced them.

In August of 1922 Eberhard Arnold had not had any choice: to side with the majority would have meant betraying everything that mattered to him, everything that had guided his life for so many years. Who would have profited? Nobody. Who would have been harmed? All who had linked their hopes for a practical, genuine discipleship of Jesus to the Sannerz community experiment, and all those who looked to Eberhard as a personal example of such discipleship.

Some may possibly be disturbed, even repulsed, by the pathos in Eberhard's 1935 recollection of the 1922 Neuwerk crisis:

On the very first stretch of our way we encountered times of testing, of hostility. Groups of friends – some closer than others, but all friends who had been very dear to our hearts – turned away from us and became enemies of the way…Even if the majority of our friends deserted us right and left, even if there was mass desertion from the lifted banner of unity and freedom…it could make no difference: with our own children and with the children entrusted to us we had to go forward, and ever forward – we had to push through to the goal![9]

Enemies of the way, mass desertion – this sounds harsh and exaggerated. But from an objective viewpoint it is neither. In this respect Eberhard had once again taken Jesus and his message in earnest and had reckoned with meeting difficulties and making enemies. The gospel polarizes. It demands a wholehearted yes. A halfhearted yes amounts to a no. The Sannerz community began with a group of people who had said yes. They had dedicated their lives to a common cause. Together they had felt the presence of the risen Christ in the Sannerz community household, and they had rejoiced in it. They had established such a degree of mutual trust that they could not go back on it without inflicting deep wounds on each other and injuring themselves. Indeed, some who left turned into embittered critics and opponents. Others simply erased the communal episode at Sannerz from their biographies. What better words to describe this than "desertion" or "flight," or even, as Gertrud Dalgas put it, "treason"? Eberhard's disappointment was justified. At the same time some relief can be sensed: they had overcome, after all, and weathered the crisis. Life once more moved forward "toward the goal" – a great goal, one that compensated for all trials and testing, one that could be lived out every day: "unity and freedom."

A Moral Victory?

A look at what happened to former companions and to the Neuwerk movement is revealing. The community attempt by Heinrich Schultheis and his supporters failed within a few months. Under Hermann Schafft's direction, the periodical *Das Neue Werk* continued with a slightly altered name, *Neuwerk.* Schafft kept it on a respectable and economically sound basis, but the magazine never regained its wide influence or provoked the level of discussion that it had raised during the stormy beginning years.[10] The Habertshof, highly praised by the "realists," evolved into a resident adult education center. Certainly it still carried out an important task, one that Eberhard supported, but the ideal had turned into an institution, the movement into a business. As a result in May 1931 Eberhard would retire from the Habertshof board. Ultimately, in 1934, the National Socialists would annex the Habertshof for the Hitler Youth, placing it at the service of their new social order.

Eberhard never felt any sense of triumph or even satisfaction over these developments. Malice and self-justification were foreign to his nature. He had already redefined his relationship to the whole Neuwerk movement after the 1922 Pentecost conference at Wallroth, and he maintained this attitude after the crisis that August. The Sannerz community household, as Eberhard had put it, considered itself "a piece of the splintered wedge." But even these splinters sometimes had an effect. The community continued, quite officially registered as the Sannerz Neuwerk cooperative. It was perhaps the most remarkable, and certainly the earliest-formed, of all the regional and urban groups connected with the Neuwerk movement.

How Eberhard weathered the crisis personally can best be guessed from his poems. In his fourteen-verse "Twilight Deepens" he expresses the bitter experiences of those August days: hollowness, envy,

The household at Sannerz on the villa's front porch, 1924.

quarreling, poison, misinterpretations, strife between brothers. In the eighth verse, quite unexpectedly, are the words "the morning dawns." Symbolic sunrise – truth breaks in; love is victorious. At the poem's end he states emphatically, "The Lord reigns." This certainty kept Eberhard from falling into self-destructive brooding, a danger he shared with Emmy.[11] Without question he was not immune to these moments. For over half a year he fought attacks of self-doubt and depression. Not until Pentecost of 1923 would he feel free and happy enough to quote Ulrich von Hutten: "It is a joy to live; minds and hearts are awaking." Not until May of 1923 could he formulate in a poem the redeeming line: "I start again to live anew."[12]

Eberhard was no super-hero. The breakup of the Sannerz community sapped his strength and was sometimes more than he could bear. The fact that he showed such self-control to the outward eye, that his rocklike certainty always won the day, can only be explained by his faith. In ways difficult to understand he had been prepared for the controversy. He was not simply caught unawares, unsuspecting and defenseless, in the face of accusations. Eberhard had seen beyond the crisis even before it reached its peak. How was that possible? A plausible answer is that he never took his eyes off the ultimate, far-reaching goal.

The Blumhardts

One cannot speak of Eberhard's perception of that final goal without noting the influence the two Blumhardts exercised on his faith and thinking.

As a nineteenth-century pastor of Möttlingen in the Black Forest, Johann Christoph Blumhardt experienced the might of demonic forces, but still more powerfully the liberating strength of Jesus Christ.[13] "Jesus is victor" was his watchword. A movement of repentance and renewal arose in his parish, one fruit of which was healing of the sick. Blumhardt took Jesus' words about the approaching kingdom of God very seriously; the kingdom of God became the central theme of his theology. He had not developed this theology sitting in his study. It was rooted in his pastoral experiences in Möttlingen and later, when church authorities made his work there impossible, in Bad Boll, on the edge of the Swabian Alps. His son Christoph Friedrich

Blumhardt followed in his footsteps and further developed his father's theology of the kingdom of God.[14]

Both Blumhardts insisted that the kingdom of God must be effective here and now, not just in the afterlife. In their opinion, to comfort people by pointing to the hereafter narrowed and distorted the gospel. Christoph Friedrich Blumhardt went so far as to refuse to accept the inevitability of sickness, premature death, and unjust conditions. Because of his concern for the working class and its estrangement from the church he joined the Social Democratic party and was a member of the Württemberg parliament for several years. But parliamentary rules and partisan bickering and intrigue remained foreign to him. As a citizen and ambassador of the kingdom of God he felt committed to obey other laws and another code of conduct. Christoph Friedrich Blumhardt died in 1919. But in Bad Boll, the center of the two Blumhardts' activities, the witness of their lives and the spirit they embodied remained tangible for many years.

Eberhard may have become aware of the Blumhardts as early as 1910 through the writings of Hermann Kutter.[15] In all events Eberhard was at least familiar with their work and writings before the end of the war. Echoes from the Blumhardts' kingdom-of-God theology can be clearly distinguished in his arguments at the 1919 student conferences.[16] Perhaps Christoph Friedrich Blumhardt's example removed Eberhard's last hesitation about closer contact with socialism, communism, and the working-class movement. Toward the end of his days in Berlin, Eberhard tried in vain to convince the Furche Publishing House to print a book on the Blumhardts. In 1920, as he and Otto Herpel selected themes to be emphasized in the work of the Neuwerk Publishing House, they included the witness of the two Blumhardts. Eberhard easily recognized that Karl Barth had borrowed certain ideas from Johann Christoph Blumhardt and had included them in his monumental commentary on the apostle Paul's letter to the Romans. This recognition showed Eberhard his own inner affinity with Barth, which is the reason he persisted so urgently in his efforts to gain Barth's cooperation for *Das Neue Werk*.

At the beginning of 1921 Eberhard successfully solicited the pastor of Öhring, Eugen Jäckh, as editor for a Blumhardt anthology. Jäckh had been Christoph Friedrich Blumhardt's former coworker and the administrator of his literary estate. After visiting Sannerz in July of 1921 Jäckh described Eberhard as "…free from self, free from every alien admixture, whether from the political, party-oriented side, or from the mystical side (Steiner!) or any other."[17] The anthology appeared at Christmas of 1921. It was entitled *Blumhardt: On the Kingdom of God.*[18]

The Blumhardts' thoughts on the kingdom of God surfaced in Eberhard's talks and actions. They dovetailed perfectly with his own understanding of the Sermon on the Mount and the words of Jesus. Eberhard lived in vital expectation of the things to come and did more than just speak about them; he banked on the present reality of the kingdom of God. Johannes Harder, a frequent guest at Sannerz during 1923 and 1924, would later say of Eberhard, "This man literally lived in the future. His longing for a new earth made him wish that heaven would no longer be relegated to the hereafter but would become a reality in the present world. I have hardly ever heard anyone pray the petition 'Thy kingdom come' in the Lord's Prayer as fervently as this ascetic did."[19] That consciousness is one of the secrets underlying the life and faith of Eberhard Arnold.

The Fellowship of Reconciliation

Under Eberhard's leadership in the early 1920s, the "Sunheart House" in Sannerz had quickly become a center of international contacts and reconciliation. Eberhard had kept in touch with both German and English Quakers, including Walter Koch, John Stephens, and Joan Mary Fry, from as far back as the time of the "open evenings" in Steglitz. In 1914 the English Quakers had formed the Fellowship of Reconciliation (FOR). After the war the Dutch Quaker Kees Boeke had taken the lead in building up the FOR on an international scale. Under the label "Christian International," the FOR met in the fall of 1919 at Kees and Betty Boeke's home in Bilthoven, near Utrecht, Holland. The German representatives were Walter Koch and Friedrich Siegmund-Schultze. On December 19 Otto Herpel published a detailed report in *Das Neue Werk*.

Eberhard missed the second conference in July 1920 as well as the first. (The invitation was lost in the mail.) He sent a message to the conference, however, declaring his support. Not until January of 1921 did Eberhard finally make personal contact with FOR representatives, first in Sannerz and a few weeks later in Bilthoven.[20] There he came into contact with Christian pacifists from England, France, Belgium, the United States, Hungary, Austria, and Denmark. Afterwards some of them appeared as guests in Sannerz.

For his part Eberhard agreed to serve on the FOR's executive committee and to speak at its national conferences – he would do so in Freudenstadt in 1924, on the Habertshof in 1925, and in Oberammergau in 1926. But he did more than just talk: "Action speaks louder than words." On one occasion during those years of social unrest Eberhard literally stepped between two antagonistic groups – government soldiers on one side, workers on the other – armed with nothing but a white flag, his own courage, and his powers of persuasion. He held true to the example of Jesus: anyone who guards his own life is unable to be a peacemaker; a person who always stays at a safe distance will never get his message across to others.

When it came to reconciliation, the real touchstone was the life together in community. "If you want to rid the world of hate, you must stop hating and begin to love." Eberhard was absolutely clear on this point. "If love is not practiced in a small group, then pacifism is an empty term. The will for peace must be proved in daily life. We are not interested in a general pacifism, only in pacifism that will permeate a person's whole life with the spirit of goodness."[21] Eberhard himself was actually very strong-willed by nature, a born fighter. He could shout at people and hurt them with his sharp words. Gertrud Dalgas once related that at every Lord's Supper Eberhard used to ask forgiveness for his outbursts and at times hurtful behavior. He put reconciliation into practice.

Neither Eberhard's participation in the struggle for reconciliation nor the continued further development of the community household in Sannerz can be imagined without the support and friendship of Kees and Betty Boeke. Kees Boeke was born in Alkmaar, Holland, in 1884, but he had been raised in England among revivalist Quakers. There he found faith in Jesus Christ. Like Eberhard, Kees applied his faith to the world around him. He became an engineer, worked for a time at a mission school in Syria, but returned to England at the beginning of the war. In England he became acquainted with Beatrice "Betty" Cadbury, the daughter of the well-known chocolate manufacturer and social reformer. Betty brought considerable wealth with her when she and Kees married.

The Boekes went far beyond the Cadburys in their ideas of social reform. They rejected all moneymaking activities and used Betty's inheritance to set up a charitable foundation. Theirs was a radical and "militant" pacifism. They refused to pay taxes, a decision that landed Kees in jail more than once. They joined marches through Dutch cities, singing peace songs. They published their own periodical and used its pages to agitate for disarmament. In Bilthoven they gathered a "Christian Brotherhood" and built a "Brotherhood House." It was a donation from the Boekes that had helped the Sannerz household community survive in August 1922 and had enabled the Community Publishing House Eberhard Arnold to make a new start. Orders for printing the Boekes' periodical, *De Streeder (The Combatants)*, and a Christian pacifist songbook in Dutch provided work and income in the difficult days of reorganizing the publishing house.

Traces of the interaction between Kees Boeke's work in the Brotherhood House and the Sannerz community also appear in the child care at Sannerz and in Eberhard's concept of education. Although he had never studied education Kees took an intense interest in educational questions. When Eberhard first met him Kees had just removed his four daughters from the Bilthoven Montessori School and had begun to home-school them. Eberhard and Emmy followed his example only a few months later.[22] In 1926 Kees Boeke founded an alternative school. In the Netherlands he is considered one of the most original and exceptional educators of this century.[23]

Children's Community

Caring for homeless children had been one motive for beginning the Sannerz household community. After the Wallroth conference in 1922 Eberhard had stated in an article published in *Das Neue Werk* that, among other things, a specific task of the communal life at Sannerz was "to give children an education and preparation for a life open to the influence of God's spirit."[24] It was precisely the urgent need to care for children that had sparked the controversy over fi-

"Kindergemeinde Sonnherz," a watercolor by Else von Hollander, ca. 1922.

nances which led to the split of August 1922. During the new building up of the community after the fall of 1922, serving children and seeking childlikeness remained one of the primary concerns.

Eberhard took child care so seriously because he had recognized Jesus' reverence for the childlike soul and Jesus' praise of childlike faith. At the end of 1920 Eberhard had written, "Everything the young people are struggling for – absolute truth and simplicity, lasting identification with the child's world and the warm glow of wholehearted love, life in the genuine spirit of community – is only possible if Christ fills us through and through and rules over us."[25] Time and again throughout his years of community life, Eberhard would seek the childlike faith that Jesus described – to become a child, to be a child, to remain a child.[26]

"We want not an institution, but a big family – the children's community as part of the adult community," was how Eberhard described the children's place within the community household.[27] Expectations and encouragement were to be suited to the children's ages. While still small they were given simple, easily supervised tasks around the house and garden and helped care for the animals. According to inclination each could learn to play a musical instrument, or could pursue craftwork or artistic activities. The community made this possible even in lean times. The children could explore nature and discover their surroundings. In the Fulda valley surrounding the community lay a great wealth of history, and to absorb it, they had to leave the classroom and hike out – a dry lecture would not have sunk in nearly as well.

Gertrud Dalgas (everyone called her "Trudi") had a particularly cheerful and enthusiastic nature and a good way with children. Eberhard had an eye for such gifts. He himself always liked to be with the children, and especially with the foster children. To them he was just as much "Eberpapa" as he was for Emy-Margret, Hardy, Heinrich, Hans-Hermann, and Monika. Sophie Löber, for example, came to Sannerz as a ten-year-old in the spring of 1924. She remarks, "Eberhard was a completely natural person, not at all studious and learned in his manner toward us. He was very simple and went along with our childlike way of talking. Eberhard did not want us merely to repeat what we heard. He found it very important that we expressed our own thoughts, however simply we did it."

Eberhard would not tolerate coercion of conscience, especially not in questions of faith. Neither would he let anything prevent him from holding his "morning hour" to help the children understand the Bible. He insisted that they use religious words and terms only sparingly. Rudi Hildel, who came to the Sannerz community as a seven-year-old orphan in 1927, recalls that little time was spent talking about religious matters: "They were something to be treated with reverence."

Eberhard taught some of the older children Latin. He took great pains to explain to them the purpose and advantages of such studies. But he was always ready for fun and games. In winter he built a hair-raising toboggan run with the older children. "He expected us to show courage," remembers Sophie Löber. "We had to be daring. There was no flabbiness; we had to be very brave."

In spite of his commanding height the children were not the least bit afraid of him. He detested threats, compulsion, and manipulation. He shared the revulsion of the youth movement to the coercive methods of educators who wanted to force young people to be good. Eberhard considered every form of physical or emotional coercion a declaration of educational bankruptcy.[28] But he also knew how to make a point firmly – about keeping things tidy, for example: "He was an orderly person and always represented that we should be orderly," remembers Rudi Hildel. Eberhard took time for the children in the community, even when it meant adding an extra hour to his evening schedule in order to catch up on other activities. He was always up to date on the experiences, the progress, and the minor and major worries of each child. His principle: "To educate means to awaken. The innermost secret of all areas of life must be opened up to the children. Their instinct for what is essential and divine in everything and behind everything must be awakened and strengthened."[29]

Eberhard and the teachers watched in wonder as the children's group actually came to such a "free awakening of a conscience for Christ." Through this process a community developed freely under its own leadership: the children's community. And within the children's community there was yet another movement: Heinrich and the children in his age group spontaneously formed the *Sonnentrupp* ("Suntroop"), wrote songs about Jesus, put together their own code of honor, undertook responsibility, and astonished the adults with profound insights and imaginative suggestions. Theirs was an energetic group. The community children formed openhearted friendships in the village, included neighboring children in their games and singing as a matter of course, and had no trouble getting along with the students at the village Catholic school. Sannerz was only a small village, but it was not an island. No one was confined to the community household. For the children the Sunheart community of Sannerz was the freest and happiest place in the world.

Sonnenlieder

"*Sonnenlieder* is our strongest and most recent peace witness," wrote Eberhard to Friedrich Wilhelm Foerster on May 8, 1924. "A strong note of faith in peace and hope for peace runs through all our songs." This was the way the Eberhard Arnold Publishing House released the *Sonnenlieder,* a book containing a hundred songs spanning eight centuries.[30]

Hardly another document tells more about life in the Neuwerk community at Sannerz, about the spiritual directions that came together there, and about the people who came and went in the first years. If nothing else were known of Eberhard and Emmy except that this collection of songs was a product of their life and communal work, much could still be deduced from it:

Sannerz must have been an inspiring place. Twenty-five of the songs originated in the three and a half years of community life following the summer of 1920. Fiery songs that radiated boundless confidence and reflected deep experiences and difficult crises. The people who lived there must have been full of sensitivity and humor to write and sing such songs. Songs like "A wanderer's staff of gold," "Let's walk in the open country," and "Early at cockcrow" suggest that they

154   must have loved nature, been avid hikers, and been early risers.

The people of Sannerz must have had access to specialized libraries. Their songs show their deep-rooted interest in Reformation history (*Sonnenlieder* contains Anabaptist songs from the sixteenth century, as well as the original arrangements of chorales by Luther), in the Moravian Brethren, and in believers and saints and mystics of every century (St. Ambrose, St. Francis, Tersteegen, and others).

Sannerz must have had connections with modern pietism and the revival movement. This is proved by songs they reprinted from a range of songbooks including *Reichslieder (Kingdom Songs)* and *Rettungsjubel (Joy in Salvation)*. The people of Sannerz were active in social issues, opposed war, and loved peace. They demanded the overthrow of class differences and looked forward to the coming of God's kingdom.

Pages from *Sonnenlieder*. Edited by Emmy Arnold and published in 1924, it contained songs from a vast spectrum of movements and sources.

Sonnenlieder is probably the only songbook in the world in which the combative socialist song "Brothers, strive for the sun, for freedom"[31] is happily bound together between "Come, thou bright and morning star" and "Work, for the night is coming."

The book sold extremely well in spite of, or perhaps because of, its unique selection and presentation of songs. Its effect cannot be overestimated. Even Carl Franklin Arnold expressed appreciation to his son:

> I am very happy that this beautiful, pleasing volume has made its appearance in the world. Thank you for this valuable present; the binding, the paper, the type, the way the music is engraved, and the illustrations are all a delight. The wealth of meaning behind the symbols brings the character and aims of the Sannerz household to the eye of the beholder...I must admit, however, that much in the book is alien to me and will always remain alien. I respect your tendency to all-embracing love – only it should not be an offense to others.[32]

This letter shows that Eberhard's father had come to peace about his son's way of life, even though he still could not reconcile himself to "pacifism, communism, empathy with the Jewish people, rejection of the church, compulsory abstinence," and even though Carl Franklin still prayed every evening for the salvation of his unbaptized grandchildren's souls. In the academic field he had long recognized his son as his equal. Since Eberhard's days at the Furche Publishing House they had kept up a regular exchange of bibliographic information, books, articles, and reviews.

Regrowth

Eberhard continued to present lectures that were held in high regard. His venues included Frankfurt, Hannover, Leipzig, Stuttgart, and Nordhausen in the Harz Mountains. In Nordhausen an active group of young Baptists had gathered around a married couple named Adolf and Martha Braun. They were part of a wider youth movement among the Baptists which had taken the name *"Weggenossen"* (literally, "companions along the way"). Adolf Braun, born in 1893, was a surveyor by profession and ran a small farm. As a soldier during World War I, he had read Eberhard's *War: A Call to Inwardness.* He was a friend of Heinrich Euler, a Baptist pastor and an original member of the "Early Church" movement.[33] Since January of 1923 Adolf Braun had been in correspondence with Eberhard and had visited Sannerz a number of times, both by himself and with other young *Weggenossen* members. In January and March of 1924 he had asked Eberhard to speak in Nordhausen and had opened the door for further meetings in Baptist circles in Saxony. What motivated him and what he heard from Eberhard came from one and the same source. "The world is crying out for acts, not tracts," Adolf Braun wrote in his invitation to a June 1924 conference:[34] "It is not important that we know a lot or that we organize and achieve a lot – the motivating power is what counts."

Eberhard spoke at this conference too.[35] The main part of his speech, however, consisted of readings from the old Hutterian confessions of faith and from directives for church order.[36] Afterwards Adolf and Martha Braun accompanied the guest speaker back to Sannerz. Then and there they decided to join the community, and they moved to Sannerz with their two little girls in 1924.[37] The Brauns were the first family to join the community after the 1922 crisis.

Chapter Eleven

"Humanity must turn around. What good are all its religious practices, what good are all its church services, what point is there in all its devout singing if God's will is not done and hands remain steeped in blood? What does people's faith mean if injustice is done to the poor as casually as one drinks a glass of water? What good is it to profess the divine if not even a little finger is lifted when countless children and poor people die?"

From "God and the Future of Humanity," a lecture given in October 1924, in Lichtenstein, Saxony.

Die Wegwarte

When Adolf and Martha Braun moved to Sannerz they brought along not only their children but also their connection to the Baptist youth group *Weggenossen* as well. And indirectly they brought *Die Wegwarte,* the magazine of the Baptist Youth Movement.[1] Begun in 1923, *Die Wegwarte* was published and edited by Maria Grossmann until she withdrew on friendly terms in May 1925. From June on the Eberhard Arnold Publishing House issued the magazine, with Adolf Braun as editor. At last the community had regained the means to supply information to their friends, to win new supporters, and to present the community's concerns for discussion. They did not inherit a very large circulation, and it certainly never equaled that of *Das Neue Werk.* Few articles bear Eberhard's name, but his characteristic style is often noticeable in articles by the "community household at Sannerz."

Die Wegwarte carried traces of Eberhard's development, just as *Die Furche* and then *Das Neue Werk* had in earlier years. But now these were not only tracks of his personal development; more frequently he spoke on behalf of the community. It is significant that in speaking

Die wegwarte

Monatsschrift der Weggenossen, des Freideutschen Werkbundes und des Sannerzer Bruderhofes
Herausg. von Eberhard Arnold, Adolf Braun und Gertrud Dalgas

3. Jahrgang. 8./9. Heft   Mai/Juni 1927

for the community Eberhard did not consider himself the leader of the community per se, but rather simply "word leader." He was the spokesman who expressed the common conviction of the community. He summed up whatever inspired, burdened, or moved the community. Almost imperceptibly his own person stood out less and less. Nonetheless what he now said and wrote was important and sharply defined. It is as though Eberhard merged more and more into the community, but without losing his own personality.

Gemeinde

Gemeinde takes center stage as the great, overarching theme of Eberhard Arnold's fourth decade. What is *Gemeinde*? It is church-community. What is the true character of *Gemeinde*? How, where, and when does it come into existence? It would be erroneous to say that Eberhard had not had any conception of *Gemeinde* in his earlier years. Very early on, in fact, he had formulated an understanding of what *Gemeinde* is not: "Not an institutional church, not a sect."[2] He already considered *Gemeinde* as something supernatural, beyond and above the natural world – something that surpassed the bounds of human understanding.

Eberhard never presumed to have plumbed this mystery. He was simply a chronicler, a spokesman seeking for words to express what had transpired in the community life at Sannerz. Where the mystery of the church-community was concerned, no comparison was too colorful for him: *Gemeinde* germinates and blossoms in secret; it is an unspoken reality. It is "the noblest and tenderest form of all possibilities of community on earth."[3] He coined the phrase *"werdende Gemeinde"* – "*Gemeinde* that is coming into being"[4] – and spoke of "a fellowship of voluntary dedication that strives for *Gemeinde*." *Gemeinde* is always in the process of being birthed and, therefore, demands intense struggle. "Life in community cannot be confused with the church of Christ itself…The mystery of *Gemeinde* is different and greater." It penetrates the community "whenever open and willing hearts are granted that indescribable strength of longing which God needs if he alone is to act and speak." *Gemeinde* cannot be compelled into being, nor is it at our beck and call. When it actually occurs, it is both a mystery and a gift.

At Easter of 1925 Eberhard described such moments in a circular to the community's friends and supporters: "Sometimes people were so deeply struck and shaken that an element of God broke in. It led to community experiences of the most profound kind. We felt our guilt and at the same time the grace that comes to us from Christ himself. We sensed something of what it means that 'the kingdom of God is among you.'"[5]

Eberhard realized that this *Gemeinde* experience was not limited to any particular form, not even to a particular lifestyle such as community of goods. In the same connection he spoke of the "unheard-of riches and variety of tasks and gifts." He was open to every movement and group so long as such a group "leads toward Christ and truly serves the whole, the *Gemeinde,* the coming kingdom." The more he sensed the "invisible reality and unity of *Gemeinde*" in Sannerz and elsewhere, the more reverence he felt for the *Gemeinde* and its members.[6] With holy awe and restraint Eberhard sought to impart this reverence to others. Towards the end of his life this task became increasingly important to him.

Attempts at Uniting

In keeping with his expectation that the kingdom of God would spread through small cell groups, work fellowships, and settlements across the country, Eberhard always took a great interest in movements spiritually akin to Sannerz. He envisioned that God's kingdom would come into being through such community cells, which would "quietly and without fanfare establish living relationships" in even the smallest details of life and would finally grow together organically as "the community of members in one single body." He was not worried that this "single body" might be artificially tacked or glued together. When unity arose, it would be through God's spirit alone. The "gift of perfect unity" could only be granted "through the Creator's spirit of love."[7]

Once again Eberhard was not content with philosophizing. The Habertshof offered the nearest possibility for an attempt at uniting. From the very first day in Sannerz, Eberhard had tried to work with the Habertshof leader, Max Zink, to find opportunities for more contact and cooperation between the two communities. In February of 1922 the Habertshof cooperative received Eberhard's proposal for an "immediate, unconditional uniting."[8] "Unconditional" meant that Eberhard actually put his own future and that of the Sannerz community into the hands of the Habertshof. At this point the Sannerz community was sincerely ready to move there lock, stock, and barrel, to integrate its work with the work of the Habertshof, and to fit in and fall in step. But the Habertshof rejected the suggestion, and the Neuwerk crisis of late summer 1922 put an end to the question.

The next opportunity to pursue uniting came in August of 1924 after the *Weggenossen* conference. Adolf and Martha Braun were with Eberhard as he composed a letter to the *"werdende Gemeinde"* of Neusonnefeld. "We are sending you the urgent request that you live and work in community with us so that, from now on, we act in unanimity with you in our daily life and in everything else. All questions of detail are subordinate to the profound awareness of our oneness of heart. Unanimity will be given to us in everything," Eberhard wrote. Once again there were no conditions, nothing held back; for the sake of unity the Sannerz community was willing to put everything on the line – be it a move from Sannerz to Neusonnefeld or vice-versa, or the establishment of a completely new community in a third location.

But this attempt met with no response either. Both proposals to unite can hardly have been rejected on practical grounds. Possibly, though, Eberhard himself presented a dichotomy: as the chief proponent of uniting, he also may have been the primary obstacle to it.

Who would have led a combined Sannerz-Habertshof settlement? What role would Eberhard have played in a united Neusonnefeld-Sannerz youth group? Would there have been any place for Neusonnefeld's leader, Hans Klassen? On other occasions Eberhard's special gifts and character prevented closer cooperation with similarly strong personalities.[9] Yet, undaunted, he made such attempts time and time again for the sake of the cause.

The Free Germans

What was sought in vain with other Christian communal settlements – a unity of aim and action – was almost attained with sections of the Free German Youth.[10] In order to understand the glowing enthusiasm of Eberhard's involvement with the Free German movement, it is necessary to look back at 1920. At that time he defended his contacts with the Free Germans by saying, "I relate to them as a missionary in Japan would relate to groups in that country that are spiritually awake and interested in religion…I am grateful for every door I can find open among relatively honest, simple, and receptive people, and there is such a door for me here."[11] It is no longer possible to establish the date Eberhard became a formal member of the Free German Fellowship.

A brief ten years after the first Festival of Free German Youth in 1913, the Free German Fellowship and related movements again sent out invitations for a Hohe Meissner youth conference at the end of August 1923. Eberhard served on the planning committee.[12] About twenty-five hundred young (or young-at-heart) people accepted the invitation. The conference took place during the struggle against the French occupation of the Ruhr district. The popular sentiment of the gathering echoed the national outrage: "Our Germany, profoundly humiliated and mistreated, shall show the newly emerging world that it wants to help in constructing a better order for humanity." All the previously touted unity soon evaporated, however, when the meetings actually took place. Young representatives of the Communist party broke up several workshops. At times the conference was chaotic.

Nevertheless, in an article for the SCM newsletter, Eberhard commented that "deeply divided and fragmented as it is, the youth movement in all its sections lives and continues as an arena where the ultimate powers strive for decision…Truly the whole movement displays a religious striving and seeking." He appreciated the Free German creed of truthfulness: "There is no decision for truthfulness without God himself having a part in it. A person who lives by the truth will experience that moment when he hears the voice that is truth." Eberhard felt certain that the Free German movement was on a sound course. The "Communist drive for the last battle"[13] had been rejected at the Meissner conference, as had the attempts of "old leaders" to tie the movement down to a particular political agenda.

As an outcome of the conference a document was composed containing a number of significant passages in Eberhard's handwriting. "The Challenge to Us," as it was titled, voiced a call to action in response to the need of the time:

> We believe in a future of fellowship among nations and among all humankind prompting a responsible freedom of the individual for the whole…We believe that when all has been shattered, inner authority must be born from the ultimate depths of existence, for without it our activity is pointless and ineffective…We therefore believe the most important task…of the Free German Movement is to live in the light of eternal truth, even though it is as yet incomplete…It is vital that groups are formed to go out to bring brotherly help wherever needed…and to proclaim the coming eternal order![14]

Four other conference leaders signed their names to this "challenge" along with Eberhard – but one organizer, Knud Ahlborn, did not. Ahlborn rejected the call for a "different order in public life"; he wanted to hold a tight rein on the younger generation as it surged ahead and to ensure that the influence of the original founders – especially his – remained intact. By the time Eberhard and Erich Mohr, leader of the Free German Fellowship's Berlin group, called a New Year's Day emergency meeting of the Fellowship's executive committee, the battle lines had been drawn. Ahlborn and his supporters boycotted the meeting. The final act of this tragedy took place at Easter of 1924, when two Free German Fellowship conferences met simultaneously: Ahlborn and his supporters gathered separately, while Erich

Mohr and the other "challengers" met on the Jugendburg at Ludwigstein (about twenty miles east of Kassel). There on the mountainside the Free German Union was born.

But Eberhard did not attend. He celebrated Easter in the Sannerz community. A few days after Easter he resigned from Ahlborn's Free German Fellowship. And at Pentecost he and all the adult members of the Sannerz community joined the new Free German Union. In July, Eberhard was asked to lead the "circle of elders." This put him at Erich Mohr's side, building up the Union.

What drew Eberhard to this group? What kept him in it for over seven years? Did this group offer anything besides an ever-deepening friendship with Erich Mohr? For one thing, Eberhard could always count on finely tuned ears in that circle – and lively, frank, and controversial discussions as well. He found a common urge to "become true men." It seems that adherents of the Free German Union refused to sidestep any question, religious or political, however difficult the consequences might be. These were the same type of people who had left their mark on the Neuwerk movement's stormy beginning. Among these idealists Eberhard saw an opening for the same task he had described back in 1920 with respect to the Youth Movement: "It is tremendously important that we find the right way of pointing these people who seek God to the one and only way, which is Christ."[15]

The Free German Union agreed to the Easter 1924 statement of purpose: "We want to model ourselves on the great figures and heralds of eternal powers." They reckoned Lao-tze, Tolstoy, Goethe, Gandhi, and others to be these role models, and they repeatedly included Jesus Christ in this list.[16] Eberhard seized this willingness to listen to the voice of Jesus in addition to the many other voices, doing all he could to help these young people learn of Christ's nature and way of life.[17] Eberhard organized conferences and projects at Sannerz. In the spring of 1925 the Free German Union considered buying a house in the village of Sannerz and setting it up as a fellowship house, but the idea was scrapped for lack of funds. In January of 1926 the Free German Union ceased publication of its newsletter and accepted

Eberhard's offer to publish its future announcements in the *Wegwarte*. Groups and individuals in the Free German Union sponsored foster children in the Sannerz community household. This growing interaction with the Free German Union coincided with Eberhard's attempts – most of them futile – to achieve an understanding of the Sannerz community among churches, SCM, and other religious groups. Even in the Neuwerk movement the Sannerz community was being pushed further and further aside during this time.

Spiritual Fight

When Eberhard Arnold looked at the youth movement he saw a raging battle that transcended the merely visible forms: "A most profound spiritual battle is being waged here, a preliminary skirmish between the vanguards in the great, decisive battle between the coming Christ and the anti-Christian glorification of man."[18] This same battle surfaced on occasion in the Sannerz household. In the summer of 1921, for example, Eberhard wrote to Normann Körber, "The stream of visitors that flows through our house brings to us much that is demonic and much that is divine. We are continually engaged in crucial struggles."

Eberhard stood watchful. He did not tolerate behavior or words that offended the spirit of community. When visitors introduced unhealthy spiritual elements to a conversation he opposed them immediately and decisively.[19] Demons, or unclean spirits as the Bible calls them, were not simply a figment of the imagination for Eberhard. He took them just as seriously as he took the victory of Jesus Christ over such powers. Experiences similar to those of the Blumhardts in Möttlingen and Bad Boll were not lacking in Eberhard's life. In her memoirs Emmy would write of visitors who could not bear the frank and truthful atmosphere in the community. In moments of worship and deepest gathering they would make compulsive disturbances, their faces twisting into uncontrollable grimaces. Eberhard tried firmly and lovingly to help such people. Some would not accept help and were asked to leave the community. Sometimes it took days or even weeks of struggle before the demonic elements were overcome. Then this victory would be reflected in Eberhard's poems, as in March 1925:

Up, join the battle now!
Up, with the hosts of Light,
United all!
Demons of darkness smite,
Break through a path for light!
Give all for truth and right,
Fighters to be!

Eberhard and the Sannerz community waged their longest and hard-

est battle on behalf of Lotte Henze, a young woman who came to
Sannerz in 1924 from the Braun's Baptist youth group. Eberhard's
report omitted all details that could have satisfied a thirst for
sensationalism:

> It was a great help to our little community that we saw the power
> to overcome demons demonstrated not only by the Blumhardts,
> but still more by the Christians of the first centuries. The dark ap-
> pearances and terrible blasphemies, the turmoil and raving mad-
> ness, the grip of evil on tormented people, the attack against faith
> and against the believers – all this can be broken only through the
> name of Jesus Christ, through witnessing to his story from the vir-
> gin birth and his words and deeds, to his crucifixion and resurrec-
> tion; only through the power and authority of the Holy Spirit.
> People are powerless here. Individual counseling is completely in-
> adequate. The church alone – no matter how small the gathering
> of dedicated believers who represent it – is empowered and given
> authority to command these spirits...When God's victory took
> place among us...some of us came to an experience of faith in
> God and a recognition of our human insignificance such as we
> had never known before...We became more and more certain of
> the power of the kingdom of God.[20]

Once more, *Gemeinde* had been at work – and this was not achieved
or merited by any one individual. It was God's victory, not Eberhard's. The community's struggle on behalf of Lotte Henze marks the
only instance that Eberhard would speak openly of "demonic possession." Eberhard approached such events with great caution; he found
them far too serious for anything less. Most importantly, Eberhard
grasped that such "preliminary skirmishes" were not isolated, remote
instances, but fit into a much larger context. A few years later this

helped him and the community recognize the demonic posturing behind the National Socialists' torchlit parades while most other Germans were still roaring their *Heil Hitlers!*

Sources

In 1924 Eberhard embarked on a tremendously ambitious publishing project, implementing an idea he had nurtured for many years: source books *(Quellen)*. He described the concept as "a series drawn from the living testimony of Christian witnesses across the centuries." He pictured a one-hundred-volume series that would give voice to Christian thinkers and writers of every hue, from the early church fathers to present-day luminaries. No one would be excluded – regardless of how contradictory or apparently irreconcilable they seemed:[21] the founder of the Jesuits, Ignatius of Loyola, side by side with "heretics" like John Huss and John Wycliffe. Pietists, mystics, reformers, and defenders of the faith. Each volume was to mirror "Christ in his holistic church." This concept inspired Eberhard to bind the volumes in all the colors of the rainbow. The project exceeded by several times the capacity of the Eberhard Arnold Publishing House. So Eberhard engaged the Berlin Hochweg Publishing House to undertake the production and business elements. He himself assumed the role of general editor and at first tried to win over Karl Barth as an advisor. Otto Herpel's existing volume on Zinzendorf was included in the series on the spot, and a new edition was published. So it came about that *Zinzendorf: On Faith and Life,* source book VII, was finished before any of the others.

For authors, Eberhard solicited competent theologians and highly specialized scholars. The volumes on the early seventeenth-century mystic Jakob Böhme, on Swedish theologian Søren Kierkegaard, on St. Francis of Assissi, and on others appeared between 1925 and 1926. In December of 1926 Eberhard added Volume I to the series, *The Early Christians after the Death of the Apostles.*[22] He had collected, translated, and written the commentary on these early Christian writings himself.

For the Sannerz community the source books project provided an assured occupation for many years to come as well as a literally inexhaustible supply of spiritual thought and inspiration. Everyone in the community was drawn in. Galley proofs were read aloud during jam making or potato sorting. Eberhard even had the community participate in selecting the passages to be included in *The Early Christians.*

In point of fact the groundwork necessary to assemble and prepare texts for consideration was a work demanding exceptional diligence. Eberhard and Else von Hollander evaluated hundreds of apocryphal writings and collected dozens of so-called "Lord's sayings" (words attributed to Christ but not included in the four Gospels). They tracked down obscure references from the writings of third- and fourth-century church fathers. Ultimately the most challenging undertaking for Eberhard was to put into understandable form the scholarly editions of apocryphal writings – previously all but inaccessible to the lay reader. Eberhard preceded the documents with a breathtaking summary of early Christianity between the years 70–180 A.D.

Even today this book has the power to transport the reader back to the time of triumphal arches and colonnades, to the time of Christian persecution and martyrdom – the time when the church was coming into being. A person with no prior interest in the beginnings of Christianity will find in the pages of *The Early Christians* a vivid portrayal of the immense power of the early Christians' faith and of the movement that flourished as a result of this faith. Eberhard himself was affected in this way: "For the editor, a clearly defined faith and way of life emerges from the manifestation of God in earliest Christian times. In contrast to later rigidity and shifts, this way continues to be a vital force today because it comes from the wellspring of living truth."

This attitude of faith and way of life is easily recognizable in Eberhard's own life: nonviolence, baptism of faith, and community of love and community of goods, the missionary status of believers.

Eberhard dedicated *The Early Christians* to his parents; the preface contained a special declaration of his love for his father.[23] Carl Franklin Arnold died on April 23, 1927, only a few months after the book was published.

Bruderhof

In addition to his occupation with the community, the Free German Union, and the work on the source books and on *The Early Christians,* Eberhard still found time and concentration to study the Anabaptists of the Reformation, and the Hutterian Brethren in particular. It is no coincidence that this intensive search for Anabaptist writings coincided with his strengthened interest in the secret of the *Gemeinde.*[24] As it comes into being a *Gemeinde* needs some kind of order. A communal life needs guidelines. But why, of all the possible groups to look to for direction, was Eberhard interested in the guidelines and way of life of a group that had disappeared from Middle Europe two centuries before? Perhaps, on second thought, this is really not so surprising. After all, he had gone back farther than that, finding models in the early Christian church. And he had already drawn inspiration from the Moravian Brethren, the Quakers, the Waldensians, and other movements.[25]

By the beginning of 1926 it was obvious how strongly Eberhard had come to identify with the Hutterian Brethren, and it was clear that his research on the life and fate of the Hutterian Church after

1528 probed far below the surface. In a letter from 1926 Eberhard spoke of a "Bruderhof" for the first time – in reference to the Sannerz community. Bruderhof, meaning "a place where brothers live," was the name used to describe the Hutterian Brethren's community settlements in Moravia, and later in Transylvania, in Russia, and, most recently, in Canada and the United States. For Eberhard to refer to the Sannerz community as a "Bruderhof" must have been the result of lengthy consideration. Moreover the community members must have **169** come to unity on this direction; they must have carefully and thoroughly evaluated the stony and demanding Hutterian way of *Gemeinde*, which requires that members submit themselves completely and crucify every bit of self-will.

"The secret of true self-determination lies in the freedom that results from surrendering oneself to the whole," wrote Eberhard in the name of the community household in October 1925. "Martyrdom by fire is the essence of community life: the daily sacrifice of all powers and all rights, and all the other claims that people usually make on life and take for granted." To the skeptical question of how anyone can voluntarily accept such a life, Eberhard provided an illuminating and complete answer. "The motivating force does not come from us as people. We were driven – and we continue to be driven. We act and continue to act because we are compelled to do so."[26]

Move to the Rhön

After the Brauns' arrival in 1924 the Sannerz community continued to grow. Soon the villa had become too small. "We want to move from here and to move quickly," Eberhard wrote to a friend early in 1926. "We do not yet know where to go, but we see clearly that our time and our task here are coming to an end. We hope to find a place in the Jena district or, in all events, in central Germany."[27] The search for a new home was underway. For a while Eberhard eyed a property in Schätzendorf on the edge of the Lüneburger moors, but this came to nothing.[28] On a visit to Sannerz a certain Traugott von Stackelberg offhandedly mentioned to Eberhard that the spa house at Bad Boll was up for sale. Von Stackelberg was enthusiastic about the idea of the Sannerz household carrying on the work of Christoph Friedrich Blumhardt, but Eberhard rejected this idea: "There are plenty of

Adolf Braun and
Eberhard Arnold
discuss a work
project at the Rhön
Bruderhof, 1928.

Christian institutions. What we want is a community of families that is founded on Christ."[29]

Not until late summer did hopes solidify into concrete reality. Near the small town of Neuhof a few miles northeast of Sannerz a large but neglected farm was for sale, the Hansehof. It was the largest of a group of seven farms in the Rhön region, known as the Sparhöfe.

The Sannerz community decided on the purchase without having any idea where the full payment of 26,000 marks would come from. Eberhard declared it "a step in faith" when he signed the contract in Fulda on November 19, 1926, with only the ten thousand marks for the down payment in hand.[30]

As far as Eberhard and the other members of the Sannerz Neuwerk cooperative were concerned, the move to the Rhön was not the most important event to take place that winter. More important, because of its irrevocable nature, was the commitment made by the members at a solemn meeting in the Sannerz community held the evening of December 5, 1926. The representative committee especially named for this purpose appointed Eberhard and Emmy Arnold, Gertrud

Dalgas, and Adolf Braun to the "life-long conduct of the community's work…at the Bruderhof…parish of Veitsteinbach, district of Fulda." They set down in writing the characteristic features and components of the communal work and life: an open door, the community of life and goods as practiced by the early Christian church, publishing, and, no less important, the children's community. In the future only people "who want to hold to this communal way of life forever" would be considered for membership. The long-winded statement was designed to satisfy the German laws for contracts of association, a legal framework poorly suited to the nature of the association formed that night. More than three centuries after the expulsion of the last Hutterites from Moravia, a Bruderhof patterned after the first Hutterites once again took root in German-speaking central Europe.

Chapter Twelve

"Our fate is inextricably bound to that of the oppressed and disadvantaged who suffer under the present order...We do not want to avoid even the worst extremes of need. Our own insufficiency shows us every day the guilt we bear for this distress. But we oppose the murderous powers of destruction by our witness to a new life, the witness to the peace that is not of this world, yet is for this world."

From the "Statement of Belief" of the Free German Union, January 9–10, 1926.

Many Mouths, Not Much Money

At the turn of the year 1926–1927 the first group from the Sannerz community moved to the Rhön Bruderhof, led by Adolf and Martha Braun. The children followed on May 15, 1927. Until the end of September, however, people still lived in the Sannerz villa, continuing the publishing work. Eberhard and the community now had to deal with a new problem: how could they preserve spiritual unity and "complete community" over a distance of thirteen miles without a telephone? Doing so was not easy. Everyone was happy when this time of separation ended. September 29, 1927, saw a last major celebration in Sannerz: the engagement of Georg Barth and Monika von Hollander. After that the Sannerz remnant moved to the Rhön.

Eberhard had been correct. Purchasing the Hansehof was a step in faith. In their dire poverty he and the community needed to draw on this faith daily. Thanks to their stores of provisions the community survived the harsh winter, but by the spring of 1928 food had grown scarce. When it came to money matters the Bruderhof members lived from hand to mouth. Some initial supporters of the Rhön Bruderhof suddenly got cold feet, demanding their loans back just when it was least convenient for the household. Often the community could only meet its bills at the last minute. The sheriff, Herr Schreiner, made almost weekly visits to the community to take a piece of furniture or a farm animal as security for the community's debt. Eberhard joked that Herr Schreiner would be able to enter straight into the brotherhood without the standard year's novitiate since he seemed to be a permanent guest. Another frequent visitor to the community included in his memoirs the following account of living conditions at the Rhön Bruderhof: "Seldom can a bible quotation be applied so literally. Up there they 'ate their bread in the sweat of their brows,' coaxing it from the meager soil. If the community work departments ever produced a surplus, it was given away to others who were still poorer...Since the days of the Ebionites in the land east of the Jordan, there has surely never been another community that operated so totally against reason."[1]

Eberhard would never have chosen to beg, but during the years of building up the Rhön Bruderhof, beg he did. Every single letter Eberhard sent out contained a poignant description of the community's need and an appeal for support. But Eberhard never asked for himself – only for others: for the foster children; for the publishing projects; and for the care of guests, whom the Bruderhof, out of inner

From 1926 to 1937, when the Nazis expelled the community from Germany, the Arnolds lived at the Rhön Bruderhof.

conviction, could not possibly turn away. On behalf of the cause he petitioned old and new friends at every opportunity. Emmy did not escape this humbling burden either. When Eberhard formulated a proposed list of household rules he included in the shared tasks of housemother and word leader: "They must solicit money to cover our most urgent needs and to pay our debts, without in any way becoming dependent on people…But it remains our firm intention and our prayer to God that such begging from friends can and must stop as soon as the work and development of the Bruderhof reach a stage to provide a simple livelihood for us, our guests, and our increasing number of children."[2]

Under no circumstances should the "open door" be shut. Even so Eberhard never disguised how much he had to overcome in himself in order to beg and solicit donations: "It went against our natural feelings and was exceedingly difficult for us to accept that we were forced to practice Franciscan beggary on such a grand scale."[3]

Remarkably it was during these years of harsh economic need and insufficient nourishment – "too little fat, too little protein" – that many people felt drawn to live in the community.[4] Between 1926 and 1930 the community grew from thirty to seventy people. Eberhard baptized fifteen new members and married several couples.

Life during the early years at the Rhön was certainly not devoid of joy. For example, when someone donated a horse and carriage, the community suddenly discovered an ardent horse-lover in their word leader. "He was a daring driver, and his wife was often nervous of riding with him," recalls Sophie Löber. "He couldn't go fast enough – that was how he was."[5] Fairness demanded that what gave him pleasure should be enjoyed by the children too – and so Eberhard declared horse-riding part of the Bruderhof educational program.[6]

Without a doubt children were the community's number one priority. In spite of the poverty there was always room for them, and not a penny spent on children was ever considered wasted. Cooking the children's meals took precedence in the kitchen; milk and eggs were always there for the children even when the adults' empty bellies rumbled. The first new house, officially opened in 1928, was built for the children. It seemed almost typical that on the opening day of the children's house an unexpected donation once more saved the Bruderhof property from compulsory auction.

Bruderhof Education

One cannot overemphasize the importance of children in the mind of Eberhard Arnold or in the life of the Rhön Bruderhof. Any attempt to assess the significant achievements of Eberhard's life must examine not just his writings and publishing work, but must also include his development of the Bruderhof method of educating children. Certainly he was not the only one who influenced the community's approach to education. But the basic direction, principles, spiritual foundation, goals, and methods of Bruderhof education unquestionably trace back to Eberhard. The problem is that, as successful and convincing as the Bruderhof pedagogy may be, it is nontransferable to other environments. A few isolated aspects can be copied, but not the main features, because Bruderhof education is so inextricably interwoven into the fabric of communal life. Eberhard had nurtured this educational method in Sannerz.[7] On the Rhön Bruderhof, it blossomed into full flower. Even the school officials accepted it. In January of 1928 the Bruderhof received official permission to establish a private school for elementary and middle-school grades. Up until that time the children had been unofficially home-schooled.

Eberhard wrote: "Our educational work depends on the faith that the living Christ will arouse from within each person all his or her resolve and capacities for good. All of a child's best powers are latent inside, waiting to be awakened. True education is achieved only when a fellowship of trust exists between teachers and students. Such an education must take place in community. Not only parents and teachers are to be educators, but the whole lifestyle surrounding the child must act as an educational example of a happy life. Children must grow up in a broad context of life."

Whether the educators were parents or teachers or fatherly or motherly friends, Eberhard insisted that, before they could teach the children, they must first learn from the children:

If we really love children and really share their lives, we will see that they have a capacity which we have lost: the child's capacity to become completely absorbed in sights and experiences even when he or she seems to be "only playing." The true child…is free of any self-consciousness…It could be said that only children can be our leaders; for we want to become like genuine children. And so we share the children's joy in flowers and woods; in horses, dogs, cows, goats, and rabbits; in the deer and the birds and every living thing…We rejoice when they play at working or work at playing. While happily occupied in play, a child learns to be creative, to cultivate values, to create culture. Not unless we educators are so moved and struck by the divine mystery of the child that it fills us heart and soul…will we be able to educate a child to be orderly, clean, truthful, loving, and to have spiritual interests or physical control.[8]

Eberhard repeatedly emphasized that responsibility for children is a holy task. He wrote, "Educational work is a work of worship. It is a matter of reverence for the mystery of the divine, for the likeness to God which is not yet extinguished here." That is why Eberhard forbade coercion and mistrust in dealing with children. The educator should not be petty-minded, but neither should he or she be careless. Force is never an option, though firmness may very well be required. Positively expressed: "Educating children means trusting, inspiring, and encouraging."

Eberhard set no store on uniformity or keeping pace:

Instead of a uniform education we respect what is personal and distinctive in each child…We must never force a child into something that is not inborn, which does not come from that child's inner being as he or she awakens to spiritual life…It must be recognized as early as possible whether children have a predisposition to physical work or mainly to intellectual activity, where they can best make a contribution, and what kind of work best suits them. Only then will it be possible for them to develop their capacities. In the very early years a child's particular character is already revealed in his or her play.

In keeping with many other educational reformers Eberhard also insisted that all children, whatever their gifts, should be treated as of equal worth.[9] Manual skills should never be considered inferior to intellectual achievement. Therefore it was taken for granted that "manual work must be given an important place in our educational community." When twenty-two-year-old Georg Barth arrived at the community in 1923, his skills as an arts and crafts teacher helped satisfy this educational requirement. A workshop was set up exclusively for creative activities with the children. There they could whittle and carve, saw and hammer, and learn wood turnery. The candlesticks, lamps, wooden dolls and animals, lanterns, bookmarks, letter openers, and puzzles the children produced added a small but not insignificant contribution to the support of the communal life.

Agreeing with the seventeenth-century religious philosopher and scientist Blaise Pascal, Eberhard asserted that an interrelationship existed between all school subjects. It must be possible "to trace the uniting spirit of the creation and of the new creation" in all subjects – from mathematics to music, from languages to sports.[10] The children should grasp "the coherence of nature and the coherence of mankind, the unity and communal character of all life."[11] This was also Eberhard's remedy for tiresome repetition. "Instead of amassing facts and learning them by rote, the underlying sense of coherence between

The Arnolds at the Rhön Bruderhof in 1927. From left: Hans-Hermann, Emy-Margret, Emmy, Monika-Elisabeth, Eberhard, Heinrich, Hardy.

the facts will be shown...Here there will be no attempt to reach what is spiritual by way of what is material, but the material will be understood through the spiritual."[12]

The success of an educational method – or of an educator – may best be determined by the students who have experienced the particular type of education. Take Rudi Hildel, for example. He remembers coming to Sannerz in May of 1927 as an apprehensive seven-year-old: "I had been in two orphanages and was desperately unhappy at coming to a third. But within the very first days I felt completely at home. Eberhard was rather tall and he made a great impression on us children. But I never felt afraid of him."

"Eberhard was very fatherly. He had real authority but never forced us into anything," recalls Lotti Magee, who was seven years old when she and her mother came to the Rhön Bruderhof in 1931. "I was never afraid of him, for I simply felt that a great love was at work in him. If he ever gave us a row – and he could certainly raise his voice at times – we knew we deserved it. But then the issue was cleared up and we felt free. I always had the feeling that he could see into my heart."[13]

This illustrates the most distinctive characteristic in Eberhard's ideas of education. He had rediscovered the "untouchable" quality of the child.[14] In this respect his teacher was neither the innovative educator Pestalozzi, nor the father of the kindergarten, Fröbel,[15] but Jesus of Nazareth, who said: "If anyone leads one of these little children astray, so that he can no longer be childlike, it would be better for that man to be drowned with a millstone around his neck." And: "Be careful that you never despise a single one of these little ones, for I tell you that their angels always come into the Father's presence."

Eberhard had read these words of Jesus with breathtaking earnestness. At the age of forty-five, with an almost grown-up daughter, two half-grown sons, and two smaller children, he testified that "only wise men and saints are fit to be educators":

Our lips are unclean. Our dedication is not without reservations. Our truthfulness is broken. Our love is not perfect. Our kindness is not free of ulterior motives. We are not free from the self-will and possessions that oppose love...So it is the child who leads us to the gospel. The task we have for the child shows us that we are too evil to be able to educate one single child in this holy sense. We can educate children and live with them only when we ourselves stand like children before God.[16]

Hutterian Writings

Back in January of 1926 Eberhard had received the address of Elias Walter, elder of the Dariusleut among the Hutterites in North America. It was forwarded to him by Robert Friedmann, a Viennese historian and specialist in Anabaptist research.[17] This address enabled Eberhard to pick up the trail first set for him in 1921 when Professor J. G. Evert had provided him with the names of certain Hutterites in North America. Eberhard sent a long, typewritten letter across the Atlantic. It was probably dispatched in the summer of 1926. Elias Walter took nine months to respond. When his reply finally arrived, it covered all of two small sheets of stationery. Everyone at the Rhön Bruderhof found this somewhat disappointing. But, to their delight, a bundle of old Hutterian writings soon arrived from Canada – and that was only a beginning.[18]

For years Eberhard and Else had been hunting through university libraries and archives – anywhere they thought there might be a chance of uncovering Hutterian writings or other Anabaptist documents. The whole community had been drawn into this journey of discovery. Once Eberhard noted: "We have finished copying the Disputation at Worms, the 1637 version. Original, 1557." The original 355-page manuscript contained the court records concerning Peter Riedemann, Jakob Hutter's successor in the spiritual leadership of the Moravian Anabaptists.[19] Each page was copied by hand with painstaking accuracy on the Rhön Bruderhof – page after page after page. This laborious method was often the only way to secure the contents of such extremely rare documents. Even the school children practiced copying old manuscripts. It was only later that Eberhard realized that the community was unconsciously following another old Hutterian tradition. The "forefathers' writings" had been – and still are – copied repeatedly in the Hutterite communities. Testimonies to a rich and inspiring spiritual history came alive in the Rhön Bruderhof: diaries and letters from the dungeons of the Inquisition, catechisms, sermons and bible interpretations, and songs that had originated in times of severe persecution. The Bruderhof received gifts of valuable documents from a variety of sources. On one occasion the community even purchased a number of original manuscripts, despite the fact that they lacked the money for absolute necessities. (But what are necessities to a community that relies on Jesus and witnesses to outsiders that "man does not live by bread alone?")

Early in 1928 Eberhard commenced an all-out search for old "Hutterian Orders," guidelines pertaining to schools and to craftsmen. This was primarily dictated by circumstances: it was essential to organize the common life and work of fifty adults and children. But it also came from Eberhard's childlike curiosity: if he could compare the daily life on the Rhön Bruderhof to the old Hutterian traditions, would he find the same astonishing similarities he had discovered in the great spiritual concepts of community of goods, baptism of faith, and refusal to bear arms?

Issues of *Die Wegwarte* from that time period provide quite a few glimpses into the communal life at the Rhön and its involvement with historical Hutterian writings. Two of the finest gleanings were printed there: The December 1927 issue carried a poem from Vogler's catechism of 1625; and, beginning in January 1928 and continuing in several later issues, a pastoral letter "On Brotherly Community: The Highest Command of Love," written in 1652 by Andreas Ehrenpreis.[20]

Distinguished Friends

Among Eberhard's hundreds of friends and correspondents during the 1920s, several are worthy of mention. Prince Günther von Schönburg-Waldenburg was well-known in his day. When Eberhard first made his acquaintance the prince was still young but already a widower. In October of 1923 he allowed the National Union of the YMCA to use his Waldenburg Castle for a youth leaders' conference. Wearing corduroy knee britches, Eberhard stood out as a bizarre figure among the middle-class gentlemen (many were friends from his prewar student days) in their formal black suits. Perhaps it was for this very reason that the prince singled him out. Shortly after the conference Prince Günther visited Sannerz. Eberhard took great pains to prepare Konrad Paul's villa to welcome the guest, not because he wanted to appear better off than they really were – there was really no way to hide the poverty – but out of consideration for the prince. Eberhard said that the prince was not accustomed to such crowded living conditions or such scanty meals. But Prince Günther von Schönburg-Waldenburg enjoyed the frank and natural company, and from the time of that visit on a large parcel arrived for the children every Easter. Sometimes, when money was tight, he even helped with loans and generous donations (as for the purchase of the Rhön Bruderhof). He took a lively interest in the ups and downs of the Bruderhof. Whenever Eberhard was scheduled to lecture in Saxony a room at Waldenburg Castle always awaited him and Emmy. Through the prince, close and long-lasting contacts were made with socially concerned pastors in the neighborhood; no other town in Germany invited Eberhard as frequently during the 1920s as did Lichtenstein in Saxony.

Eberhard's friendship with Martin Buber was on an entirely different level. Eberhard had studied Buber's writings during the war, and in 1918 he had described him in *Die Furche* magazine as the "prophet of the new Jewish movement." The two had already met at that time, a contact revived once more in 1921. True, Buber's help on Eberhard's planned book on Landauer never materialized – and, consequently, neither did the book. But Buber's curiosity about the Neuwerk movement was aroused. On July 28, 1921, Buber and

In 1924 an evangelical conference of youth leaders convened at Prince Günther von Schönburg-Waldenburg's castle in Saxony. Eberhard is fourth from the right; the prince is seventh from the right.

Eberhard had a long talk at Sannerz. From a theological point of view the two held exactly the same reservations about Karl Barth, and they shared a nearly identical understanding of the kingdom of God and of the mystery of *Gemeinde* – the sole exception in their mutual understanding was Jesus of Nazareth: for Buber, an inspired prophet with power from above; for Eberhard, the Lord of the *Gemeinde* and of the world. After 1924 Martin Buber met Eberhard several times at Neuwerk conferences, and the two helped to organize the August 1927 World Youth conference meetings on religion and world views. Their relationship was always one of great mutual esteem – a respect almost too great to permit a close friendship.

A robust, man-to-man friendship linked Eberhard to the poet and literary critic Hermann Buddensieg. Buddensieg, a *Wandervogel* member, was ten years Eberhard's junior and had been at the 1913 Hohe Meissner conference. He fought in the war and, as a result, returned home to Germany disabled. The two met in 1923 at the second Hohe Meissner conference. Hermann Buddensieg had just started a newspaper, *Challenge to Change.*[21] Here was a Free German in the best possible sense of the word – sharp-tongued, good-humored, and keenly perceptive. Though not a Christian, Buddensieg enjoyed Eberhard's company and regularly sought his advice.[22] As a result the *Challenge to Change* was published for two years by the Eberhard Arnold Publishing House. When Hermann Buddensieg had a son in the late 1920s, he named him Tilmann-Eberhard, and Eberhard became godfather. No other contemporary described Eberhard in so eloquent a manner as did this word artist, Hermann Buddensieg: "I will never forget the roguish glint in your eyes, your mischievous smile, with your waggish beard, your cheerful laugh when peculiarities and all-too-human elements forced themselves on us. We were often wearied with dull, commonplace talk. And then a witty remark, sometimes even ironic, was just what we needed – not at anyone's expense, but to stimulate and wake us up…We often laughed freely and heartily, in gales of truly Homeric laughter."[23]

Another person who deserves mention is Leonhard Ragaz. Ragaz had studied under Hermann Kutter and after the war had become his successor as the leading intellectual force behind the religious-socialist movement. He gave up his position as a theology professor in order to pastor a parish in a working-class district of Zurich. Eberhard first became acquainted with Leonhard Ragaz in 1921 through an exchange of articles and letters. Ragaz's book *The Fight for God's Kingdom through Blumhardt and His Son* came as a revelation to Eberhard, and he expressly told Ragaz this.[24] They corresponded at sporadic intervals of weeks and months, their exchanges evolving from polite to friendly and, finally, to brotherly greetings. By 1926, as far as can be judged, almost complete spiritual unity existed between Eberhard and Leonhard Ragaz. In an article in *Die Wegwarte* entitled "Our Way," Ragaz expressed the wish "to join with all who follow a similar direction as part of the church of brothers here on earth – this great church, although it will always seem small to the world." Eberhard stated in the same issue that the Rhön Bruderhof stood "hand in hand in brotherly fellowship" with Leonhard Ragaz, Kees Boeke, and the Hutterian Bruderhofs, among others.

On his sixtieth birthday, July 28, 1928, Leonhard Ragaz received a telegram from the Rhön: "Sixty coworkers and children are grateful for the living witness of their pioneer." Complete unanimity, it seems – and yet the relationship had several peculiar aspects. For example, Ragaz promised half a dozen times to visit Sannerz, and later the Rhön. He often traveled through the immediate neighborhood, but he never visited. The relationship between Ragaz and the Bruderhof lacked a true spark and it never really caught fire. Unfortunately the story ends in the ashes of discord.

Companions along the Way

Friendship is one thing. Sharing one's life with another person is something altogether different. And so it goes without saying that the young men and women who found their way to the community after 1923 were more important for Eberhard's life, and were for their part more deeply affected by him, than all the distinguished friends and well-intentioned supporters on the outside. Many people lived in community with Eberhard and his family for at least a few years. Many others, like the following three, joined Eberhard and the Bruderhof community for the rest of their lives:

Irmgard Wegner belonged to the Neuwerk group in Hannover in

1921. Her introduction to Eberhard came through reading his articles in *Das Neue Werk*. Then she heard him lecture at the Hannover YMCA. After attending the Pentecost conference at Schlüchtern in 1923, Irmgard came across an advertisement for help in the publishing house, and she applied for a job. Committing herself for one year, she became responsible for Eberhard's correspondence. "He was thorough and exact, but without pedantry," she said. Eberhard expected of her, as of all other coworkers, a complete dedication and joy in the work, but at the same time she came to know him as a considerate and observant friend. Later, Irmgard Wegner married Karl "Roland" Keiderling, who had come to Sannerz in November 1922. She worked as a secretary at Eberhard's side until his death. To the very end of her own life in 1995 the memories of her twelve years of work close to Eberhard remained fresh and alive.

Arno Martin worked in the Dresden YMCA, where he belonged to a youth movement group. In February of 1925 he heard Eberhard give a lecture at St. Ann's Hall in Dresden – and what a message he heard! Eberhard spoke straight from the heart, sometimes leaving the podium to go into the audience, take a doubter by the shoulders, and ask him face to face what he thought. Finally Eberhard became so heated that he took off his jacket – an unheard-of thing to do in those days. Eighteen months later at a Free German conference Arno and Eberhard met again. Eberhard invited the young man to help with the construction work at the Rhön Bruderhof. Arno accepted, knowing immediately that there would be no turning back. During Advent of 1926 he arrived in Sannerz with only a rucksack and the clothes he was wearing. By 1927 he was already a brotherhood member, and he was baptized on July 27, 1928, at the Rhön Bruderhof. Arno often drove Eberhard in the carriage to and from the railway station. The half-hour trip was long enough for heart-to-heart talks. Soon Eberhard was simply "Papa" to Arno Martin, too.

Born in Zurich, Switzerland, Walter Hüssy originally belonged to the *Freischar*, a religious-socialist youth group that had been in contact with the Neuwerk movement since 1920. He had already passed through several attempted communities and communes before coming to the Bruderhof in 1929. He was looking for "down-to-earth, joyful brotherhood in an early Christian way" – and he found it at the Bruderhof. Walter was a skilled gardener, but he had a hard time raising vegetables in the harsh Rhön climate. In December of 1931 Walter Hüssy and Gertrud Dalgas were married by Eberhard. Theirs was the sixth wedding at the Rhön Bruderhof.

Walter's memories of Eberhard are happy ones: "He wanted the brotherhood to keep awake and alive and to concern itself with contemporary questions as well as with movements throughout the centuries. And that was immensely inspiring." Walter shared experiences with Eberhard that, even sixty years later, he could not recount without a noticeable tremor in his voice. "The greatest thing is the forgiveness that you could feel from Eberhard. I once hurt him very deeply, but the way he could forgive is almost beyond description. It was overwhelming. He gave up his own feelings completely."[25]

Irmgard Keiderling, Arno Martin, Walter Hüssy: three out of the total of seventy-one people who shared their lives with Eberhard and Emmy and remained true to the way of brotherhood.

Free German Brotherhood

Of all the relationships Eberhard had maintained since the early 1920s, his friendship with the Berlin teacher Erich Mohr bore a special quality. Both thought highly of Gustav Landauer and his farsightedness, and they shared a common love for the socially disadvantaged and a dedication to young people. Like Eberhard, Erich Mohr had worked for postwar reconciliation since the early 1920s; reconciliation with France especially concerned him. In the years after the Free German Union was founded Mohr had received Eberhard's ideas more eagerly than anyone else. Eberhard had made sure that the Sannerz community household, and then later the Rhön Bruderhof, participated as active local groups in the Free German Union. And Erich Mohr, for his part, had pointed to the community as a working model for the Free German Union. At a January 1926 conference Mohr formulated this concept as a statement of shared conviction for all Free German Union members:

> We believe in the ultimate reality of the living *Gemeinde*. In and through this *Gemeinde* we await the kingdom that is to come…It is essential to live with eyes fixed on the eternal truth – not yet in

its fullness among us – and to rouse and strengthen on all sides the understanding for justice and truth...We believe in the victory of the creative powers of love.[26]

At the same time Mohr introduced for discussion a statement attempting to define the relationship between the Free German Union and the community then living in Sannerz. He cited the collaboration between the two groups: "The Free German Union has entered into close cooperation with the work of Eberhard Arnold and the Sannerz group. The Free German Union believes the hour has come to witness to the contemporary world by work and deed to the ultimate reality of the living church." This achieved a previously inconceivable agreement and degree of trust. It enabled Eberhard – actually, it compelled him – to go a step further.

In the summer of 1926 Mohr suggested the formation of a Free German Brotherhood, "which would bring together all Free Germans who confess a living faith in Christ."[27] This step was intended to overcome the lack of commitment and the deliberate haziness in the basic principles of the Free German Union – to get down to brass tacks and to be able to say not just "church," but the "church of Jesus Christ"; not just "kingdom," but "the kingdom of God." Moreover, this step would extend beyond the narrow circle of the Free German Union. As Eberhard envisioned it the Free German Brotherhood would be open to Free Germans in other youth movement groups too. It was a stimulating and highly interesting proposition, but also a provocative one: a Free German Brotherhood would mean a fellowship within a fellowship – shock troops, an elite guard.

Next to Erich Mohr, seventeen-year-old Hans-Joachim Schoeps was Eberhard's fieriest supporter of the proposed Free German Brotherhood. Schoeps was a German Jew and, despite his youth, was already a driving force in the Free German movement. In the next few years he would find his Jewish identity and would later be acknowledged as a notable scholar of religion – all by way of the Free Germans and the "spirit of Christian love" that he encountered while with Eberhard in Sannerz and the Rhön Bruderhof.[28]

The Free German Brotherhood took shape at an October 1926 meeting. Hans-Joachim Schoeps promoted it among the Free German youth groups, declaring that "all who feel spiritual affinity with the Free German Brotherhood must feel themselves pledged to bring the spirit of brotherhood and love into all areas of life...I ask you to see the Sannerz community as a focal point where the spirit of brotherhood has found *one* of its possible outward expressions..."[29]

Carried to Extremes?

Even at its finest the Free German Brotherhood never amounted to much more than a loose network of individuals. Unavoidable disagreements arose within the Free German Union about the role of the Free German Brotherhood and about the witness to *"werdende Gemeinde."* Karl Sachse, a founding member of the Free Germans, had already clarified the dichotomy at the January 1926 conference: "A fellowship can never be more than a human endeavor, but *Gemeinde* is the work of God. *Gemeinde* is organic; fellowship is a human attempt at practical expression."

A short while later the Bruderhof community and the Free German Union parted ways. The turn of the year 1926–1927 marked the last time a group from the Free German Union gathered for a conference at the Rhön. In 1928 factions developed, and accusations ensued, targeting both Free German Union and Free German Brotherhood leaders, as well as the "Sannerzers." During 1929 the Free German Union gradually ceased to function. By its January 1930 conference the story ended with the crucial ultimatum: either the Free German Union or the Free German Brotherhood; either action or contemplation. Eberhard's protests against these extremes fell on deaf ears. Erich Mohr still hoped that the corpse of the Free German Union could be resuscitated. But Eberhard responded, "Not every death leads to resurrection. The decisive question is whether it is the death of the crucified one; this death leads to resurrection." Proposals for the dissolution of the Free German Union followed quickly. The Free German Union breathed its last even while everyone stressed their good will.[30] At this point Eberhard's connection with Erich Mohr came to an end.

In the final analysis it was painfully apparent that the Bruderhof's lifestyle based on faith and commitment would never be compatible with the Free German Union's uncommitted "community of principles."

Chapter Thirteen

"Only in the spirit of unity will we encounter Christ in his purity. It is in this spirit alone that we come to faith in the almighty Creator-God of all worlds, suns, and earths; the God who became our Father in Christ, who poured his spirit upon his *Gemeinde;* the God to whom we belong and whom we trust to provide us with everything we need.

Letter to the Rhön Bruderhof, November 26, 1930.

On the Trail of the Past

Perhaps Andreas Ehrenpreis's pastoral letter "On Brotherly Community: The Highest Command of Love" provided the final spur to action. Perhaps it was "The Hutterian Communities," an article by Bertha W. Clark about life in the Hutterian communities in America. Or perhaps it was the advice and insight from the seventeenth-century Hutterites, and the descriptions of the ongoing vitality of the communities still in existence in North America, all of which corresponded completely with the Bruderhof's inner experiences.

Whatever the case, the proposition to get down to business came not from Eberhard but from the ranks of the brotherhood: "What prevents us from uniting with these Hutterian brothers?" This prompted Eberhard to compose a letter to Elias Walter on August 22, 1928. In the name of the brotherhood Eberhard declared "in perpetual and resolute certainty our firm and irrevocable will" to unite with the Hutterian communities.[1] In addition the letter suggested that the American communities immediately send two "servants of the Word" (the Hutterian term for a minister) to Germany to assume the spiritual leadership of the Rhön Bruderhof.

It soon became clear that all this would not be quite so simple. Elias Walter explained that the North American Hutterites lacked a united leadership. He proposed that letters should first be sent to the ministers of a few other communities. This was done immediately – but with no results. If any reply came, it only came in the form of another communication from Elias Walter. In May of 1929 Eberhard drafted a short "epistle," written in true Hutterian style, to all the communities in South Dakota, Manitoba, and Alberta. The crucial sentences were:

> We give ourselves first to God, and now to you. We want to be yours in the obedience of faith, love, and discipline. As we prayed to God, so we now ask of you: Accept us! Give us a commission! Just as we can do nothing without Christ, so we want to do nothing without you.[2]

Two other documents accompanied the epistle across the Atlantic: Eberhard's ninety-page manuscript entitled *Foundation and Orders* and his recently revised *Living Churches: The Essence of Their Life*.

Elias Walter received the letters from the Rhön very favorably. In the fall of 1929 Eberhard wrote to Robert Friedmann, informing his friend that Elias Walter had given the Rhön Bruderhof the task of publishing Bertha W. Clark's article in book form, as well as "other writings of the Hutterites," and that Elias Walter had donated funds for the publishing work. Clearly a great trust had gradually developed between the two; the old Hutterite minister asked Eberhard to put together, among other things, a scholarly edition of *Das Klein Geschichtsbuch* (*The Small History Book*, documenting early Hutterianism) – a major undertaking requiring several years of work.[3]

For his part Eberhard had become a heart-and-soul advocate of the Hutterian communities. He wrote to Robert Friedmann: "The tremendous thing about the Hutterian *Gemeinde* is that it puts faith into deed so that here and now – in the practical, communal life of the church – the kingdom of God is shown as justice, peace, and joy in the Holy Spirit (Romans 14:17)."[4] And to the American Mennonite scholar John Horsch he wrote: "Although a centuries-old tradition may all too easily lead to a gradual loss of faith, love, and the direct experience of Christ, I find absolutely no hindrance to seeking and believing in complete unity with the present-day Hutterites…Their prayer for the Holy Spirit proves that the truth is still living and active among them, and is not and cannot be extinguished."[5]

Meanwhile Elias Walter had outlined the steps to unity: Eberhard would have to travel to America, present himself to the elders of the

Hutterian communities, and allow himself to be searched – mind and heart. He must be prepared to answer questions about his hopes and desires, the history of the Bruderhof in Germany, his personal faith, his knowledge of the Bible, his family life, and his opinions. At the end of all this – maybe! – uniting would take place.

But there was a great deal to be done first. In June of 1929 Eberhard traveled to Austria to discuss with Professor Johann Loserth the editing and publishing of old Hutterian writings. In November Eberhard gave a series of lectures at Robert Friedmann's "Tolstoy Club" in Vienna, and had another meeting with Loserth.[6] Afterwards he traveled to Sabatisch and Velké Leváre, early sites of the peaceful Anabaptist movement.[7] There he encountered secularized descendants of the Anabaptists, visited the sites of old Hutterian Bruderhofs, searched through archives, and returned home with all kinds of interesting documents. Even on his return journey he discovered, to his surprise, a valuable Hutterian writing in the Herrnhut archives of the Zinzendorf Brethren.[8]

In the spring of 1930, as his American journey drew near, Eberhard's high spirits and enthusiasm inspired the entire Rhön community. On May 19, days before his departure, he jotted down that "two to four of us are continually at work copying and comparing the old Anabaptist books and manuscripts."[9] On May 27 another great, and very appropriate, celebration took place on the Rhön Bruderhof: the baptism and acceptance into the brotherhood of eight novice members.

Eberhard Arnold at the Rhön Bruderhof, shortly before his departure for the United States and Canada, 1930.

Across the Ocean

On May 30, 1930, Eberhard boarded the Atlantic liner Karlsruhe at Bremen and embarked on the first leg of what was to be a long journey. He sent the following personal description beforehand so that the reception committee in New York would recognize him: "I can be identified by my Hutterian garb, and I am six feet tall and not particularly thin." On June 12 he telegraphed home from Brooklyn, New York: "Landed safely. Thinking of you all. Eberhard."

For the first few days he felt like an alien from another planet. The Americans laughed behind his back at his knee britches and sandals. He found American cities insufferable, the small towns in bad taste. He wrote home that the country was held firmly in the grip of mammon. Seldom did he feel inspired to take a stroll, and his damaged left eye was causing him difficulties once again. He had spent most of the crossing in bed. Reading was a great strain, writing even worse. Nonetheless, he wrote, "I believe in Christ, who will make the inner light into a light for my body and will restore my physical eye for me to continue on my way." And a very long way still lay before him. First he went to Scottdale, Pennsylvania, to meet the Mennonite historian John Horsch. Then on to Chicago, and into the midwest.

As Eberhard was making his way west, on the Hutterian communities (at least on some) his visit was eagerly awaited. For example, Peter Gross, the servant of the Word at the Iberville community in Manitoba, wrote to Elias Walter, speculating about how the late "old Schmied Michel" would have responded to Eberhard.[10] "Were he still living," Peter Gross wrote, "he would be so stirred in spirit that he would use every means and opportunity to reach the Bruderhof in Germany and would get to know it, every aspect of it, both spiritual and temporal."[11] But some others held aloof. Eberhard, on his part, was generally confident but somewhat apprehensive about what the brothers might require of him. He wrote to Elias Walter that he did not expect to meet angels.[12] In fact he was received in Tabor, South Dakota, by men of flesh and blood: white-haired Michel Waldner and his son Paul took him to Bon Homme, the oldest Hutterian community on American soil.[13]

Dariusleut, Lehrerleut, Schmiedeleut

There were only four Hutterian communities in South Dakota in 1930. All the other communities had moved to Canada after the war in order to avoid military conscription.[14] The four remaining communities in South Dakota formed a kind of Hutterian microcosm. All three branches of Hutterianism were represented within a small area – one Schmiedeleut community, one Lehrerleut, and two Dariusleut. Eberhard recorded his first impressions:

> The brothers and sisters at Bon Homme are very, very loving to me...The spirit and reality of contemporary Hutterianism far surpass anything any of us expected...Joy and cheerfulness are expressed in a fun-loving disposition born of deep inner contentment, and in still deeper words of faith from the Scriptures, from proverbs, and from experience. Simplicity of life is still fairly well preserved in their culture...The prayers, teachings, and songs are wonderfully clear and objective, as are the community decisions...But it is hard for us to understand their wealth both in property and in the lavish standard of living.[15]

The Hutterites were no less impressed by Eberhard Arnold. Everyone, young and old alike, wanted to hear over and over again about the Rhön Bruderhof and the beginning of the Sannerz community. Within a week, however, he had to seek medical care. His eye had become inflamed and forced him to spend three weeks in bed. The Dariusleut at the Wolf Creek community surrounded him with loving care. It would be a long time before he would rest so well again. In retrospect, it can be seen as a pause to catch his breath – a gathering of strength before an incredible marathon. Six months and over twenty-five hundred miles of travel by train, car, and horse-cart lay between him and his goal of uniting the Rhön Bruderhof with the Hutterian *Gemeinden*. But at the time, of course, he could not know any of this.

Eberhard now confronted his first hurdle. He had to win over David Hofer, the gray-haired elder of the Lehrerleut and minister of the Rockport community. This man commanded much respect for his faithfulness to principle and his forthrightness, but he was also feared for his obstinacy and the sharp, gruff manner in which he represented his views. When Eberhard arrived at Rockport on June 21, 1930, the old man did not so much as glance at him. The rest of the brothers and sisters at the community were just as loving and as full of curiosity as those at the other communities had been. But it was days before David Hofer finally deigned to exchange a few words with his guest. To put it more accurately, he gave Eberhard his opinion in no uncertain terms. Eberhard recorded the conversation in his diary. Superficially it seems no more than an interesting anecdote. Looked at more closely, however, it reveals an important turning point.

Mention has already been made of the soaring expectations on the Rhön Bruderhof before Eberhard's departure. He wrote in a letter of May 19, 1930, "We believe that this is once more an historic hour when the complete truth of the gospel...is to be revealed far and wide."[16] A day later he wrote again: "Now is the hour when the great and mighty event, the experience that came from God to the brothers at the beginning, is taking place anew."[17] In other words he ascribed historically redemptive significance to the rediscovery of Hutterianism. Eberhard in the course of his lifetime had been frequently and unjustly accused of fanaticism. Now he was really in danger of being swept off his feet. A letter he wrote to the Hutterian communities on June 14, during his stay with John Horsch in Scottdale, Pennsylvania, stated that "because of adherence to the Hutterian way of faith, the brotherhood on the Rhön Bruderhof has been completely deserted by all those in Germany who call themselves Christian." That was, to say the least, an exaggeration, and perhaps it bore a shade of self-righteousness.

Now Eberhard stood in front of the stern patriarch David Hofer and brought forward his request for complete unity with the Hutterian *Gemeinden* on the basis of the directives given by Jakob Hutter and Peter Riedemann: "It would be a sin on our part and have no blessing from God if we tried to continue on our own initiative."

The venerable and wrathful old man's reply was hard to take: "You are quite mistaken there. The Lord has his people all over this vast earth, even where we do not know it – wherever people recognize the truth and act on it." In a nutshell, David Hofer told Eberhard that it was not necessary to become a Hutterite in order to be a Christian.

Giving him a further piece of his mind, he said, "Instead of turning to our forefathers, you should turn to the apostles and prophets as did the Hutterian Church of the early days." That was a warning against the pitfalls of tradition and sectarianism. Only the Bible can bring a common basis in faith – nothing else. "You want to unite," David Hofer went on, "but unite with whom? We are no longer united ourselves. Here is Dakota, there Manitoba, there Alberta. Here we are Lehrerleut, there Schmiedeleut, and there Dariusleut. Where is their bishop? Who takes any notice of the elders? If you want to unite, you must try to unite thirty-three times with thirty-three different communities." (And that is exactly how it would turn out for Eberhard.) Finally the old minister concluded, "If God has given you the true spirit, zeal, and faith there in Austria, you had better stay there and make do without us." This can also be understood to mean that the Rhön community should, in David Hofer's opinion, remain self-sufficient rather than allow the obvious defects of the old Hutterian communities to infest it.

After this brief and blunt instructive session David Hofer said little more. Nonetheless he grew more friendly. Right up until the day of Eberhard's departure from the Rockport community, David Hofer gave no indication as to whether he would support or reject uniting with the Rhön Bruderhof. But he drove Eberhard to the railway station himself and, at the last minute, he came out with his answer: David Hofer would support any decision reached by the brothers in Canada. This was not an agreement, but it did show his belief in unanimity. At least he would not hinder the unity Eberhard sought.

Just as Eberhard's three weeks of medical care at the Wolf Creek community had treated the infirmity in his eye, so too old David Hofer from Rockport had cured him of another, different infirmity: he took away all Eberhard's illusions and helped him to see things in their true perspective. He pointed Eberhard back to the source of faith. Who else would have had the authority to give the forty-seven-year-old doctor of philosophy such a dressing-down? In his diary descriptions Eberhard certainly paints other Hutterian ministers and elders in a more sympathetic light, reflective of the more heartfelt relationship he found with most of them. But in important and critical situations Eberhard often went back to the advice he had received from David Hofer.[18] A year after their meeting in Rockport he commented on a particular occasion, "As so often before, old David Hofer has proved to be a prophetic figure among the brothers."[19]

For the time being Eberhard's community-to-community travels in South Dakota continued. He received both pampering and strenuous demands wherever he went. To please him the housemothers made his coffee with "plenty of beans and little water." Almost ashamed as he thought of the monotonous fare back home at the Rhön, he described in his diary all the wonderful things that were served up for him – for the breakfast menu alone: "fish, cheese, sausage, honey, white bread, butter, coffee, porridge with cream, and a glass of wine…" The abundance did not suit him at all after so many years of the Rhön's meager diet.

But the treasures he found in the communities' libraries fueled him with enthusiasm. Bearing a wealth of old teachings and other writings given to him as presents, he traveled further north on August 7, 1930. Joseph Stahl, minister at the Lake Byron community, wrote to Elias Walter:

> At six o'clock this morning dear Arnold left on the Great Northern for Winnipeg, Manitoba, to visit the brothers. He had stayed with us four days. Each day he studied our old books and made notes for himself on them all, and every evening he told us about their own beginning. The whole community, old and young, big and small, gathered in front of our house until twelve every night…It is beyond description what joy and inspiration the man finds in our forefathers' writings. It puts us to shame…In everything he attempts, Arnold seems to me like a second Jakob Hutter, especially in his opposition to greed and to having one's own money in the community.[20]

Manitoba

All ten communities in Manitoba were Schmiedeleut. "The love the Schmiedeleut here have for me and for all of us is, if possible, still greater than that of the oldest communities," wrote Eberhard in his diary, where he also bemoaned having still less quiet than in South Dakota. The Schmiedeleut elder particularly impressed him. "Josef Kleinsasser, Milltown, is the most outstanding and deeply spiritual man and Christian I have met so far…He speaks sparingly, but what he says carries great weight, and everyone hangs on his words…A small figure with a very loving face and a patriarchal character…he could and should be bishop and elder of all the communities…He is a man of faith and of the Spirit, and he depends completely on God."

In Manitoba, Eberhard discovered little of the reputed carelessness of the Schmiedeleut communities. He certainly thought that the proximity of a big city like Winnipeg presented all kinds of temptations, but wrote that "the overflowing love and gratitude with which I am welcomed here shows the direction of their will and their longing, their faith and pulsing life." At the same time the Manitoba community leaders each formed their own view of Eberhard Arnold. David Hofer, second Schmiedeleut elder and minister of the James Valley community (not to be confused with David Hofer, Rockport community), wrote to Elias Walter, calling Eberhard "a true child of God, full of love and Christian virtues. There is no question of us teaching and instructing him; it is rather we who have to learn from him, for his only longing is for the welfare and uniting of our *Gemeinden* in God's honor…"[21]

On September 14, at the Rosedale community, the matter of unity was taken up officially. With Joseph Kleinsasser as chairman, the Schmiedeleut servants of the Word discussed what historical precedent to follow in responding to the Rhön Bruderhof's longing to unite with the Hutterian communities, and also whether earlier baptisms at the Bruderhof could be counted valid. They asked in exact detail whether the brotherhood had appointed Eberhard to the service of the Word "in apostolic power," and, finally, they told him their decision. "We have unanimously decided to agree to your request. We are all in favor of uniting." Joseph Kleinsasser, as elder, addressed a letter to the communities in Alberta informing them that "Eberhard Arnold from Germany has spent a considerable time with us here in Manitoba. During this time we have had many godly and blessed talks and discussions with him and found, as far as we could ascertain and learn by inquiry, that he agrees completely with the Hutterian Brethren in matters of faith. We therefore see no obstacle to the union he desires and seeks with us."

Alberta

With Joseph Kleinsasser's letter safe in his pocket Eberhard arrived at the Stand Off community, Macleod, Alberta, on September 24, 1930, and wrote in his diary, "I feel a warm love for Elias Walter, the venerable champion who has guided our path...He at once had Joseph Kleinsasser's letter typed and sent to the twelve nearest communities in Alberta." Elias Walter was at least as impatient as his guest and thought it a waste of time to wait any longer for the incorporation and confirmation of Eberhard's service of the Word. He would have preferred to send Eberhard to preach to the individual communities immediately. On October 5 Elias Walter wrote to John Horsch: "It is impossible to refuse his acceptance as a Hutterite, for he is such a Hutterite that there is not another like him in these days." But everything had to proceed according to good Hutterian order.

Two Hutterites required exact information: Andreas Gross, servant of the Word at the Lehrerleut community of Old Elm Spring, and the Dariusleut elder, Christian Waldner, of the West Raley community. Christian Waldner grilled Eberhard for five and a half hours and then abruptly dismissed him without giving any indication of what he thought. Eberhard's diary reports: "Christian Waldner displayed the well-known Hutterian sharp mind, objectivity, clear-mindedness, thoroughness, caution, and – yet again – caution. He is undoubtedly a very capable leader." A little further down the page: "Through the grace of God I came very close to Christian Waldner as the days went on."[22]

But Eberhard's original timetable was soon completely disrupted. At the beginning of October he still hoped to be home for Christmas, but in a letter of October 23 he asked for patience and understanding. "Every fiber of my being is urging me homeward. But the goal of this costly and strenuous journey must not be endangered by our impatience and longing...Continue to have faith and to pray. God will hear everything." And on November 12: "It is extremely important, this venture I have undertaken. Now I must carry it through, or rather hold out, until the Creator of all things has brought it to a good end." The crux of the matter was that all eighteen communities in Alberta were expecting a visit. A final decision on unity with the Rhön was impossible without this. So Eberhard was required to make another round of visits, traveling in a closed carriage to protect his inflamed eye.

Eberhard spent his days copying old manuscripts and conversing by the hour. He met amazed disbelief whenever he spoke of the Rhön Bruderhof, a place where "even clergymen learn to work." And always, curiosity about the children and questions about his wife: "Is she very plump, your Emma?" – the centuries-old Hutterian standard for health and beauty. Wherever he went Eberhard was immediately surrounded by listeners. In his diary he notes that "if I go to another house…then the whole group of those who have been listening to me follows me. And if I have been in one house and have said 'good night' and shaken hands with everyone, and then go over to the word leader's house, within five minutes the same people are all gathered there, filling two rooms…And so it has gone almost without exception on each of the twenty-six communities I have visited up to now, so that the evenings are always very late, and at six o'clock in the morning I am again hailed with 'Arnold Vetter, are you getting up?'"[23] Several times, in desperation, he had to rent a hotel room so that he could write at least the most urgent letters in peace and quiet.

In Manitoba, Eberhard had been among recently founded communities that were still becoming established and were burdened with debt. In contrast, he found great wealth at some of the Alberta communities. Once he crossed five neighboring communities, an area two to three miles wide and fourteen miles long – a "state within a state," a "communal principality," he called it. He could not understand how

Surrounded by curious onlookers at a community in Alberta, Eberhard meets Hutterites during his American travels in 1930–1931.

the rich communities could look on quite undisturbed while poorer communities struggled for economic survival, and he did not hide his feelings. At several communities he told them, "Today the devil is using much subtler ways to lead you astray with his accursed property. Instead of tempting you with private property, he is getting at you through collective property...Only one thing can help you: transfer any rights of ownership to the whole group or body – fully, entirely, and forever." The brothers and sisters listened to him with intense interest: "The sharper my words, the happier and more thankful they are," he wrote. But of course nothing changed overnight.

This was all a part of the contradictory impressions Eberhard received from the Hutterian communities in America. In general they were extremely hardworking and thorough, full of exuberant life, and a living tradition. Yet in a few areas he sensed weariness, sluggishness, and fatalism. This was connected with such details as the fixed amount of petty cash given to travelers – money they did not have to account for. Eberhard saw this as a loophole for the little devil of private property to wiggle through. This lukewarmness also showed up in the failure to appoint a common elder for all three groups. The servants of the Word were simply unable and unwilling to revive the bishop's office. It also showed in the Hutterites' complete neglect of and indifference to mission work during the seventy years since their emigration to America. As a result the thirty-three colonies were now peopled by the descendants of only fifteen clans and extended families. In vain Eberhard called them back to the first centuries of Anabaptism, the days when Hutterian communities had devoted great effort to mission. "You urge us to do mission, but your Bruderhof with its guests is already a mission station," they responded. The American Hutterites had no understanding at all of Eberhard's words on this topic.

Ordination

If Eberhard's eye had not grown worse his circuit through the communities might well have continued for several more weeks. Ironically it was Eberhard's painful sickness that caused the Lehrerleut and Dariusleut elders to realize that he had been tested sufficiently. This brought them to sit down together at the same table for the first time in twelve years. On December 8, 1930, the elders and leaders of the Alberta Hutterites met at the Stand Off community and agreed to unite with the Rhön Bruderhof. The next day Eberhard Arnold was incorporated into the Hutterian Brethren by baptism, with the pouring over of water, according to Hutterian practice. Christian Waldner and Elias Walter performed the ceremony.

Here the question may arise, why a second baptism? All the servants of the Word essentially agreed that Eberhard's baptism of faith by immersion was just as valid as the baptisms performed at the Sannerz and Rhön Bruderhofs. They simply wanted to proceed with the assurance that none of the absent servants of the Word could dispute the new unity because of doubts on this point. After some hesitation Eberhard accepted the pouring over of water, referring to it as a sign of the "baptism of the Spirit, which comes from above when the Holy Spirit is poured out, flooding, surrounding, and blowing through and through." With him, the entire brotherhood of the Rhön Bruderhof was received into the Hutterian Brethren.

A few days later more than twenty servants of the Word assembled for Eberhard's ordination. This shows that they did not consider it necessary for him first to be appointed to the service of the Word – he was, after all, already word leader of the Rhön Bruderhof. What took place now was his confirmation in this task. The official record stated:

> On December 19, 1930, Eberhard Arnold was confirmed in the service of the Word of God with the laying on of hands by the elders Christian Waldner, Elias Walter, Johannes Kleinsasser and Johannes Entz…With this the church appoints Eberhard Arnold to the task for Germany, to proclaim the word of God there, to gather the zealous, and to establish the Bruderhof near Neuhof (Fulda in Hessen-Nassau) in proper order.

Eberhard wrote to Emmy, "It should be seen as a divine confirmation of the task I was given for this journey that we are now the first Bruderhof to belong at the same time to the Dariusleut, Schmiedeleut, and Lehrerleut." Some days earlier he had sent off a Christmas parcel with symbolic contents: traditional Hutterian kerchiefs (most of them second-hand, to avoid import duties) for all women and girls on the Rhön Bruderhof, a present from the women at the Elm Spring community. Eberhard enclosed a note with these head coverings, explaining that "by wearing the same style of dress, you will show that you love them and belong to them."

In all his joy Eberhard could not hide his disappointment that the question of economic support had not yet been dealt with. At the torturous expense of his health, he determined to go once more from colony to colony to gather help for the Rhön Bruderhof's economic survival. The fundraising journey through the Alberta and Manitoba communities alone took a full three months. Some communities were very hospitable and proved generous. Others – and those not the poorest – skirted the issue, offering good wishes but contributing very little. Here was further evidence of the "collective egoism" that Eberhard had denounced so passionately. Nonetheless he was able to send a few hundred dollars home to the Rhön Bruderhof each week.

An urgent matter pressing on Eberhard's mind during those weeks was the future of the Rhön Bruderhof. The catalyst was a a suggestion by Josef Stahl, minister at the Lake Byron community in South Dakota: move the Rhön Bruderhof – every man, woman, and child – to America. Sooner or later the Lake Byron community was intending to relocate to Alberta. This would allow the Rhön Bruderhof to take over the lease of Lake Byron. Of course Eberhard and his community would first have to finish the scholarly work on the Hutterian manuscripts, and the gathering of "the zealous." The suggestion was raised again – this time officially – when the Rhön Bruderhof and the Hutterian Brethren were formally united in December. Would the Rhön Bruderhof be ready to move to America if the elders decided that they should? Eberhard answered yes without hesitation. But the elders had appointed him as servant of the Word for Germany and had commissioned him to the task of building up the Bruderhof there. Taking all this into account, Eberhard wrote to Emmy in February, "I have been deeply confirmed in the conviction that we should remain as long as we possibly can in Europe, in our Germany that is once more struggling and suffering so severely."

In spite of the prolonged strain of his quest for unity Eberhard never questioned whether the prize was worth the effort. Four years later he would reflect, "The Hutterian communities convinced me deeply that in this communal life the three articles of the Apostles' Creed are brought together in unity: the creative life, the redeemed life of complete forgiveness for all sins and deviations, and the life of the Holy Spirit coming with its goodness from the powers of the future world. This was manifested in the wonderful unity among them, in a way I have simply not found in Christian circles in Europe today."[24]

Homecoming

At long last, on May 1, 1931, Eberhard embarked on his return voyage. The Atlantic liner Berlin docked in Bremerhaven on May 10. Emmy and Hans Zumpe were waiting to welcome him. On the way home to the Rhön, Eberhard stopped to buy some "cobble stones," a special kind of gingerbread that he had promised the children eleven months earlier for their help in paving a road to the Rhön Bruderhof. He had not forgotten.

Eberhard's arduous journey bore immediate fruit. First there was the notarized document officially recording the union with the Hutterian Brethren in Canada and the United States – only a sheet of paper, but in just two years it would be of incalculable importance. In addition Eberhard's experiences among the North American Hutterites provided enough to talk about for weeks and months to come, and plenty of illustrative material, as well: Hutterian garb for men and women (including the women's head coverings), hand tools, and photos.

The harvest from a scholar's point of view cannot be overestimated. In the course of just under a year Eberhard had shipped home more than two dozen packages containing hundreds of Hutterian writings, epistles, teachings, pastoral letters, and books – treasures that the individual Hutterian communities had guarded so carefully that not even their fellow communities were aware that the documents existed. The Rhön Bruderhof suddenly found itself housing the most comprehensive library of Anabaptist writings in Europe. It would take years to sort, compare, and evaluate all these documents.

Only a fraction of the hoped-for twenty-five thousand dollars – the sum needed to pay off debts and further build up the Rhön Bruderhof – had been collected. In this regard the journey was certainly a disappointment. But as Eberhard made clear in one of his first reports to the brotherhood: "Even if we had found the communities completely impoverished there would not have been a moment's hesitation about uniting with them."[25]

On the first evening after his return home, the community gathered outdoors. The children's community performed a play. Afterwards torches were lit. Irmgard Keiderling recorded the gathering in detail:

> We formed a big circle around the little circle of torches. Then Eberhard spoke about free and voluntary unity and about freedom in unity, in opposition to all rigid rules and halfheartedness. He said that just as he had reunited with Emmy, the two becoming one, and just as the Hutterites in America had bound themselves to us in Germany, two becoming one, so Christ and the church are bound together in true unity and freedom, without any law. He spoke in such a living and powerful way.
>
> When only two torches remained alight, Eberhard went to the middle of the circle and leaned them together so that they blazed twice as brightly, and he spoke of our uniting with Hutterianism, a union in which both groups, with their own particular characters, must complement each other in order to become completely one, as is the case in a true marriage.[26]

"When we pray for God's kingdom to come, we should pause for a moment and ask ourselves if we are ready to accept and to live out all the changes that God's rulership brings with it."

Innenland, "The Peace of God."

How Hutterian Should a Hutterite Be?

Union with the Hutterian communities in North America merged Eberhard and the members of the Rhön Bruderhof into a four-hundred-year-old spiritual stream. The spiritual waters of this old stream, freshly found in the New World, now poured back into the land of their source, flooding the little German community with energy and life. It was everything Eberhard had hoped for. Quite literally, a new world opened before them.

Upon his return Eberhard made it crystal clear to the gathered community that uniting with the Hutterites had been a consciously chosen step:

> Apart from the brotherhood known by the name Hutterian there is nothing in all the world, not even in the community groups existing in our day, that could correspond more closely to us in its very essence, in character and spirit, and could deepen us and give us more strength to go forward in our life. And so, while giving full recognition to our origins in the Youth Movement, to what we have found in the practice of communal living and in the Sermon on the Mount, I can affirm that this is the way we want to go...to the end.[1]

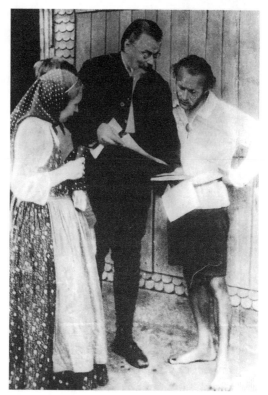

After Eberhard's return from his travels among the Hutterites in North America, letters strengthened the bonds of unity and provided rich food for thought and discussion.

Eberhard himself had no wish to deny the formative influences on his life, his past, or his spiritual development; nor did he want the community simply to forget the years of growth it had shared. All this made it a miracle that two such different movements had found one spirit to unite them: the one, a communal movement centuries old, mature and strong in numbers in North America; the other, a comparatively tiny, new, life-reform group spawned from the religious revival and youth movements in Germany. And this small group had rediscovered original Hutterianism to an extent unequaled anywhere else – even in the North American Hutterian communities themselves.

This fact had not escaped Eberhard during his time in America. After only a few weeks in South Dakota he had written in his diary: "The difference between our Bruderhof and American Hutterianism consists largely in this: we seek our spiritual nourishment and foundation in the joyfully combative first and second Hutterian periods of

1525–1533 and 1533–1578, whereas in the American communities it is the late period (1650–1700) that serves this purpose."[2] After his return Eberhard told the brotherhood, "We don't want to become Hutterian in the sense of 1692; we don't want to become Hutterian in the sense of 1780; neither do we want to become Hutterian in the sense of 1930–1931; but we do want to become Hutterian in the sense of those first sixty years, from 1529–1589."[3] At the same time Eberhard was aware that the Rhön Bruderhof could never link up with this history without reservations regarding some of the outward forms. A purely literal interpretation would have meant, among other things, a farewell to photographs and pictures, to the much-loved musical instruments, and to the songs and dances of the Sannerz community's joyful beginnings.[4] A cheerless caricature of the dynamic life of the earliest Hutterites would have been all that remained.

In fact during the years after uniting, impulsive fits of iconoclastic picture-purging sometimes broke out in the brotherhood – one or another member occasionally sought to be more Hutterian than the Hutterites. This always made Eberhard's blood boil. Even in the last months of his life he could be heard thundering, "If we are to go along with no one but the old Hutterian brothers and insist on everyone accepting our beliefs…then I will have no part in it but will protest against it as long as I live." He would pound his stick on the floor, punctuating each word with agitation.[5]

To the end of his days, however, Eberhard stood unshakable in his conviction that uniting with the Hutterites in North America came at just the right time, that they provided the German Bruderhof with important guidelines for survival and gave it legitimacy. With firmness he would say, "It is important to me that the source of our blessings is with the brothers and arises from the tremendous witness of the apostolic mission through the centuries. Our blessing comes only in this way, and in no other."[6] Eberhard tried to instill a reverence for Hutterianism, not an idolization of it. This is why the Rhön Bruderhof adopted a number of old Hutterian traditions, and why many songs from the sixteenth and seventeenth centuries are found in the second volume of the *Sonnenlieder*, published in 1932.[7]

Second Generation

Perhaps even before his American journey Eberhard had sensed that his time was running out. Openly, and more and more frequently, he considered what would become of the community after his death. He wrote in his diary at Christmas 1930:

208

> That unspoken concern was one of the primary motivations urging me to make this extremely demanding and strenuous journey. Our fellow fighters and coworkers have shown unprecedented trust and self-sacrifice. For their sake, instead of the will a rich man would leave, I want to establish our community on as deep, strong, and firm a foundation as possible, to ensure its continuation beyond my death.[8]

While still in America Eberhard had for the first time pondered over who should succeed him. He was hardly home before he suggested that Hans Zumpe be appointed as his assistant and that, after a time of testing, he should be appointed to the service of the Word – expressly in the case of Eberhard's own sudden death.[9]

Eberhard arranged with the Hutterian elders that as soon as possible two servants of the Word should visit the Rhön Bruderhof and take over its leadership, either in whole or in part.[10] All this can be seen as answers to urgent practical questions.

At the back of these concerns were far-reaching questions of principle. For example, what was to happen to children who had grown up in the community? They could not automatically become members anymore than anyone else. They too must one day make a conscious decision regarding the communal way of life. This problem first arose toward the end of the 1920s. Emy-Margret Arnold was already in college. Hans Grimm and Gerd and Liesel Wegner, three of the foster children, were taking their final school exams. What was to happen to them after that? In August of 1929 the brotherhood reached an agreement that "older children should remain in the Bruderhof only if they can honestly accept and bear witness to the foundation of faith, the structure, and the order within the church of God."[11]

Both Eberhard and Emmy represented that young people, even those who felt drawn to stay, should experience life outside the Bruderhof for as long as necessary to form their own views and to consider the communal life from a distance. They made no exceptions for their own children. Hardy began a course of study at Tübingen, and in 1934 Heinrich started his training at the Strickhof near Zurich, an agricultural school of excellent reputation.

To Eberhard and Emmy's great joy, all their children found their way into the community. Emy-Margret became a teacher, and after her studies she took over the children's extracurricular activities on the Rhön Bruderhof. Hardy showed, even at quite an early age, a marked gift for explaining the essence of the gospel to others. Of the five siblings, Heinrich was the contemplative and mystic. He loved people, and would later develop a rarely equaled ability to judge character. The two youngest, Hans-Hermann and Monika-Elisabeth, were also growing up firm in character and in faith. Eberhard wrote in the summer of 1934: "How grateful I am to my Emmy for what she has done for our children through her love and especially through her daily prayers for them! And how many prayers from our beloved parents and our long-deceased ancestors have been heard."[12] Even his nephew, Hermann Arnold, came to the Bruderhof in 1934 – "my only brother's only son." All this encouraged Eberhard to have trust for the future of the children's community. But he never gave in to the wishful thinking that every child would be happy in the Bruderhof life, or that each would be called to it.

A further question that increasingly concerned Eberhard was what would happen when the founding members were no longer living. He was well aware that decay often set in during the second and third generations of a movement. "It is true that this has often happened," he said in a discussion with guests at the Rhön Bruderhof, "but that is not proof that it is inevitable." And, "This question can be answered only through faith in the Holy Spirit." He pointed to the history of the Hutterian Brethren, "who throughout the centuries were again and again in danger of extinction, yet revived again and again and were repeatedly brought new strength by constantly renewed mission."[13] Of course he did not know for certain that the Bruderhof would confirm this experience, but he was ready to believe that it would.

Eberhard refused to accept that fossilization and decay were inevitable. On the contrary, he repeatedly astonished the brotherhood and even his wife with daring visions of the future. In the summer of

**Else von Hollander:
1885–1932.**

1932, for instance: "It often seems as if a life with one thousand people, to say nothing of one hundred thousand, in complete unity and peace is something that still lies far ahead…Whether there are few or many who are moved to leave the old life and seek the new, we are determined to unite with them in the expectation of the kingdom of God, which is not limited to only one hundred thousand people."[14] The brotherhood, then numbering just about fifty adult members, listened in disbelief. Many of them experienced later how the brotherhood, after periods of crisis and revival, grew to a thousand and more members. Some of those who heard Eberhard speak with such undaunted vision are still alive today and give a vivid account of it.

Else von Hollander would have had no trouble with this picture of the great "city of peace." Whereas Emmy was a realist, Else was a visionary. Else was a strong pillar of the community life. She shared Eberhard's most daring ideas and foresaw, perhaps even sooner than he did, what would develop over the following years – the growth, the struggles, the menace of an anti-Christian state. Next to Emmy, Else was Eberhard's most loyal friend. Of all the brotherhood members she was certainly the one most at home in his spiritual and intellectual world. Else was a theologian without a diploma – and a fiery fighter, just like him. Their common way ended on January 11, 1932. Else von Hollander died after a long, difficult illness; even in death she still gave a powerful witness. Her bequest to Eberhard and the brotherhood was a steadfast and boundless confidence in the course that they had pioneered.

Burdens of Authority

Eberhard and Emmy's natural authority had long been recognized. Both of them had shouldered spiritual authority before Eberhard's appointment in America as servant of the Word and Emmy's confirmation as housemother. And yet Eberhard, by his own recognition, seems to have been infused with an added power through the laying on of hands by the Hutterian elders. His words gained greater authority. His manner grew firmer, his judgment more decisive, his watchfulness keener. The brotherhood noticed this first. One of his former foster children recalls that "his great concern was for us to have an understanding of all the movements of our time. But he always said we must not be infected by these movements." Another Bruderhof sister recounts, "If Emmy said, 'Oh, he didn't mean it like that,' Eberhard could get quite worked up. It was crucial for him that the Holy Spirit came to expression clearly and that we did not get lost in human feelings. That was why he could be so pointed."

To people from outside the community Eberhard could seem quite intimidating. When a group of young Baptists came to the Bruderhof for a volunteer service project in the late summer of 1932, there were heated confrontations. A few of the young men flared up in opposition to Eberhard. He held out resolutely and told one of them to leave the Bruderhof because he had offended the spirit of community to an intolerable degree.[15] Some thought this to be highly authoritarian – almost dictatorial. Eberhard, however, made no attempt to hide his disappointment: the young people completely lacked "reverence for what is holy." By this he meant the sanctity of life in general, but also the spiritual dignity of the task of leadership. He did not claim this respect for his leadership on his own account; it had been passed on to him by the Hutterian elders according to New Testament example.

This dignity and authority also gave him the freedom to challenge the consciences of the brothers in America. For example, he repeatedly attempted to restore the bishop's service to the Hutterian communities. When he heard of the death of David Hofer, the difficult but wise elder of the Lehrerleut, he advised his successor, Johannes Kleinsasser, and the two other elders from the Schmiedeleut and Dariusleut to meet regularly to strengthen their unity.

In the years following his journey to America, Eberhard acted on the strength of this authority. He conducted twelve Bruderhof marriages, baptized more than sixty people, and accepted more than fifty into the brotherhood – among them a whole list of Bruderhof children: Hans Grimm, Sophie Löber, Liesel and Gerd Wegner, and all five of his own children.

But this authority came with a burden. While on his journey to America, Eberhard wrote to Emmy, "It is such a heavy and agonizing burden to have to be a word leader or something similar. Anyone who desperately wants such a service does not know the suffering that this

Emmy Arnold wearing her Hutterian head covering, ca. 1935.

all-too-holy imperative brings to us weak men. Happy are those who are not burdened with it."[16] In his talks with the North American Hutterites, Eberhard discovered this problem over and over again. The entry in his travel diary for April 10, 1931, reads: "The Hutterites here often say, 'Those who sit at the back of the church cannot know how hard it is to have to stand at the front.'" Later he experienced this himself, and this spiritual responsibility weighed down on him more heavily than ever. Rudi Hildel recalls, "He was saddened when he felt we were narrow-minded or were absorbed in self-concern. It hurt him when we did not share the breadth of Christ's vision with him."

This authority and its burden came without medals or ribbons. Eberhard wore no cassock, no clergyman's collar – no sign of any kind to distinguish him from the other Bruderhof men. Emmy stood out just as little from the other women of the community. The English Quaker John Hoyland, who later translated Eberhard's introductory survey to *The Early Christians*, wrote after only one visit to the

Rhön Bruderhof: "These two leaders are simply ordinary individuals among all the rest and have no outward authority. Yet they have the gift to understand, put into words, and accomplish the things to which the Spirit of God is leading the whole community." Hoyland went on to describe the "humility of true parental love" that he had observed in the Arnolds. "Their leadership shows itself in kindness, not in giving orders."[17]

In all this Eberhard always explicitly stated that spiritual authority and the aptitude for spiritual tasks can never be attained by human efforts. It can literally only be granted. He chose his fiftieth birthday as an opportunity to make a statement to the gathered brotherhood:

> On this day I have been especially conscious of my lack of ability and how unsuited my own nature is to the work I have been given. I remember how God called me when I was only sixteen years old and how I have stood in his way, with the result that much of what God must have wanted to do through his instruments has not been possible...Another thing concerns me very much: the powerlessness of men, even of the man who has been entrusted with some task. Only God is mighty; we are actually powerless. Even for the work that has been given us, we are entirely lacking in power. But I believe that just this is the only and deepest reason why God has called us to this service: we know we are powerless...[18]

This is the attitude in which Eberhard Arnold led the Bruderhof. Longtime friends and fellow workers watched from near and far as he matured into a bishop-like figure. He frowned on admiration of every type. "Away with all honoring of men!" was one of his most notable pronouncements.[19]

Inner Land, Revisited

It is not known exactly when Eberhard began a complete revision of *Inner Land.* Perhaps he was considering a new version even before his journey to America. But it was not until 1931 that the revisions took book form. At first glance not much is left of the 1918 edition – only the book's skeleton, the general outline, and a few particularly striking pictures. Even though this new rendition of *Inner Land* is still subtitled *A Guide to the Soul of the Bible,* it also gives insight into Eberhard's soul and mirrors his inner development after 1918. It reflects, as well, the theological conflicts of the 1920s. The dispute with Karl Barth and his "totally other" God takes place both in and in between the lines.[20] Liberal, intellectual theology is challenged.[21] Ideas from Sigmund Freud's psychoanalysis are taken into account.

The revised edition of *Inner Land* can also be read as a record of approaching disaster. From one page to the next Eberhard's premonitions grow sharper, his warnings clearer. His farsightedness is stunning: months before Hitler seized power, before the whole of society was forced into National Socialist conformity, long before the hellish aspect of Nazism was recognizable, Eberhard prophesied the collapse of any kind of national self-redemption. He castigated race idolatry and foresaw the approaching evil, bloodshed, and death.[22] Naturally his capacity to predict the future had its limits. Eberhard could have no idea of the crimes the National Socialists would later commit. A state that trod justice underfoot and set up injustice as its norm defied even his powers of imagination.[23] After January 30, 1933, when reality surpassed imagination to the most horrible degree, he had no desire to expend his energies on describing the terror; he did not want to direct any more attention to evil than was absolutely necessary. Eberhard chose an altogether different approach: look away from the dangers, focus on the mystery of *Gemeinde,* and draw strength from the spiritual powers that help the believers to withstand persecution and face the enemy.[24] Here once more he anticipated his own personal experiences and the experiences of the Bruderhof.

By the end of 1932 the revision of the chapter "Light and Fire" had been completed. It served as a statement of belief for Eberhard and the brotherhood at the Rhön Bruderhof. After January 30, 1933, the day that Hitler became chancellor of Germany, any attentive reader of this chapter of *Inner Land* must either have been alarmed for the fate of its author – or else have been on the other side and have recognized immediately that the new state could never expect the support of such a man.

Eberhard included in "Light and Fire" a short history of the swastika, the eastern symbol of sun and fire that the National Socialists had chosen – in error, Eberhard asserted – as the symbol for their movement. He pointed out that this symbol, which dates back to the Stone Age, has a universal significance for all humanity. He claimed the swastika for all peoples, regardless of race or color, and quite specifically for the Jews. With Eberhard's insights into the universal nature of the swastika in mind, the horrors of the holocaust, meted out under this very symbol, seem all the more perverse.[25] In this same chapter he wrote of a new community of people to be gathered from all the nations – the church of Jesus Christ – thus repudiating the idolization of the nation state. Eberhard went on to speak of Jesus Christ as the "opposite of all earthly rulers," and declared the inherent conflict between exercising governmental authority and living the likeness of Christ. He called upon people to refuse military service, to be conscientious objectors who reject all participation in war, and to love their enemies.[26]

"Light and Fire" carries Eberhard's statement: "Whoever gets ready for the expectation of his kingdom – Jesus' kingdom – prepares himself in spirit for martyrdom's baptism of fire." With the early fourth-century martyr Methodius he said:

Fleeing the cunning Serpent's
thousandfold flatteries,
I endure the firebrand's flame
and the dread onslaught of wild beasts,
to await Thy coming from heaven.

Jesus Christ, Eberhard declared, is the "one and only leader" for Christians to follow – their one and only *Führer.*

Only a few months after the chapter was published ("Light and Fire" first appeared as a separate booklet) Eberhard's stand would be put to the test. Would it prove to be nothing but empty words and wasted breath, unable to withstand the storm of evil engulfing a whole society? Or would it be a conviction built on rock, strong enough to stand firm against the wind?

Today the Jews, Tomorrow the Christians

Even today, decades after World War II, many people still assert that right until the end of the war nothing was known about the crimes of National Socialism, that the true character of Hitler's regime was hidden from ordinary people. Either this assertion is a conscious lie or else it is psychological denial. How else could it be explained that in a remote settlement at the edge of the idyllic Fulda valley everyone knew what was going on two months after Hitler seized power?

Good Friday 1933 came two days after the Reichstag had passed the so-called Enabling Act, and two days after Adolf Hitler's address to the Reichstag in which he finally dropped his mask of respectability.[27] On this day the brotherhood of the Rhön Bruderhof gathered to celebrate the Lord's Supper. Each member had a chance to speak, as was the usual custom. Everybody in the circle could express his or her own impressions. Here is a short extract from the transcript of this decisive meeting:

> *Emmy Arnold:* We must know exactly what is actually happening. Nothing is being written about it. Herr G—— from Heubach… said that a line is being drawn through the parish – those with Hitler on one side, and on the other those who are unable to cooperate on grounds of conscience. He said no one could risk using the word "justice" for fear of immediately being labeled a communist. He is surprised he hasn't been taken away yet. A Heubach woman's father-in-law was beaten to death in Fulda. Now the Jews are being persecuted, next it will be the Christians."

In Nazi Berlin, crowds pack Unter den Linden below the Ministry of Interior to demonstrate their allegiance to Hitler.

Else Boller: It is urgently necessary for us to make perfectly clear to the authorities why we live as we do and what our purpose is. Hitler says terrible things in his speeches.

Eberhard Arnold: We want to put all our efforts into building up this place, as long as we have it, as a memorial to God's honor, so to our last moment here we want to do the very utmost that can be done...It is inherent in *imitatio,* in being Christlike, that we are ready for imprisonment and death. We are prepared to leave here; we are also prepared to remain. We shall not flee without an especially valid reason. We shall stay firmly in this place that was shown to us until God sends us a direct call to leave it. And so we continue with our building and daily work...We carry on working as before so that no one can say, "The Bruderhof has changed its way of work because of the change of government." If that can be said of us, then it would be right to accuse us of cowardice and unfaithfulness...

I believe it possible to speak very plainly to this government... So we must ask God that an interview will be possible and that we are granted a completely frank exchange. Then we must take up the cause of prisoners and those in distress, inquire at places where we can get authentic information, do our utmost and be extremely active, even without the magazine. We cannot publish a magazine at this moment. So we must follow the Hutterian example, speaking person to person, the way of personal contact.[28]

In saying this Eberhard gave the community its marching orders for the following years. Hold out. Do not be intimidated. Do not yield one inch without just cause or need – that would remain the Bruderhof's directive until 1937. By taking the offensive and meeting the authorities openly, Eberhard and a few other brothers gained access to people at the top levels of the National Socialist government and succeeded in getting an ear. Here, personal relationships played a key role. For example, Norman Körber, the nature lover and friend from Berlin and early Sannerz days, who had more recently worked as a government lawyer, provided Eberhard with important information from within the administration, which now, under the Nazi policy of forced conformity *(Gleichschaltung),* had to toe the party line.

To help prisoners and the destitute proved scarcely practicable. All the same in the years after 1933 the Bruderhof became a refuge for several people who could not have evaded the grasp of the National Socialists in any other way. For example, Friedel Sondheimer, a young Jew, found his way to the Bruderhof in 1931. For him and others, Eberhard put his own life on the line.

The dire premonitions of the first months of 1933 were not off base. Already by September 1933 Eberhard had heard from a university pastor about concentration camps, arbitrary arrests, mistreatment of innocent people, and denial of basic human rights.[29] A short while later the state began to show official interest in the Rhön Bruderhof. The so-called Reich Bishop, Ludwig Müller, tried to sound out the Bruderhof's attitude through a letter of October 11, 1933:[30] "It would interest the Reich Bishop to know what position you and your community take toward Christianity and the church."

Eberhard's answer was plain and direct: "Never, in four hundred years, have the brothers named after Jakob Hutter taken part in the power struggles of state politics, political parties, parliamentarianism, and class distinctions, just as they have never had personal property and have never used weapons." In the Hutterian communities "real community of the people is realized on the basis of community of faith." In closing Eberhard wrote: "Our whole brotherhood wishes and prays that the Reich Bishop of Germany may be granted grace from Jesus Christ and enlightenment from the Holy Spirit to do the will of God, who wants to reveal his love and unity to all men." Müller, a compliant henchman of the Nazis, can seldom have been admonished in so elegant yet so plain a manner. Enclosed with the letter was a copy of "Light and Fire." This was the first and only time that the "German Christians" sought contact with the Bruderhof. Obviously Eberhard's letter had told them everything they needed to know.

A Letter to Adolf Hitler

Eberhard wanted very much to meet Hitler face to face. During the brotherhood meeting on Good Friday 1933 he had actually said, "I believe that this government would be glad to hear a deepgoing and clear word. If I could have a talk with Adolf Hitler, I would approach it full of confidence. I look forward to the day it happens." He left no stone unturned in his efforts to gain an interview with Hitler.

On November 9, 1933, in anticipation of the plebiscite on Hitler's policy scheduled for November 12, Eberhard wrote a letter in the name of the brotherhood addressed to "Adolf Hitler, Chancellor of the German Reich, Berlin." It opened with the words, "We greet our beloved Reich Chancellor Adolf Hitler for November 12 with an affirmation of our loyalty to the government and representation of the German Reich committed to him by God." The form of this initial greeting alone needs careful consideration. Without it, Eberhard's attitude is inevitably misunderstood, as it was by the Swiss pastor Leonhard Ragaz, who was still furious years later because "this expression of love betrayed a *reservatio mentali* [mental reservation] that even the Jesuits have seldom equaled."[31] But Ragaz never had to risk his life, nor did he ever have to test his theological understanding of magistracy on a dictator like Hitler, as the Christians in Germany did. Safe in Zurich, it was very easy for him to pass judgment.

Yet the question remains: how could Eberhard possibly speak of "his beloved rulers Hindenburg and Adolf Hitler?" How could he call Hitler his "beloved Reich Chancellor?" He called him "beloved," and he told him why he loved him: Eberhard saw even Hitler's chancellorship as "appointed by God" in the sense of Romans 13:2. He explained his expectations of Hitler and under what conditions Hitler would deserve to be loved: Hitler should "establish peace and justice." Eberhard rejected every arbitrary act and every claim that went beyond this God-given mandate. In one breath he declares his love to Hitler, in the next he lectures him!

Eberhard courteously told the "beloved Reich Chancellor" that, in accordance with the Bruderhof's confession of faith, the brothers could not serve in the military. He tried to get Hitler to promise the freedom of conscience and religion that the Prussian kings Friedrich Wilhelm and Friedrich II had once accorded to the Mennonites. With the letter he enclosed the *Inner Land* chapter "Light and Fire" for closer study. And finally he let Hitler know that the community was praying to God with all their hearts that he, Adolf Hitler, "at the time granted by God, would become an ambassador of the lowly Christ."

Unlike many Bruderhof friends abroad, the National Socialist officials – Hitler's subordinates – understood the letter perfectly. (Hitler presumably never laid eyes on it.) Their answer was not long in coming.

It is important to keep in mind that Eberhard's frank explanation of the Bruderhof's attitude to the National Socialist state came months before the Confessing Synods were formed in the Protestant church, and half a year before the Barmen theological declaration – each in opposition to the Nazis. Eberhard's conviction of 1918 held good in 1933. Christians were to be a "corrective to the normative" and were duty-bound to give their first allegiance to God rather than to men. No one belonging to the Bruderhof ever lifted a hand in the German salute. Not one member ever shouted *"Heil Hitler!"* Not one of them ever became a storm trooper.

Subtler points deserve mention as well: Eberhard never addressed Hitler as *"Führer,"* much less "beloved *Führer,"* and therefore, by definition, Eberhard never acknowledged Hitler as a leader. Always, he kept it to "Reich Chancellor" or "Chancellor." Even in his letter to Hitler, Eberhard spoke with consistent clarity about only one Leader: Eberhard spoke of discipleship to "our *Führer* and liberator, Jesus Christ."

Chapter Fifteen

"The mystery of the kingdom of God is that it encompasses both polarity and universality. All questions come together into one central question."

Spoken to Winifred Bridgwater.

A Church or *The* Church?

Hitler and the new state challenged the Bruderhof and faced it with questions. At almost the same time, the community had to deal with a question of quite a different character. Leonhard Ragaz wrote a letter on February 22, 1933, addressed to "Eberhard Arnold, Hans Boller, and their closest friends." Ragaz sounded genuinely disturbed. He asked point-blank, "Isn't it the case that you are not simply 'a' church, but 'the' church?…Do you believe that the Hutterian brothers, taken as a whole today, constitute 'the' church?" – and, in the same breath, he urged them to "holy sobriety" and strongly warned against "fanaticism."

What had happened? On the face of it the question seemed to have been provoked by the disintegration of the Werkhof, a Swiss Christian community settlement. The Werkhof was by no means the first community experiment of its type in Switzerland. Earlier a religious-socialist group had lived in community near Lake Zurich. Ragaz had identified very closely with these settlements, all the more so because, out of consideration for his wife, he had never taken the step of joining their communal life.

The Werkhof had been founded in 1930 by three young married couples. Max and Eva Lezzi knew the Rhön Bruderhof; they had stayed there for some time and had gathered much valuable experience about community living. When another young couple, the Kyburg pastor Hans Boller and his wife Else, made plans to join the Werkhof in 1931, the Lezzis advised them to spend time at the Bruderhof first. The Bollers went to the Rhön and after a few weeks decided to remain there. This meant that the Bruderhof had deprived Leonhard Ragaz of both a zealous disciple and a friend – or at least that was how he felt about it.[1]

After a period of inner tensions – apparently unavoidable in Christian community settlements – two of the Werkhof's founding members, Peter and Anni Mathis, left in the late summer of 1932, bound for the Rhön Bruderhof. Finally, Hans and Margrit Meier made the move to the Rhön as well, depriving the Werkhof of two more of its founders. The possibility of unity between the two communities, though seriously considered in the past, had shipwrecked.

In light of these developments Ragaz's question can well be understood. The assumption behind it was not so far off the mark either. Even a reader without ulterior motives could find much in the old Hutterites' choice of words and forms of expression that sounds very exclusive.[2] Whether it is meant exclusively is another question. In his enthusiasm for the old Hutterian writings Eberhard had adopted a number of very emphatic terms that, without further explanation, were bound to lead to misunderstandings. For example, he often spoke of the *Gemeinde* as the "ark of the Last Days." After a series of further misunderstandings Ragaz later countered with the comment that, for him, this ark had too many holes in it.[3] First of all, however, he waited for a reply from the Rhön Bruderhof. It came in two letters written March 9 and 11, 1933, in which Eberhard put it quite clearly:

> When we are asked whether we…are God's church, the *Gemeinde,* we have to say, "No, we are not. We are an object of God's love, just like all other people, and we are unworthy, powerless, and unfit to follow the Holy Spirit's promptings, to build up the *Gemeinde,* or to go on mission into all the world." But when we are asked, "Is the church of God among you? Does the church of God come to people where you are – is the church of God there in the sense of the Holy

Spirit, who is alone able to bring the church of God?" Then we have to answer, "Yes, that is so. Wherever believing people are gathered and have no other will than the one, single will that the kingdom of God may come and that the church of Christ may be revealed as the perfect unity of his spirit – then the church is in every such place because the Holy Spirit is there."

This answer satisfied Ragaz at first. But the matter of the Werkhof, which actually did not directly involve him, continued to nag at him. And Eberhard? In the following years he rigorously resisted any shadow of arrogance or elitism within the brotherhood. He continued to cultivate friendships and fellowship with Christians of the most varied beliefs and creeds. At a later opportunity Eberhard would again make it unmistakably clear that "the witness of the communal life is one decisive witness in our day; this does not mean, however, that no other witnesses exist."[4] Scarcely anyone else could express the earnestness of an inner call as clearly as he continued to do. He wrestled without reservation for the sake of certain individuals. And sometimes he lost.

Do You Want to Go Away, Too?

On July 15, 1933, a novice member deserted the Bruderhof, abandoning his wife and children as well. Eberhard was deeply affected. So were all other brotherhood members. It was not so much the act of desertion of the brotherhood – at times other companions of the way had left the community for a wide variety of understandable reasons. Rather it was the circumstances that Eberhard found so shattering. The brother who left had made his decision entirely on his own and had disappeared without a word of explanation. This, Eberhard felt, was a breach of trust. "We certainly cannot expect that everyone stays with us," he said to the assembled community. "People can remain here only if they have surrendered unconditionally and forever to the gathering, uniting power of Jesus Christ. Nothing else can keep them here. When people leave us, we are saddened as we think of the individuals themselves, but for the sake of the cause we are glad if those who do not belong to us part from us. I mean in the sense that they show no sign of a unifying power at work in them…It is a question of what they really want in their deepest hearts."

From a purely objective standpoint, a thousand excuses and arguments could easily be formulated on behalf of this novice who left the community: the material need, the inner tension, the Nazis' very real political pressure, the prospect of being crushed between the millstones, the obligations of community life. And always the demanding – necessarily so – order of the life together. Certainly it seems understandable that not everyone would be equal to such demands.

But Eberhard chose that event to present the crux of the matter to the brotherhood:

> This morning we must once more ask: are we ready? Do you wish to leave, too? Who wants to go away? If anyone does, let him say so; let him have the courage to explain why he is leaving. We ask anyone who wants to go away to stand up and tell us. Only those may stay who have chosen without reservations and forever Jesus' purpose of drawing people together; who have chosen the spirit of reconciliation, unity with the perfect sacrifice of Jesus, the unity of the body of Christ, and the peace and unity of his kingdom – only those may stay who are ready to live and die for all this. Everyone else should leave.

Shocked silence.

Eberhard had voiced nothing less than the meaning and seriousness of a vow. All or nothing. Then, as now, this aspect of Eberhard's thinking may have presented the greatest stumbling block for others. From the perspective of our day and age Eberhard's attitude is undoubtedly anachronistic – out of sync with our times. It is rare enough in today's world for someone to vow lifelong faithfulness to another person without a prenuptial agreement in the back pocket. But Eberhard was talking about a lifelong pledge to a cause – an unquestionably noble cause, but a cause all the same.

More than a few would trip over this stumbling block. Only two months later the wife and children of the novice who had left also departed, together with another novice member. For Eberhard this was further cause to speak of the holy seriousness of the decision for life in community:

> When a person gives his or her word to God and to God's *Gemeinde*, it is binding. It must determine the whole course of that person's

future life. Such a promise can never be taken back or annulled, for it is not a question of giving one's word to people…No one should take up God's cause out of human goodwill or without first counting the cost, without being clear what this cause is about and what loyalty, what perseverance to the very end, is demanded by this discipleship. Once again, it is not demanded by people, but by the One who called us to follow this way.

Eberhard was not demanding something humanly impossible. He knew how far to depend on human decisions, or rather how fragile they are. According to him the secret of a spiritual pledge consists of trusting in God. He is the one who makes it possible. He is the one who establishes it. God must give the strength to keep it. God gives the calling for a life in community; no human being can call himself to it. God gives the strength to live in community. Only through trust in God can anyone dare to take this step, to enter this life.

Over the years many people found their way to the community – first in Sannerz, then in the Rhön. Eberhard shared months and years of his life with many of them. During his lifetime eighty men and women promised lifelong faithfulness and became brotherhood members. Later on nine of them would become unfaithful. But only one of these members turned back while Eberhard was alive: Suse Hungar left the Bruderhof in 1930 while he was in America.[5] Others, in effect, used the novitiate as a time of testing, then left after recognizing that they could not promise single-minded loyalty.

Eberhard tried for years to win certain individuals to the communal life. He persisted only if he felt strongly that a person was actually called to life in community. Then he fought for them with much ingenuity and perseverance. Sometimes his efforts fell short. But sometimes he succeeded. Marianne Hilbert, for example, came in 1932 to teach at the Bruderhof school for a trial period. Eberhard noticed how she struggled to make a decision. Her mother was a strict Lutheran and regarded Eberhard as a fanatic and a sectarian. Marianne felt torn between her love for her mother and her calling to community life. When she told Eberhard about her mother's reservations he advised her, as a start, to study Luther, out of love for her mother. "Eberhard never forced anyone against his or her inner convictions," Marianne recalled later.[6] To others, such as Erich Mohr and Hermann Buddensieg, he simply extended a friendly invitation, with the unspoken hope that God's call would one day reach them.

There is only one case recorded where Eberhard pushed and pulled and urged with every means at his disposal and possibly made a great mistake in doing so. This was the case of Robert Friedmann, the Viennese researcher on Anabaptism. Friedmann had an intimate knowledge of Hutterian history and had been deeply impressed by the Hutterian way of life. He made his first visit to the Bruderhof in April of 1929 and was fascinated by Eberhard.[7] Friedmann called Eberhard "quite an exceptional and compelling leader, full of love and a source of spiritual inspiration," and acknowledged that he and Eberhard "became good friends, truly brothers in spirit." Eberhard knew that Friedmann's wife was a practicing theosophist and that she did not share her husband's leanings toward Christianity. In spite of this he endeavored to win Friedmann through years of intensive correspondence. "Leave your middle-class existence," he wrote in June of 1929. "Give up your useless efforts in social democracy and in the all-too-individualistic dabbling in scholarly work, which doesn't put into practice what it puts into print."[8] In February of 1934 Eberhard wrote even more emphatically, "Leave all worthless efforts made by human power politics. Humble yourself and be a simple member of a small, despised unity."[9] In the meantime Friedmann had made it plain that he felt more closely allied with the religious-socialist activities of Leonhard Ragaz than with the Bruderhof experiment. Eberhard answered this with unusual sharpness, saying that Ragaz appeared to be "still much too optimistic in his assumptions about the possible development of leagues of nations and their governments...Peace and justice, God's kingdom? In this way? People should have recognized at long last that such evolutionary thinking has totally collapsed." In a thoughtless moment Friedmann told Ragaz about this letter, and as a result the always mistrustful Swiss professor cut ties with Eberhard once and for all.[10]

Not that Friedmann always heard favorable reports from Ragaz about Eberhard – as early as 1929 Ragaz had shared his objections to the Bruderhof idea and had sown seeds of doubt, so that in the end

Friedmann did not know what to believe.[11] The bottom line of the problem was that both Eberhard Arnold and Leonhard Ragaz stumbled into a tug-of-war, each trying to win Friedmann over to their respective viewpoints. Friedmann wanted to be a friend to both and did not want to hurt either of them, and so he became their unwilling buffer, hearing complaints from each side about the other. Unable to bring about reconciliation between Ragaz and Eberhard, he instead played an unhappy role in the already puzzling and contradictory relationship between these two men.[12] Robert Friedmann later joined the Mennonites; after 1937 he taught in the United States at the Mennonite college in Goshen, Indiana. He remained in contact with the Bruderhof for many years.

Wise as Serpents

The uncertain future presented another reason for Eberhard's demands of absolute single-mindedness and dedication from his brotherhood companions. That, of course, is only one side of the coin. The other side is that the community backed up every single member, a commitment that soon proved necessary. After about half a year's respite the Nazi authorities began to harass the Bruderhof. The community had to do battle on three fronts, one after the other: for the independence of the Bruderhof, for their children, and against an economic stranglehold. Eberhard led these battles for over two years.

The National Socialist harvest festival, celebrated on October 1, 1933, served as the prologue to the drama to come. The Bruderhof had received threats beforehand – "You'll catch it if you don't join in." They sent a harvest wagon laden with vegetables for winter relief and so came out of the affair honorably.[13]

A few days later, on October 25, Eberhard Arnold broke his left leg. It was such an awkward break that he had to spend the next few days in the Fulda hospital. Only a mishap, a minor incident, one might suppose. But as time went on the accident had tragic consequences.

Around this time the brotherhood began using code names in their letters in order to shield the identity of friends and correspondents. Their principle was to stay open about their aims, but to keep names confidential.

For the November 12 plebiscite on Hitler's government policy the brotherhood worked out a short statement, more or less extracted from Eberhard's letter to Hitler. They printed it on gummed paper, and each brotherhood member stuck it on his or her ballot:

> By conviction and will, I am pledged to the gospel and the discipleship of Jesus Christ, the coming kingdom of God, and the love and unity of his church. This is the one and only vocation God has given me as my calling. Out of this faith I intercede before God and all people for my fatherland and above all for the Reich government as men with another and different vocation, which is not mine, but a vocation given by God to my beloved rulers Hindenburg and Adolf Hitler.

The reaction was not long in coming. On November 16 about one hundred fifty heavily armed policemen, Storm Troopers, and *Gestapo* officers surrounded the Bruderhof. Under the direction of a *Gestapo* official they ransacked every room, even tearing up floorboards. They took away all books with red covers from the library, and in addition took special interest in meeting transcripts and mail from abroad. Eberhard lay in bed with his broken leg, unable to be moved. He tried in vain to dialogue with the officials.

The Bruderhof people suddenly became aware of the value of their foreign members: Walter Hüssy and the families Meier, Boller, and Mathis from Switzerland; and Nils and Dora Wingard, Swedish members who had been married by Eberhard in October of 1932. With the exception of Walter Hüssy all had found their way to the community during the two years before Hitler seized power. As long as they were on the Bruderhof, Hitler's foot soldiers had to maintain at least a semblance of decorum. In the following period, when members of the brotherhood needed to visit officials, Eberhard never sent a German member alone; it was the rule for at least one foreign member to go along too. Only he himself risked going alone to the authorities, and then he always carried letters and documents from the Hutterian brothers in North America. Here too his line of thought was clear and proved itself: the world should and would know what transpired. This message was understood. In October 1934 Eberhard found open doors and ears even within the Ministry for Foreign

Affairs in Berlin.[14] International contacts and the bond with the Hutterian communities in North America became a life insurance policy for the whole Bruderhof.

Eberhard fought against the Nazis' racist ideology. It was, at least at first, a lonely fight. Long before the Nuremberg Laws on race were issued in September of 1935, Hitler's government strongly recommended that all inhabitants of the German Reich prove their Aryan heredity. That, of course, was more than a little difficult for the Bruderhof. In the brotherhood there were not only people with somewhat complicated biographies, but also some from Jewish families or ancestry. What should be done? Eberhard decided on a daring plan. During 1934 he drew up the combined Arnold/von Hollander family tree and introduced it with the words, "The purely Aryan, exceptionally Germanic, heredity and family history of the brotherhood of the Neuwerk Bruderhof Inc., in particular its directors." Strictly speaking, of course, only its "directors." Then he expanded on this heritage in rapturous, operatic style, naming every highborn personage, every prince, every princely court, every prominent name that had ever played a part, however insignificant, in the family histories of the Arnolds and von Hollanders. He brought in everything and anything that could somehow make an impression: doctoral degree; SCM; his Excellency Reich Chancellor Michaelis; articles in reference books such as *Kürschner's Calendar of German Scholars, Religion in the Past and Present,* and the *Mennonite Encyclopedia.* Eberhard compiled an impressive array of advisors to the consistory, professors, deacons, superintendents, chief executive officers for miscellaneous dukes, and so on and so forth – not to mention Peter Poelchau, the last bishop of the German Evangelical Church in Latvia. Still more astonishing were the personages with whom all these von Hollanders, Voigts, Arnolds, and Drachenhauers had associated: Queen Amalia of Greece; the Royal House of Württemberg-Oldenburg; Johann Lavater; and, of course, Heinrich Pestalozzi; as well as a healthy sprinkling of knights from various German orders and German-Baltic nobility.

This composition was a desperately audacious attempt to protect the people of the Bruderhof, with its haphazard assortment of itinerants, Jews, anarchists, and former middle-class citizens. *Pars pro toto –*

a small part was to stand for the whole. It is, of course, doubtful whether all the glitter of aristocratic names would have produced an effect for even a quarter of an hour had push come to shove – but that is hardly the point. Only the principle counts: Eberhard wanted to dazzle the racial ideologists and to hide the endangered members of the community without being untruthful. Quite apart from this it cannot be denied that the "genealogy" gave him considerable enjoyment, even though the reason for drawing it up was deadly serious. By the time the Nuremberg Laws on race went into effect the endangered community members, such as thirty-two-year-old Friedel Sondheimer, had already been moved to safety.

At the end of the day the Bruderhof would win its fight for the integrity of the community. In five years under Nazi rule the National Socialists failed to daunt or divide the Bruderhof, failed to induce individual members to leave, and failed to force the brotherhood to make concessions to the Brownshirts' ideology. But it is true that during this same time the Bruderhof grew more isolated. Good friends such as Friedrich Siegmund-Schultze had gone into exile. In mid-December 1933 the Dahlem pastor Martin Niemöller, cofounder of the Pastors' Emergency League, refused to stand shoulder to shoulder with the Bruderhof members because of their attitude toward military service. The Confessional Church was still absorbed, year after year, with itself and with its understanding of government authority.[15] Relatively few people showed the courage to admit friendship with the Bruderhof. Karl Heim was one of the few. Throughout these years the Arnolds kept up a brisk correspondence with him and his wife, and he in turn wrote recommendations and letters in favor of the community.

The Fight for the Children

On November 22, 1933, a few days after the Nazi raid on the Bruderhof, Eberhard felt obliged to write a letter to the school authorities in Kassel, applying for a young teacher for the Bruderhof's elementary and middle school – "a teacher with state qualifications and a supporter of National Socialism." Evidently the local authorities had threatened to close the Bruderhof school because it did not provide an education oriented to National Socialism. There are only four possible explanations for the wording of Eberhard's letter:

The first is that the brotherhood had actually become reconciled to letting the children come into the hands of a loyal follower of the party line. But that would have meant a betrayal of their convictions, and as such it is an unthinkable idea, considering the community's background.

The second possibility is that the brotherhood hoped to keep some part of the responsibility for the school and so be able to exercise an influence on the children and even on the "young teacher." That would have been an unpredictable game of chance and hardly consistent with the clarity that Eberhard had always demanded in other matters.

A third conjecture is that the brotherhood wanted to wring a bearable compromise from the authorities through negotiation. That is at least credible.

The only other possible explanation is that the brotherhood wanted to buy time and was striving meanwhile to find an entirely different solution. This supposition is supported not only by the events that took place following Eberhard's letter but also by a report from Hans Meier. Already in the last days of November, Hans, his luggage crammed with shorthand notebooks (the verbatim records of many public gatherings and confidential brotherhood meetings), had been sent out by the brotherhood with the task of finding a safe place for the school children.[16]

On December 5 the Fulda Inspector of Schools, Dr. Hammacher, arrived at the Bruderhof. He inspected the school and was very much put out that the children did not know any National Socialist songs, and he openly threatened that the foster children would not be able to stay. This was the very same Dr. Hammacher who had visited the Bruderhof in December 1930 accompanied by fifty assistant teachers, all of whom had left very much impressed by the Bruderhof's standard of education.

Still, despite this struggle over the school, the joys and sorrows of day-to-day Bruderhof life continued. There was a burst of joy when, on December 20 (Eberhard and Emmy's twenty-fourth wedding anniversary), Emy-Margret gave birth to her second child, a son who was named Hans Benedikt.

Eberhard, now the grandfather of two, wrote to Zacharias Walter in James Valley, Manitoba, and eleven other Hutterian ministers.[17] The letter is noteworthy because it contains the first reference to plans for a second Bruderhof – a Bruderhof outside of Germany. In so doing Eberhard openly refers to the advice given to him by David Hofer, the late Lehrerleut elder: "Stay in Germany as long as you can keep the control of the school in the church's hands."

On December 29 a letter arrived from the chief government official in Kassel: the school authorities found themselves obliged to withdraw permission for the maintenance of a private elementary and middle school.

On January 4 Eberhard politely informed School Inspector Dr. Hammacher that the Bruderhof school had been dissolved. The children of school age had moved to another place, Eberhard explained, "…so that there are no longer any school-age children of German nationality resident on our Bruderhof." In fact the children had already been in Switzerland for days, staying at the invitation of a Frau Anna Schmidt in a children's holiday home in Trogen, Apenzellerland.[18] They were safe – for the time being. But the Swiss officials were unwilling to provide them with papers for a permanent stay.

Eberhard was led to the next step by an inspiration. It must have occurred at a mealtime toward the end of January 1934.[19] He asked for someone to bring a large atlas, then opened to a map of Austria and Switzerland, and pointed to the inconspicuous little principality of Liechtenstein – a mere sixteen miles long and seven miles wide. "That's the country we are going to move to," he said.[20]

Liechtenstein

When Eberhard started out with Emmy on a journey to the Alps on February 26, 1934, he had nothing definite to go on – no fixed destination, no recommendation in his pocket. His leg was still in a plaster cast. In fact the whole journey was almost beyond his strength.

In a solemn meeting two weeks previously Eberhard had appointed his son-in-law Hans Zumpe and Hans Boller as servants of the Word through the laying on of hands. He did not know when he might return, and in the meantime the Bruderhof must not be left without spiritual guidance.

Time was growing short; Anna Schmidt was expecting the first spring guests at her children's home in Switzerland and the Bruderhof children could not stay there much longer. After visiting a few friends in northern Switzerland the Arnolds traveled to the principality of Liechtenstein on a hunch. One day in early March, Eberhard and Emmy were sitting in a village inn at Schaan on the right bank of the Rhine. They asked whether there was a suitable house in the vicinity that they could buy or rent and were told of a resort house standing empty on the Alm mountain pastures known as "Silum," located above Triesenberg, almost forty-five hundred feet above sea level and three thousand feet above the Rhine Valley. After a breakneck ride by sleigh and a few hundred yards of toiling through knee-deep snow (Eberhard with his cast!), they reached their destination. The view to the west compensated them at least in part for their trouble: some of the finest peaks of northwestern Switzerland lay directly before their eyes, and the Rhine Valley lay at their feet. They soon made a rental arrangement with the owner. Now all they needed was money.

Returning to Switzerland, Eberhard and Emmy visited a number of friends including Julia Lerchy. As they were leaving she pressed an envelope into their hands. Contents: sixty-five hundred Swiss francs – more than enough for the beginning of the Alm Bruderhof in Silum.[21] That

Members and children of the Alm Bruderhof enjoying the alpine air on the high pastures of Silum, ca. 1936.

was on March 12. On March 19 the children and their teachers moved to Silum. Eberhard and Emmy were there to greet them. Emmy returned to the Rhön Bruderhof in April. Little by little a few experienced brothers and a few young couples moved to the Alm. Eberhard remained until mid-May and supervised the building up. Once again that year, and five more times in all, he took on the difficult journey to the Alm from the Rhön.

Novices from Britain

Hardy Arnold spent the summer term of 1934 in England at the invitation of a Quaker friend, John Stephens, and aided by a grant from the Boeke Foundation. Within a very short time he had made a great number of contacts. Hardy had the ability to describe the Bruderhof in a way that held fellow students and socially committed English Christians spellbound, and he was soon recommended by one group to another. As an aside it may be mentioned that in London he became acquainted with Dietrich Bonhoeffer, then twenty-eight years old.[22] Bonhoeffer had been minister of two German-speaking congregations in South London since October 1933. He was very much interested in communal living and, with a few friends, had formed ideas of practicing a type of evangelical monasticism. More than once during the summer of 1934 he announced his intentions to visit the Bruderhof, but he never found the time.

More exciting for the Rhön and Alm brotherhoods was Hardy's news that a few young Britishers wanted to get to know the Bruderhof. By now the German authorities had tightened up on residency permits for foreigners, so Hardy's friends planned to travel directly to the Alm Bruderhof.[23] At the beginning of August, a few days after Eberhard's fiftieth birthday, they reached Silum: newlyweds Arnold and Gladys Mason, both twenty-six; and, shortly thereafter, Kathleen Hamilton, a twenty-seven-year-old Scotswoman from Edinburgh, accompanied by another young woman, Winifred Bridgwater.

There on the Alm Bruderhof a kind of Pentecost miracle took place. The British guests did not speak German. Eberhard spoke no English. At first either Hardy or Susi Gravenhorst, a young teacher, translated. But that was too slow for the guests. They wanted to comprehend the meaning more rapidly and precisely. Eberhard, for his part, sensed immediately when the translation was inaccurate, when it missed his exact meaning, and he would then ask for a second translation.[24] "He was such a warm-hearted, loving person," Kathleen Hamilton reports. "We felt at home at once."

The four guests from the British Isles had certainly come with a number of serious questions. Arnold and Gladys Mason were unsure about the position of man and wife in the church community. "Eberhard answered our questions completely and convincingly," Arnold Mason would recall. Kathleen Hamilton was a vegetarian and asked how people could justify killing animals. Eberhard disarmed her with the argument, "You can eat meat with a good conscience as long as you yourself are ready to sacrifice your life."[25] One evening she put forward a purely hypothetical question: "If there were no poverty in the world, would we still have to be poor?" A brotherhood member who had suffered great poverty in his childhood admonished her sharply, asking, "How can you be so loveless?" She felt deeply distressed and ashamed. Next morning Eberhard came to her and asked how she had slept. She had not slept a wink, she admitted. "Neither did I," he replied, "I was with you as you battled your way through."[26]

Meeting on a railway platform in London, Winifred Bridgwater *(left, with child)* and Kathleen Hamilton traveled together to the Alm Bruderhof in 1934. They were among the first British members of the Bruderhof.

Within a few days the newcomers had grasped what they wanted to learn and had reached complete inner unity with the brotherhood. By October of 1934 all four were simply treated as novices. Nothing in Eberhard's last years inspired and encouraged him as much as the encounter with these young people from England and Scotland. When another young English woman, Edna Percival, visited for a few days, he was so enthusiastic about her name (in the legends of King Arthur, it is Perceval who wins sight of the grail, a story told in Wagner's *Parzifal* as well) that in the next evening meeting he referred to the holy grail and the cabala. When the young woman had to leave he said to her in parting, "You have seen the grail glimmering from afar. Don't give up the search until you have found it." Turning to Arnold and Gladys Mason he added, "I believe we will see that girl in green again." He was right.[27]

Incidentally, Hardy had prepared the British guests for the inconceivable poverty on the Bruderhof. "They live on prayer and potatoes," he told them. But they found that at first Eberhard provided them with more substantial food than was given to the rest of the brotherhood. "The British guests are not accustomed to our meager diet," he reasoned. Here, too, the way to the heart lay through the stomach.

Arnold and Gladys Mason, with baby Jonathan, at the Rhön Bruderhof in 1935. Joining the Bruderhof in those days meant joining a life of poverty in a politically unstable country.

"When we come to the end of every-thing that we ourselves have done and can do, then God begins."

From a meeting held November 9, 1935.

No One Starved

The period of 1933–1935 is remarkable for its amazing juxtaposition of seemingly contradictory events. During the months and years after Hitler seized power Eberhard found himself responsible for a con-tinually growing group of adults and children. There seemed to be a mysterious connection: the more insufficient the means and the more miserable the menu, the more people were drawn to the life in com-munity. During the years 1933 through 1935 Eberhard took more new people into the novitiate, accepted more new members into the brotherhood, and baptized more brothers and sisters than ever be-fore.[1] Space grew tight and the community had to make do with closer quarters. Each loaf of bread had to stretch further, so the slices grew thinner. To make matters worse, the National Socialist officials initiated harassments to strangle the Bruderhof. Even before the Bruderhof moved the children, the Nazis had cut off all subsidies for the school and for agriculture. The consequences were keenly felt. In

December of 1933 the community could not even afford candles. (Emmy begged some from her relatives.) In February of 1934 there was often nothing to eat except potatoes and vegetables.

It was hardly necessary for the officials to introduce special measures to repress the publishing work. At the beginning of the Nazi regime the publishing house was still printing books, but in the prevailing atmosphere of fear and anxiety hardly any book dealers had the courage to put works with pacifist ideas on their shelves, much less place them in their display windows. Itinerant booksellers could move around only with caution under the suspicious eyes of the Nazi police. Needless to say, book distribution was greatly reduced, leaving Switzerland as the only market worth naming.[2] The brotherhood decided to send brothers there to sell books. Eberhard's attitude toward selling books door to door is particularly noteworthy: "Love compels us to do this. We are not doing it for economic reasons. Our motive is not to get money, but we have always prayed to God to be able to go out to the people. That is our task…We can make the sales only on the condition that the whole community works like busy bees. You are taking the sweat of your brothers with you, decades of dedicated life!"[3]

Eberhard emphasized that book sales and fundraising were to be kept strictly separate. He regarded book sales and book distribution as a part of mission, and so the brothers sent out on these journeys were commissioned with a special blessing for their task. Since books were intended for mission they were to remain affordable, even if it meant a smaller financial return for the community. People were to buy the books for their message, not out of sympathy for those suffering from hunger on the Rhön and Alm Bruderhofs. Begging journeys were necessary too, but Eberhard reminded the community to make a clear distinction between begging and book selling.

Selling the workshop's turnery and wood carvings, such as bowls and candle holders, was a different story again. Eberhard worked out a marketing strategy and even formulated an imposing goal for their sales: every table and sideboard in Germany should have its Bruderhof bowl. Better to sell handicrafts than simply to beg. (Eberhard never actually said "beg" but used a more elegant expression: "to travel in Franciscan style.")[4]

From the beginning it was clear to Eberhard that revenues from sales alone would never give the Bruderhof an assured livelihood. And they were not meant to do so. Eberhard remained true to his conviction that "our economic life, too, must be guided by the Spirit...To this day we have not suffered harm through keeping to this faith, and we never will if we remain true."[5] In actual fact the Bruderhof's means were always sufficient for survival. At the right moment friends and well-wishers were always at hand, mostly with small contributions, occasionally with larger amounts. No one starved on the Bruderhof. Speaking of hunger, Eberhard pointed out that "the greatest danger to central European Christianity is not a shameful death...nor even economic ruin and the literal starvation that often follows...The greatest danger lies simply and solely in the threat of a compromise between God and the devil, hate and love, fear of men and fear of God!"[6]

Struggle for Unity

The tension that the young brotherhood members (the average age was about thirty) lived in after 1933 can hardly be imagined: the hard work, the outside pressures, the struggle for daily bread, and on top of all that, the many newcomers who arrived full of idealism and goodwill but very little practical experience. Strong-willed, original characters. Totally different personalities. Artistic types, thinkers, hardworking women, laborers with rolled-up sleeves, introverts, and cheerful natures – all rubbing shoulders in the minimum of space. Though the brotherhood had hardly had the time to draw together as one body, it was now split into two groups, one at the Alm, the other remaining at the Rhön. Eberhard had to fight as energetically for the inner unity of the community as for its outer existence.

The first crucial test of the strength of that unity came in the summer of 1934 on the Alm Bruderhof. Not long before, Eberhard had put together a fundraising brochure for the Alm Bruderhof in which he wrote that life in community demands a struggle from every individual against anything that could destroy the community. All must aim at "consensus in small and very small concerns, and unity in great and very great matters."[7] This goal could be attained only when all members preserved the deepest reverence for the character and reality of the communal life. That is how it was written down for anyone to read. In daily practice, however, it proved very difficult. Hans Boller had been the responsible servant of the Word for the Alm Bruderhof during Eberhard's absence in the summer of 1934, but at the direction of the brotherhood he laid down his service after only three months. Eberhard engaged in an ongoing struggle against legalism at the Alm – too much concern about petty matters, and loveless behavior among members. He waged this battle both long-distance from the Rhön and on the scene. The summer crisis was not completely overcome until September of 1934, when a new pledge of commitment was celebrated. At the year's end Eberhard drew up a sobering balance sheet: "We have become spiritually dull. We are on the point of losing the movement of the Spirit...As long as we have community with God, we must be inwardly moved. As long as we are moved, it is impossible for us to go to sleep."[8]

Over and over again Eberhard had to admonish, rouse, and encourage the brotherhood. On some occasions, when even his eloquence had no results, outside events helped to expel any sleepiness and apathy that might have settled upon the brotherhood. One such event was the reintroduction of compulsory military service in Germany on May 16, 1935. It was announced on a Saturday. Eberhard, at the remote Rhön Bruderhof, learned of the new circumstances through a telephone call from two brothers on a sales trip in Switzerland. At once he sent two community members to Fulda by bicycle to find out what was happening. When the news about conscription was confirmed, the brotherhood met and, after a brief consultation, decided that their only recourse lay in sending the young brothers of military age out of Germany to the Alm Bruderhof in Liechtenstein. There they could continue to witness, and they could help with the building up of the community. The alternative would have been for the young Bruderhof men to remain at the Rhön and to refuse military service – a choice tantamount to going without resistance into a concentration camp. The brothers left the Rhön Bruderhof that same night, traveling by separate, and in some cases dangerous, routes to Liechtenstein.[9]

Only a few days earlier in Zurich, Eberhard Arnold and Leonhard

Ragaz had met for what would be their last personal encounter. Members of the Werkhof were also present. Ragaz aired reservations that he had held for years (attitude toward Hitler, friction over Friedmann, etc.), along with a slew of objections dragged up from the past (over the understanding of *Gemeinde*) and fresh complaints (about the visits of brothers traveling in Switzerland, and alleged agitation against the religious-socialist movement). Others in the meeting added one thing or another to the list. It was a proper tribunal. Eberhard asked for some understanding of the economic and political pressures in Germany, explained and made corrections, and tried to bring some order into the confusion of questions and complaints. But his answers went almost unheard. Many issues had to remain unresolved because of lack of time. Leonard Ragaz had already formed his opinion and held to it, and so Eberhard and Hans Meier, who had accompanied him, left without really achieving anything.

Search for Refuge

Two weeks after this meeting in Switzerland, and only one week after the young men had left Germany, Eberhard once more embarked on a long journey. This time he headed for the Netherlands and the British Isles, with a twofold purpose. Initially the word leader of both Bruderhofs had undertaken the journey in an effort to raise twenty-five thousand marks to help build up the Alm Bruderhof and to alleviate the worst of the economic need. But as the days went by, a second motive for the journey came more and more to the fore: to search for a permanent home for the community outside of Germany. The Alm Bruderhof at Silum was not a long-term solution. It was too small to take in all the community members if worst came to worst. And two Bruderhofs were one Bruderhof too many for people who felt called to complete unity. "We feel we need to draw together," was Eberhard's simple explanation. If the Bruderhof had to leave Germany, then at least it should regain its outward unity.

Apparently from time to time Eberhard had looked for another, larger house in Liechtenstein. A note about a telephone call on October 9, 1934, reads, "We either buy the Gutenberg-Balzer property or take a ten-year lease with first option to purchase."[10] But could

Liechtenstein really offer security for any length of time? A large portion of its citizens sympathized with the powerful new Germany. The brothers and sisters at the Alm Bruderhof had already heard this plainly enough. It came down to the Netherlands, England, or Scotland.

Hardy Arnold accompanied his father on the journey because of his English contacts and his grasp of the English language. Traveling first to the Netherlands, they visited representatives of the Mennonite churches in Amsterdam and Utrecht, and rummaged through the Mennonite archives. The talks with the Mennonites resulted in a few gulden and the promise that more would be done for the Bruderhof, an offer that Eberhard later took up. In the Netherlands, Eberhard discovered a remarkable proposal: the government was looking for settlers for its land-reclamation project in the Zuider Zee and was ready to finance the Bruderhof's beginnings there. Of course the government required guarantees that the settlers would not later become a burden on the national welfare services.

Next, the two travelers left for London. There Hardy learned what dogged persistence his father's character contained. For five straight days Eberhard kept up the same routine: every morning he visited the Quaker office, limping up several staircases. He would knock, go in, and explain his requests to Joan Mary Fry, the General Secretary, and to the other Quaker functionaries. He made the same explanation again and again. In the end Eberhard's perseverance paid off. The Quakers agreed to give six hundred pounds sterling, earmarked for greenhouses on the Alm Bruderhof. In addition to the Quakers, Eberhard and Hardy met with social workers, university groups, and with people at the International Fellowship of Reconciliation center. Then father and son went on to Edinburgh, where Kathleen Hamilton's mother introduced them to every possible church and to international clubs, artists, politicians, and professors.

Eberhard held a noteworthy talk in Edinburgh on April 23, 1935. Speaking of the situation in Germany he said, "Human blood is put in place of the divine Spirit, the materialistic belief in race in place of the breath of God, morbid hate in place of love; the mammonistic rule and the bloody violence of the state, the triumph of private property, in place of true social justice; the merely feigned peace of the sword and preparation for war in place of a genuine will for peace…and above all, embittered hostility to the Jesus of the Sermon on the Mount – the Antichrist against Christ!"

And on the situation of Christians in Nazi Germany: "There are undoubtedly Christians everywhere who abhor this apostasy with its heathen admixture, who would rather die than consent to take part in this impure confusion. In central Europe too it is certain that such Christians can be found – but only with difficulty. The power of public enslavement, the brutal suppression of every expression of free spirit, has driven them from all public places."

Eberhard pleaded for the "necessary outer and inner help" not only for the Bruderhof but for all Christians in Germany.[11] And in Great Britain, Eberhard and Hardy had their ears filled with all kinds of well-meant but contradictory advice:

John Fletcher, a World War I conscientious objector regarded by many as a living legend, said that without a doubt the Bruderhof's young men should have remained in Germany. Rather die than yield – that would have been a witness for the cause![12] The attitude "of giving one's utmost and remaining alert and active to the end" appealed to Eberhard. At one point he seriously considered sending a few brothers from the Alm Bruderhof back to Germany "to stand firm on the question of military service as a test of character, to show their faithfulness to their promised word."[13] Fortunately he soon abandoned these ideas.

Leyton Richards, a charismatic personality and a Birmingham minister, justifiably doubted whether the Alm Bruderhof could survive economically.[14] He suggested that the community immigrate to Canada, and he was ready to make funds available for the move.

Joan Mary Fry advised them to come to England instead, but at the time land was virtually impossible to obtain. So at the time of Eberhard's return to the Rhön Bruderhof in May of 1935, the Netherlands still seemed a more likely choice.

All these ideas had a point, and many of the contacts made or renewed during this journey provided reliable support a short while later. A letter Eberhard sent to the "emigration office of the Dutch Anabaptists" a few weeks after his journey also bore fruit. In it he applied for permission to make a fundraising journey through all the

Mennonite churches in the Netherlands, and while it is true that he was never able to make the journey, his appeal for generous help and support was favorably received and rewarded two years later.[15] In October of 1935 Eberhard would still have time to speak personally with the Masons and Winifred Bridgwater to prepare them for a return to England to look for a suitable location for the community.[16] A year later the new place would actually exist.[17]

Consumed by His Task

"I would not find it too hard to give both eyes and more for the sake of insuring the inner and outer life of our Bruderhof for the next fifty to a hundred years." Eberhard had written these words in a letter home from Canada at Christmas 1930.[18] In fact, he would sacrifice more than his eyes for the survival of the community. When he broke his leg in October of 1933 the conflicts between the Bruderhof and the violent National Socialist state allowed him no time for recovery. In January of 1934 he still felt weak and was struggling with heart trouble. But in February of 1934 he limped through the Alps, leaning on two sticks, with his leg in a walking cast, on the journey that would lead to the establishment of the Alm Bruderhof. "The call to freedom is the call to a spiritual campaign that never slackens, to a spiritual battle that allows no one time to recuperate," he wrote in May 1934.[19] How true! And the brothers and sisters in the brotherhood, in particular the young ones, were not always especially considerate of his physical condition. Consequently, Eberhard remained responsible for many tasks that could have been spared him, and he had to deal with petty daily concerns to the very end.

But some of his tasks could only be done by him. At age fifty-two, a grandfather several times over, handicapped and weakened, he covered as much ground as he had in the two previous decades of evangelizing and lecturing. Now, however, it was begging journeys to Brandenburg, Breslau, and Switzerland. These were emergency missions – for fire fighting and disaster service, as it were – to negotiate, to patch up, to piece together, and to clear away misunderstandings. To persuade officials, to talk to deaf ears. He grew well acquainted with the inside of administrative offices in Fulda, Kassel, and Berlin. In late October of 1934 he visited half a dozen Reich ministries, trying to induce them to recognize the Bruderhof as a charitable institution for the public benefit. He attempted to gain exemption from agricultural taxes. He limped straight into the lions' den – into the National Socialist government administration – seeking sympathizers. He found them too, namely in the Foreign Ministry, which because of its specific task had to be concerned about Germany's global reputation.

Far more frequent, however, were the encounters with people who exhibited indifference or opposition to any type of experiment in early Christian community. "I have been hobbling around until nine or ten in the evening," he wrote home at the end of this marathon through government corridors.[20] He put thousands of miles behind him in these months. By train, by horse carriage, and, since money for transport was always short, perforce on three legs – one healthy, one collapsing, and the third the wooden prop that finally became almost a part of him. Even when he was sitting he would lean heavily on his stick, rocking it from side to side. That is how many in the Bruderhof would remember him.

Eberhard worried little about his health, or the lack of it. He was far more pained that the brotherhood often proved so negligent. He could hardly bear it when he was away on a journey and went without news from the community for several days. "Please understand how wretchedly unhappy I feel over the long delay in receiving detailed letters from you…Greet the brotherhood and ask them all to cheer and encourage me with messages of faith," he wrote. "I had not expected to be left so completely out of touch on such an exceedingly difficult mission journey."[21] Such phrases reveal a glimpse of how lonely and isolated Eberhard sometimes felt in the last months of his life. "Unity!" he wrote as the greeting at the top of one of his letters from Edinburgh. *"Unity!"* [22]

And yet at such times of extreme tension he always inspired courage and confidence in those around him. Eberhard never gave up. Tirelessly, he devised plans to overcome the economic need of the Bruderhofs, to sell more craft items, and to win new friends, supporters, and customers. Sick as he was, with pain in his leg and the weight of so many troubles on his shoulders, he could still sparkle with humor and successfully encourage the whole brotherhood. There were times when he would tell one joke after another, sometimes carrying on for half an hour.[23] He took all the time in the world for his brothers and sisters. He shared their enthusiasm and listened to their worries. And he took secret joy in observing the young, fiery idealists. He once came across August Dyroff and a guest, a communist, locked in a heated argument. He went up to the two wranglers unobserved, laid one hand heavily on each of them and thundered, "It's so wonderful when two matches rub against each other and catch fire!"[24]

Paradoxically, in these months Eberhard was fully alert to the pulse of life around him and contributed amply to it – but at the same time it seems as if he were preparing for death. Eberhard always demanded dedication to the utmost limits of capacity, and he himself always gave his energy to the last ounce of his strength. It was as though he knew that his strength would not last forever.

Rearranged Lights

In the summer and fall of 1935 Eberhard and Emmy shuttled between the two Bruderhofs, staying at the Alm for a few weeks on several occasions but always returning to the Rhön. On the Alm Bruderhof at the end of June they wrestled for the life of their daughter-in-law Edith, Hardy's young wife who was in extreme danger after the birth of her first child. Almost defiantly Eberhard affirmed his faith that "the life of God and his perfect love and his life-giving Spirit ultimately triumph over everything else."[25] Meanwhile on the Rhön Bruderhof a stagnant, lethargic spirit had settled over the community, and for months it refused to give way. Little groups and cliques formed, paralyzing the community. As Gertrud Dalgas would later express, the Spirit was in chains.

During those weeks Eberhard had a nightmare.[26] He dreamed of a seven-armed candlestick bearing seven lighted candles, and he recognized it as the symbol of the *Gemeinde*. He identified the center candle as Jesus Christ, the Lord of the *Gemeinde*. The other candles represented attributes such as love, unity, and community. Then in his dream he saw a dark hand pick up the candles and rearrange them, changing their positions. The hand moved the candle representing Christ over to one side. All at once the candle of community was placed in the center. Eberhard cried out – and the vision disappeared. He told the brotherhood of his dream, begging and pleading with them, "Don't let it happen!"[27] At the Alm Bruderhof his words were heeded. Even so, weeks of talks and meetings were necessary to clarify the situation, but then the atmosphere at the Alm cleared once again.

When Eberhard set out from Silum on October 5 at the end of his sixth stay at the Alm, he left a well-ordered and alert brotherhood with forty-four members, as well as many novices, guests, and children. At the Rhön Bruderhof, on the other hand, the situation was still not resolved. To the contrary, in mid-October the crisis broke out anew. On the surface the community presented a picture of harmony. As Eberhard described it, "nearly everyone is working hard and being nice to each other." But that was precisely the problem. There was "almost an anxiety about staying even-tempered, kind, and good-hearted toward themselves and everyone present…The spiritual horizon was growing narrower and narrower, their God and their Christ had shrunk to a very small God and a very small Christ." Apathy compounded the problem: "They don't say anything – don't do anything – not a word of agreement comes from them – not a protest, not even when the most terrible things are mentioned. No one shakes his head; no one cries out in horror." Eberhard diagnosed the trouble as the worst kind of self-complacency. He attacked it first with controlled voice, and then he shouted against it – with no results. In the end the brothers and sisters themselves found the affair so strange and inexplicable that they asked for an "unforgettable discipline."

Consequently, on November 7, 1935, Eberhard took away all appointed services for the time being.[28] Since there was no inner readiness for peace it would, in Eberhard's view, be totally out of place to wish anyone peace and blessing. Therefore during the following days no one on the Rhön Bruderhof was to give the greeting of peace. No talks, no happy singing, no brotherhood decisions. Instead, until the first Sunday of Advent, there was to be a time of personal prayer, repentance, and purification. Eberhard called only three more meetings. These were held on November 9, 10, and 12. Speaking to a silent circle of listeners during the last of these meetings, he gave a detailed report of Thomas Münzer and the Peasants' War. In the meeting two days before he had given a six-hour survey of the history of the Anabaptists in Reformation times. In contrast, the talk on November 9 had been short and impassioned. It cannot have lasted more than five minutes. Here are the last sentences, the lasting impression:

> When we come to the end of everything we have done or can do, then God begins…The Anabaptist brothers of old used to say, "The earth is the Lord's. We refuse to relinquish the earth, for God's day is near when the earth will be set to rights, and we, as his messengers, will not allow ourselves to be banned from any place on it." Seen from this standpoint, our life ought to be worth living as an advance post of the kingdom of God. We ourselves are drained and useless, but we have the hope that God will establish his perfect rule. In the face of this, what do our own petty feelings of our petty little souls have to say? Absolutely nothing. Let us turn once more to the great cause, for the earth belongs to God, and he will conquer it, and the nearer we come to his victory, the more the satanic forces will try to spread over the earth and in our hearts. And God is all the closer![29]

Then he asked them to sing the chorale "Break forth, O glorious morning light."

Three days later, on November 12, 1935, Eberhard took leave of the community without any special ceremony. He was driven in the carriage to the railway station, and from there he traveled to the Elisabeth Hospital in Darmstadt.

Last Journey

The hospital appointment had been scheduled a long time in advance. Dr. Paul Zander, a friend of the Arnolds' since their first years in Halle, wanted to give thorough attention to Eberhard's broken leg. In the two years since the accident the bone had never healed properly. A growth had developed around the break that prevented the leg from bearing weight and created a great deal of pain. At any moment the bone could break again. After examining Eberhard's leg, Dr. Zander proposed removing the unhealthy piece of bone. Eberhard phoned the Rhön Bruderhof to convey the news. In a letter to Emmy he wrote, "How very sorry I am that where you once had a dark-haired husband you now have an old, grizzled graybeard, and now even one with a shortened leg too! But I won't behave in the least like

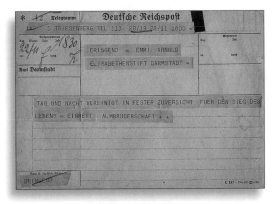

The telegram sent from members at the Alm Bruderhof to Emmy Arnold in Darmstadt an hour and a half after her husband died (the news had not yet reached the community): "Day and night united in firm confidence for the victory of life – Unity."

a grumpy, grizzly old man! Even if I am a cripple I shall dance in spirit whenever you sing your happy songs."[30]

The following day, November 14, Eberhard sent a long letter to his son-in-law Hans Zumpe in Liechtenstein. Sometimes sober, sometimes moving, the letter read like a will – which is exactly what it was. Eberhard had no false hopes. He did not count on the certainty of a successful operation, and he prepared himself for death. He gave directions about what should be done with his writings.[31] His legacy to the brotherhood was to be the strength of unity melded from authentic early Hutterianism, the active faith of both Blumhardts, and the attitude toward life of the true youth movement. Eberhard warned against "mixing Hutterianism with modern pietism." By this he must have meant the pietism that is quietism, which ignores "Jesus' fundamental intention that inner composure be the source of strength for action. If we sink spinelessly into quiet and stillness, it means we are losing hold of the life to which Jesus has called us."[32] Eberhard exhorted the brotherhood to become more missionary-minded: "We have not yet come to real mission. It is getting more and more urgent for us to pray for this." He mentioned the points in the work that should be stressed during the coming years. In the event of his death, Hans Zumpe was to take over the responsibility for both Bruderhofs, working in close cooperation with Georg Barth, Hardy, Hans-Hermann, Heinrich, and other brothers and sisters who were deeply grounded in faith. Eberhard ended his letter to Hans Zumpe: "For you personally and for all of you, I wish only one thing: *the Way, the direction!*"

Emmy came to Darmstadt on November 15. The operation took place the next day and lasted longer than anticipated. Eberhard remained fully conscious throughout the procedure. To spare his heart, the doctors administered only a local anesthetic. "They sawed me, chopped me, and sewed me up," he told his wife afterward. A second operation was scheduled for November 22. But Eberhard no longer clung to his life.

In the few hours he was awake he spoke loudly and directly to visitors and other patients about their relationship to God. When Emmy tried to calm him, he said firmly, "But I have to go on witnessing till the last moment!" In the nights he ran a fever, and he talked in his delirium about the sun and the world of stars, a realm of creation that he had always loved, one that had filled him with enthusiasm and inspired him to overwhelming thoughts about the nature of God. On the Day of Repentance, November 20, 1935, he called out repeatedly, asking if Hitler and Goebbels had repented. At another time he saw a white-robed figure sitting on his bed and told Emmy about it – but she had not noticed any such thing.

On November 21 Eberhard asked Emmy to read the first chapter of John's Gospel to him. He spoke a great deal about the Rhön, saying that he would never forget the Bruderhof there. He wanted without fail to talk once more with his son-in-law and Emy-Margret. Eberhard spent the night alone. The next morning he was still able to countersign a check from the Hutterian community at Milford, Alberta.

At ten o'clock Dr. Zander explained that Eberhard's leg would have to be amputated. Eberhard said simply, "The surgeon must know, and God's will be done." Those were his final words.

The operation took only a few minutes, but it was complicated by multiple medical difficulties. By the time Hans and Emy-Margret Zumpe arrived after their long journey from the Alm Bruderhof, the word leader and father of the Bruderhofs – their own father – was still alive, but he was no longer able to recognize them. Only when they sang the songs he loved best were they able to waken a glimmer of consciousness. Tears ran down his face. At nearly four o'clock in the afternoon of November 22, 1935, even this last link failed. Eberhard grew very still and slipped peacefully away.

Too Early a Death?

Eberhard Arnold died at the age of fifty-two – at the height of his spiritual powers, authority, and activity. According to human standards he could have had twenty, thirty, or more years to live and continue his work, if only – if only what? What had not gone well? Was this cup filled to the brim or not? Eberhard himself, in accordance with good early Hutterian theology, had believed and had taught that unity existed between the upper church of the brothers and sisters who had died and the visible church incarnate in the believers still on earth. Eberhard knew himself to be surrounded by a cloud of witnesses from every century. For him, life did not end in death.

But what about the brotherhood of the Rhön and Alm Bruderhofs? Eberhard's death did not leave them orphaned. Through the terrible shock and pain of his death and the difficulties pressing in from outside the Bruderhofs, they found a way to work together. They received help from the Hutterian brothers and sisters in America and from many other friends. They were prepared for the challenges of their time. This was what Eberhard had been striving for until his last moments. Winifred Bridgwater, one of the last of those able to tell about Eberhard Arnold from personal experience, was convinced that "he had prepared this young brotherhood for the future – consciously, purposefully, and in every conceivable way."[33]

A few months before Eberhard's death a visitor to the Rhön Bruderhof had heard him say, "After I have died, I would wish that my name be forgotten, but that the truth for which I stood should go on living through God's great spirit."[34] Two years later the marks of his decades of work in Germany were blotted out by the Nazis, leaving hardly a trace. But the truth for which Eberhard Arnold stood – this truth could not, and cannot, be suppressed. It lives on.

Postscript

More than sixty years have gone by since Eberhard Arnold's death. As for what happened to the brotherhoods of the Rhön and Alm Bruderhofs, their story appears in numerous publications. Of course Nazi Germany was not the end of the road for the Bruderhof movement, and anyone wishing to gain a personal insight may visit one of the seven modern-day Bruderhofs. The touchstones of Eberhard's legacy will suffice here.

The Bruderhof Movement Is Alive

Despite severe crises and struggles for direction during the 1940s and 1950s, the communities survived. Sadly, for a time Eberhard's nightmare came true, and the candles really were rearranged. Today, though, they are once more in their proper places and are carefully guarded. The brothers and sisters are keenly aware that the uniting spirit of Jesus Christ is not a permanent possession. It blows where it wills – but it blows continuously, or else it always begins blowing anew.

The Communities Are Dynamic

Over the years, many have joined the Bruderhof – people from every walk of life, as well as Bruderhof children. The communal life has received and continues to receive new stimuli – from the Civil Rights Movement in the 1960s, for example, and from the death penalty abolition movement today.

The Witness of Eberhard Arnold Lives On

Over the decades, Eberhard's writings, lectures, and articles have been lovingly documented and, in many cases, translated into English. *Innenland,* Eberhard's lifelong project, has been recently published in a new German edition and, as with many of his other works, is readily available in English through The Plough Publishing House. Other writings await publication for the first time or are released in new editions.

Final Questions

What enduring message does Eberhard Arnold have for all people, and especially for all Christians? His attitude towards life, his writings, and his deeds compel each and every one of us to take a stand, to examine our own aims and means:

If we do not choose to lead a life like his, with a communal table, community of goods, communal work, what sort of life do we choose?

If we do not believe in the guiding power of the kingdom of God as he did, in what do we believe?

If we do not represent nonviolence and unconditional love to our enemies as he did, what do we represent?

If we understand the requirements of the Sermon on the Mount and discipleship of Jesus in a completely different way than he did, in what way do we understand them?

As a lasting challenge from Eberhard Arnold's life and work, Jesus' unmistakable call (John 21:22) rings out: "*You* follow me."

Endnotes

Many of the citations in this book's endnotes reference original German sources. For the reader's benefit, translated titles of sources that are unpublished to date in English appear on first reference in brackets following the source's original German title. Where a cited German source exists in a published English translation, the English title is given on first reference in parentheses. All additional information (publisher, date, page number, etc.) is cited from the author's original source (i.e., in most cases, the German source).

In the interest of clarity, English translations of German book titles frequently appear in the text. Where this occurs, the German title is cited in an endnote.

Additionally, in these endnotes Eberhard Arnold is frequently referred to as "Eberhard." Likewise, "Emmy" is used in reference to Emmy Arnold née von Hollander.

The abbreviation "BA" has been used in these notes for references to sources located in the Bruderhof archives.

Chapter One

1   Each chapter in this book begins with a quotation or poem taken from Eberhard Arnold's talks and writings.

2   A poem Eberhard wrote on October 31, 1905, includes this line: "If you want to call me once more to serve your divine kingdom…"

3   According to Eberhard's handwritten account of his life, which appears in his doctorate record files.

4   b. September 20, 1852, Delmenhorst (near Bremen), Germany.

5   b. March 10, 1853, Williamsfield, Ohio, USA.

6   Clara Arnold, *Sein Weg* [His way], 1936, unpublished manuscript, BA. This account of Eberhard's life, written by his sister following his death, was originally intended as a photograph album with explanatory notes.

7   The Moravian Brethren (formally the "Unity of the Brethren" – *Unitas fratrum* – but often referred to as the Moravian Church) came into their own following Luther's Reformation. Facing persecution in Moravia and Bohemia, about three hundred Brethren fled to Saxony, invited there by Count Zinzendorf, who

allowed them to settle on his estate. Under the count's leadership, the Brethren built the settlement of Herrnhut, the first of many similar self-contained settlements, and worked for understanding and unity among Protestant churches of similar persuasion.

8   Eberhard Arnold, *Aus dem Worte Gottes und aus unserem Leben* [About the word of God and about our life], 1918, unpublished manuscript, BA. In this highly informative document, penned by Eberhard for his wife, Emmy, he gives an account of his childhood and youth. Eberhard describes himself in the third person and calls himself "Erhart." In *Sein Weg*, Clara Arnold concurs with Eberhard's account and expands on it from her own memory. Most of the events and circumstances recounted here are based on these two documents.

9   Emmy Arnold, *Aus unserem Leben* [About our life], written from 1938–44, unpublished manuscript, BA.

10   E.g., Hans-Joachim Schoeps, *Rückblicke* [Looking back] second edition (Berlin: 1963), 43.

11   Emmy Arnold, op. cit.

12   Clara Arnold, *Sein Weg*.

13   Samuel Collenbusch: 1724–1803. German mystic and forerunner of pietism in the Lower Rhine region, which emphasized mysticism and biblicism.

14   Gottfried Menken: 1768–1831.

15   The Protestant Church in Germany is virtually synonymous with the Lutheran state church. For a further explanation of the German church structure, cf. chap. 3, n. 5.

16   The circumstances themselves are remarkable. At that time most clergy looked down on the Salvation Army's sometimes simple, sometimes unusual, but undoubtedly effective methods.

17   Eberhard Arnold, *Aus dem Worte Gottes*.

18   Thomas à Kempis, *The Imitation of Christ*, Book I.

19   Presumably the meetings of a Breslau chapter of the YMCA; cf. Hannah Arnold's account in Emmy Arnold et al., *Eberhard Arnold: Aus seinem Leben und Schrifttum (Eberhard Arnold: From His Life and Writings)* (Bridgnorth, England: The Plough Publishing House, 1953), 36.

20   Eberhard Arnold, op. cit.

21   Clara Arnold, *Sein Weg*.

[22] Only at first glance is the Salvation Army organized along military lines. The "soldiers" are the ordinary members; the "officers" are equivalent to ordained deacons and ministers. Since its founding by William Booth in 1878, the Salvation Army has accepted women in positions of spiritual leadership.

[23] Eberhard Arnold to Emmy von Hollander, June 23, 1907, BA.

[24] Eberhard's account is supported by the recollections of his sister Clara in *Sein Weg*, which in turn refer to his own records. Aside from that, there is no reference to a Herr von Gürten. It is possible that "von Gürten" is a deliberate alteration of the name. Then, if von Gürten were to be identified as Ludwig von Gerdtell, the episode must have taken place in 1902 (cf. chap. 2, *Growing Responsibility in the SCM*), and von Gerdtell would have been the one who gave Eberhard the first impetus to concern himself with the Anabaptists. In any event, the description of "von Gürten" corresponds in its main characteristics with Ludwig von Gerdtell: strict Anabaptism, a low opinion of the Reformers, and an emphasis on early Christianity. Grounds for the supposition that "von Gürten" does, in fact, refer to von Gerdtell appear, for instance, in a letter Eberhard wrote to Karl Schönfeld on December 3, 1920, BA: "It has become clear to me that when we were first in Breslau there was much talk that contained a great deal of overbearing, hurtful, unfree, and humanly egocentric expressions. Gerdtell did not recognize this." In a letter to Ludwig von Gerdtell on September 6, 1921, BA, Eberhard diagnosed "a split in your character and witness."

[25] Regarding Anabaptists: unlike Luther, Calvin, and Zwingli, a few of the Reformers rejected infant baptism as an unbiblical and misleading practice, and instead insisted on an adult "baptism of faith." Prior to this time practically every child had been baptized, and therefore people who had accepted the baptism of faith now had to live with the reproach of having been baptized twice, or "over again." The "rebaptizers," the Anabaptists, were ruthlessly persecuted both by the Roman Catholic Church and by the newly-founded Protestant churches of the Lutheran and Reformed creeds. Thousands of Anabaptists died under torture or at the stake. In spite of this, the Anabaptist movement could not be completely crushed. Anabaptist churches took root, especially in the Netherlands (Mennonites), in Switzerland, and in Moravia. Jakob Hutter was the founder of the community movement that became known as the Hutterites, a major branch of the Anabaptists, discussed later in this book.

[26] German title: *Der Anabaptismus in Tirol*. Loserth's book was published in 1892. In Eberhard's library there is a heavily underlined copy that contains notes in Eberhard's own handwriting. It is clear that he repeatedly worked through it; cf. bibliography.

[27] Quoted in Eberhard Arnold, *Aus dem Worte Gottes.*

[28] In 1907, regarding the question of baptism (cf. chap. 3); in 1913, Eberhard's *Lebensbeweise lebendiger Gemeinden (Living Churches: The Essence of their Life)* (cf. chap. 5); in 1919, regarding the issue of the use of force and the appropriate attitude toward the state (cf. chap. 6); in 1926, at the beginning of contacts with the Hutterites in North America, descendants of the original Moravian Hutterites (cf. chap. 11).

[29] 1929; cf. chap. 13.

[30] Eberhard Arnold to Emmy von Hollander, June 2, 1907, BA.

[31] Clara Arnold, *Sein Weg.*

[32] According to the doctorate files of the philosophy department at Erlangen University.

Chapter Two

[1] Clara Arnold, *Sein Weg.*

[2] Inspired by the Student Christian Movement in the United States, which worked very closely with the American YMCA, a conference was held in Niesky (about 50 miles east of Dresden) in 1890. It was initiated by Graf Eduard von Pückler and Freiherr Waldemar von Starck as a logical development of the bible circles that had been in existence since 1882 in schools and universities. The German SCM was formed in 1895 as a result of these annual conferences. The World Student Christian Alliance was founded the same year.

[3] William Booth: 1829–1912. Originally a Methodist preacher, he took over the leadership of the East London Tent Mission in 1861 and over the years gave this work an efficient, "military" structure that became, in 1878, the Salvation Army. Booth was a powerful and popular preacher and a declared enemy of sin. In addition, he was very progressive and, even at an advanced age, was open to innovation.

[4] The letter itself has not been preserved. In *Sein Weg,* Clara Arnold mentions it and gives the general sense of it.

[5] From Eberhard's reports it is clear that around the year 1906 the SCM had groups in at least 21 universities and numbered about 500 members. Added to these were a similar number of so-called *Altfreunde* (alumni).

[6] Reuben Archer Torrey: 1856–1928. Torrey worked in close cooperation with Dwight L. Moody and was the first director of the Moody Bible Institute in Chicago.

[7] Eberhard Arnold to Emmy von Hollander, April 9, 1907, BA.

[8] German title: *Die ältesten Berichte über die Auferstehung Jesu Christi: Eine historisch-kritische Untersuchung.*

[9] Paul Tillich: 1886–1965. During the 1920s, Tillich, along with Günther Dehn and Karl Mennicke, belonged to the representatives of the Neuwerk group in Berlin. Cf. chap. 9.

[10] Eberhard enclosed the text of his address in a letter to Emmy von Hollander, July 1, 1907, BA.

[11] Eberhard Arnold to Emmy von Hollander, July 7, 1907, BA.

[12] Eberhard Arnold to Emmy von Hollander, March 8, 1908, BA; cf. chap. 1, n. 24.

[13] Karl Heim to Otto Schmitz. This letter is quoted in Karl Kupisch, *Studenten entdecken die Bibel* [Students discover the Bible] (Hamburg: 1964), 256.

[14] Eberhard Arnold to Emmy von Hollander, May 5, 1907, BA.

[15] Eberhard Arnold to Emmy von Hollander, June 23, 1907, BA.

[16] In 1907 Eberhard wrote a report on von Gerdtell's work using this title. The article appeared as a special supplement to the *DSCV Mitteilungen* (the SCM newsletter).

[17] Even the first series of lectures drew an audience of 600–800 men (women were not invited). On one day of the second series, so many people tried to enter that 1000 had to be turned away by the police; cf. "Aus der Arbeit der Studentenmission" [About the work for the student mission], a speech given at the twenty-second Blankenburg Alliance conference.

[18] According to Emmy in *Aus unserem Leben*. Clara Arnold wrote that Eberhard was introduced by fellow students into an already existing fellowship (cf. *Sein Weg*). However, Clara also mentions a leader of the fellowship to whom not a single reference is made in the voluminous engagement letters of Eberhard and Emmy.

[19] The Evangelical Alliance movement dates to the mid-nineteenth century, and was founded to promote ecumenism based on affirmation of nine common doctrinal articles, among them: the divine inspiration, authority, and sufficiency of the Holy Scriptures; the right and duty of private judgment in the interpretation of the Holy Scriptures; the utter depravity of human nature in consequence of the Fall; the immortality of the soul, the resurrection of the body, and the judgment of the world by Jesus Christ, with the eternal blessedness of the righteous and the eternal punishment of the wicked.

The Evangelical Alliance took root internationally, and the movement organized throughout Europe as well as in North America. Conferences, which often lasted as long as ten days, were common, not as a means of settling dogmatic disputes but rather as an opportunity for free discussion, prayer, and fellowship.

[20] For further discussion of the differences between German state and free churches, cf. chap. 3, n. 5.

[21] The first of Eberhard's articles accepted in the *Evangelische Allianzblatt* (translated as the *Evangelical Alliance Magazine* in the text) was the report "Aus der Arbeit der Studentenmission" [About the work for the student mission] on August 28, 1907, BA. This article may be identical with his speech at the Blankenburg Alliance conference that same year.

[22] Emmy Arnold, *Aus unserem Leben bis 1920* [About our life before 1920], unpublished memoirs, probably written between 1936–1937, and most likely before 1940, BA. (Though similar in content, this document should not be confused with Emmy's similarly titled account, *Aus unserem Leben*.)

[23] The respective years of birth for the von Hollander children are as follows: Olga, 1882; Emmy, 1884; Else, 1885; Heinrich, 1887; Monika, 1888.

[24] Emmy Arnold, *Aus unserem Leben*.

Chapter Three

[1] In Germany, the Baptist Church *(Baptistengemeinde)* is the largest of the recognized free churches (cf. n. 5 for explanation of "free church"). Its members are baptized into the church as adults (believer's baptism). Though the German Baptist Church shares denominational ties to international Baptists (including the Baptists of the USA), there are few similarities between them. Consequently, one should not assume that the cultural characteristics of one necessarily apply to the other.

[2] Eberhard Arnold to Emmy von Hollander, September 6, 1907, BA.

[3] Eberhard was not the only one to draw such conclusions. About the same time a fellow fighter in the SCM, Franz Spemann, felt forced to "abandon his cassock," recognizing that "the churches have turned Christianity upside down," etc.; cf. Franz Spemann, *Landeskirche oder Religiöse Freiheit* [State church or religious freedom] (Berlin: H. Walther, 1907), 9, 59, 80.

[4] Eberhard Arnold to Emmy von Hollander, September 6, 1907, BA.

[5] In Germany, the relationship between the mainstream Protestant and Catholic churches and the state has been regulated by contracts and laws

since the Reformation. The state-recognized Protestant Church (which is virtually synonymous with the Lutheran Church) is comprised of an alliance of seventeen independent regional churches (Landeskirchen). Both the Protestant churches of this alliance and the Catholic churches benefit financially from "church taxes" levied and distributed by the German government. Aside from these so-called state churches, Germany also has free churches (Freikirchen), for which the state bears no financial responsibility. These churches exist outside of the state church structure. Whereas membership in both Protestant and Catholic state churches is established through infant baptism, members of free churches join voluntarily as adults.

6 Eberhard Arnold to Emmy von Hollander, September 13, 1907, BA.

7 Eberhard Arnold to Emmy von Hollander, October 13, 1907, BA.

8 Eberhard Arnold to Emmy von Hollander, November 12, 1907, BA.

9 Eberhard Arnold to Emmy von Hollander, January 19, 1908, BA.

10 Statement to the SCM executive committee, October 1907.

11 Eberhard Arnold to Emmy von Hollander, November 15, 1907, BA.

12 Emmy von Hollander to Eberhard Arnold, August 9, 1907, BA.

13 "Blankenburg Alliance" is another way of referring to the Evangelical Alliance from Bad Blankenburg; cf. chap. 2, n. 19 and the related text, *Bernhard Kühn and the Evangelical Alliance Magazine*.

14 In July 1907, almost at the same time as the events reported from Halle, a series of meetings took place with two Norwegian women, Dagmar Engström and Agnes Thelle Beckdahl. In those meetings intense spiritual experiences occurred, including speaking in tongues and prophesying. In neighboring Grossalmerode similar prayer and worship meetings began that, according to all contemporary witnesses, proceeded from the start in an orderly and impressive manner. In Kassel, on the other hand, the evangelist Heinrich Dallmeyer failed to keep things under control. The Norwegian ladies complained that he did not intervene to check unspiritual influences, and they immediately withdrew from the meetings. Dallmeyer ignored the criticism and continued the meetings. They ended in utter tumult and in bizarre scenes. So apparently Eberhard and Emmy heard completely contradictory reports at the same time: chaos in Kassel, blessing in Grossalmerode; cf. Ernst Giese, *Und flickten die Netze* [And mended the nets] (Marburg: 1976).

15 In accordance with 1 Cor. 12, 14.

16 Eberhard Arnold to Emmy von Hollander, April 14, 1908, BA.

¹⁷ His assigned examination topic: "What are the differences between the way John the Baptist's preaching is portrayed in John's Gospel and in the other Gospels?" The text for Eberhard's sermon for the theology examination was Mark 4:26–29, one of Jesus' parables about the kingdom of God.

¹⁸ Eberhard Arnold to Emmy von Hollander, October 9, 1907, BA.

Chapter Four

¹ Mentioned by Emmy in a letter to Eberhard, June 1, 1908, BA.

² Eberhard Arnold to Emmy von Hollander, December 3, 1908, BA. In his diatribe against Eberhard, Johann Heinrich von Hollander was referring to the radical, violent wing of the Reformation connected with Thomas Münzer and to the fanatical Anabaptist movement connected with the Leyden tailor Jan Bokelson, which caused mass hysteria in Münster in 1534 and set up a bizarre and bloody despotism.

³ Toni von Blücher, the great-niece of the Prussian field marshal by that name, remained single and, after her conversion in 1875, developed flourishing, charitable mission work. The fellowship house at Hohenstaufenstrasse 65 in Berlin was built on her initiative. The Evangelical Alliance Bible School began on April 11, 1905, in Toni von Blücher's apartment in Berlin. From 1911 on, it was simply called the "Bible School." In 1919 it was moved to Wiedenest, where it still exists today as a mission house and bible school of the Brethren Church.

⁴ Emmy von Hollander to Eberhard Arnold, October 19, 1908, BA; cf. Emmy Arnold, *Aus unserem Leben*.

⁵ E.g., the article "Täufertum und Baptismus" [The Anabaptists and the baptizer movement], published in the periodical *Die Wegwarte* (Aug./Sept. 1925).

⁶ The Bruderhof archives contain a striking account by Eberhard about the work in Erfurt and the origins of the Gallery (in German, *Passage*) Fellowship. Apparently at times misunderstandings over the aim of the work in Erfurt arose between Eberhard and Ernst Modersohn (cf. *Evangelisches Allianzblatt*, vol. 19, 64). Perhaps Modersohn assumed that the work was solely for the service of Otto Mau's Baptist Church. But in fact the lectures and the follow-up work were carried out in complete accordance with the interdenominational outlook of the Evangelical Alliance.

⁷ The similarities between the contents of Eberhard's doctoral thesis and von Gerdtell's work were pointed out by Thomas von Stieglitz in his two-volume thesis *Kirche als Bruderschaft: Das hutterische Kirchenbild bei Eberhard Arnold aus heutiger katholischer Sicht* [Church as brotherhood: the picture

of Eberhard Arnold's Hutterian Church as seen from a modern Catholic perspective] (Paderborn, Germany: 1990).

8   Eberhard could not, of course, have had any preconception of the ignominious role Elisabeth Förster-Nietzsche would play in the exploitation of Nietzsche's thinking by the National Socialists. All the same, in the course of working on his thesis, Eberhard noticed that in many respects she reproduced Nietzche's views in an abbreviated and distorted fashion. She "pushed aside the Christian antithesis in a very noticeable manner."

9   German title: *Urchristliches und Antichristliches im Werdegang Nietzsches* (Eilenburg, Germany: Otto Thon, 1910).

10 From the doctorate record files.

11 Eberhard Arnold, *Urchristliches und Antichristliches*, 87; cf. Nietzsche, *Antichrist (The Antichrist)* and *Der Wille zur Macht (The Will to Power)*.

12 *Urchristliches und Antichristliches*, 84; cf. Nietzsche, *Zarathustra*.

13 *Urchristliches und Antichristliches*, 105; cf. Nietzsche, *Ecce Homo*.

14 *Millenniumsleute:* it is not quite clear what sect or movement is meant. Possibly the reference is to the Jehovah's Witnesses, since the "thousand-year Kingdom" (i.e., millennium) plays a prominent part in their understanding of the Last Days.

15 Emmy Arnold, *Aus unserem Leben*.

16 Von Gerdtell later became part of the originally American "Christadelphian" movement, which rejected the doctrine of the Trinity and denied the divinity of Jesus. During the 1920s he founded an "early Christian church" in Berlin, based on the tenets of this movement. After the 1930s he is said to have lived and worked in the USA; cf. Kurt Hutten, *Seher, Grübler, Enthusiasten, und religiöse Sondergemeinschaften der Gegenwart* [Visionaries, contemplatives, enthusiasts: and contemporary religious alternative communities] (Stuttgart, Germany: Quell Verlag, 1958), 250f.

17 German title: *Die Revolutionierung der Kirche*.

18 The daughter, Wally Rast, later married the Baptist minister Hans Klassen. Together, they founded the community settlement of Neusonnenfeld; cf. chaps. 10, 11.

Chapter Five

1   The exact date of this incident is unclear. It could have taken place in late January, February, or at the beginning of March 1912.

[2] In Eberhard's book *Der Krieg: ein Aufruf zur Innerlichkeit* [War: a call to inwardness] (Gotha, 1914), 10, he names August Hermann Francke along with Luther, Zinzendorf, and Ernst Moritz Arndt in a list of examples of "a resolute turn to inwardness." He does not, however, make reference to Francke's social or educational work.

[3] George Müller: 1805–1898.

[4] Eberhard Arnold to Emmy von Hollander, August 31, 1908, BA.

[5] Hermann Kutter: 1863–1931. German title: *Sie Müssen!* First published in 1903, Kutter's book went through many editions.

[6] The religious-socialists is the name given to the movement begun by Hermann Kutter, initially in Switzerland; cf. chap. 7.

[7] "Die soziale Not" [The social need], a lecture given by Eberhard on October 12, 1910, in the Eiler's Hotel, Oranienburg, BA.

[8] "Der Umschwung der irdischen Verhältnisse durch Jesus" [The overthrow of earthly conditions through Jesus], a lecture given by Eberhard on December 11, 1910, in Halle, BA.

[9] Quoted in Eberhard's lecture "Die soziale Not."

[10] Quoted by Johann Loserth in the first volume of *Der Anabaptismus in Tirol.*

[11] Balthasar Hubmaier: 1480?–1528. Hans Denck: 1495–1527. In 1923 Eberhard edited a book by Adolf Metus Schwindt, published by the Neuwerk Verlag, titled *Hans Denck: Ein Vorkämpfer undogmatischen Christentums* [Hans Denck: a champion of undogmatic Christianity].

[12] German title: *Lebensbeweise lebendiger Gemeinden.*

[13] In 1929 Eberhard revised the chapters "Die Liebe zu Christus" ("Love to Christ") and "Die Liebe zu den Brüdern" ("Love to the Brothers") (new edition 1934, reprint 1973); cf. chap. 13, *On the Trail of the Past.*

[14] This section of chap. 5 highlights Eberhard's preliminary steps toward his book *Innenland* (published in English as *Inner Land;* Rifton, NY: The Plough Publishing House, 1976), which he would ultimately rewrite several times over and which would constitute one of the major achievements of his life.

Eberhard took the words "inner land" from a poem by Friedrich Lienhard (1865–1929), first published in 1912. In translation it reads:

> If Germany forgets her mission,
> If Germany, after roaming the seas
> Is no longer guide of the peoples
> To the inner land of the unseen
> To God and Spirit –

If Germany neglects her holy mission
And no longer leads the way in zeal for perfection
When she no longer points
Away from hate, which holds the iron world
tense and divided,
No longer points the way toward new love –
Then know: Your happiness and rule are dashed to pieces.

It is very likely that Eberhard only discovered the words for his title during the war. Apart from the unfortunate first edition (1914), which bore the title *Der Krieg: ein Aufruf zur Innerlichkeit* [The war: a call to inwardness] (cf. chap 6, n. 5), all later editions of the book carry the title *Innenland*. Moreover, the original series of articles were written completely in the sense expressed in Lienhard's poem, and therefore the heading "inner land" seems suitable for this section (though some may regard it as premature).

15 Cf. Eberhard Arnold, *Lebensbeweise lebendiger Gemeinden*, 57.

Chapter Six

1 Eberhard Arnold to Emmy von Hollander, June 20, 1908, BA.

2 On August 18, 1914, the Arnold family was alarmed by news – afterwards proven false – that Italy had declared war on Austria. Concerned by their proximity to the Italian border, they left Oberbozen straight away. The journey home was very difficult. The only available passenger train had to stop often and be rerouted to allow emergency military and hospital trains to go straight through; cf. Emy-Margret Arnold's *Kindheitserinnerungen* [Childhood memories], unpublished manuscript, BA. Italy remained neutral at first and did not enter the war until May 25, 1915, when it joined the Entente.

3 "We sometimes asked ourselves where our duty lay and whether Eberhard should voluntarily go to the help of our nation in its need." Emmy Arnold, *Aus unserem Leben bis 1920*.

4 German title: *Das inwendige Leben*.

5 Eberhard Arnold, *Der Krieg: Ein Aufruf zur Innerlichkeit* [War: a call to inwardness] (Gotha, 1914).

6 Ibid., chap. 1, p. 10.

7 As worded in the introduction to *Innenland (Inner Land)* (Berlin: Furche Verlag, 1918).

8 Quoted from a letter written by the Jewish social philosopher Gustav Landauer to the publisher and journalist Fritz Mauthner, November 2, 1914.

9 German title: "Gottes Sprache in ernster Zeit," published in the *Evangelische Allianzblatt* (Sept. 27, 1914).

10 "Ist der gegenwärtige Krieg von Gott oder vom Teufel?" [Is the present war from God or from the devil?]; remarks on an article with the same title by S. Knappe in *Der Wahrheitszeuge* (Aug. 14, 1915), no. 33, 262f.

11 "Über den Sinn des Krieges" [On the meaning of war] in *Der Wahreitszeuge* (Sept. 1915), 281.

12 This is substantiated by various statements in the engagement letters of Eberhard and Emmy.

13 Eberhard Arnold, *Die Drei Bücher im Felde* [The three books at the front] (Gotha, 1915), 6.

14 *Der Krieg,* 8.

15 "Gott oder Mammon?" [God or mammon?] in *Der Wahrheitszeuge* (Apr. 1915).

16 "Aus der Kriegsliteratur: Der deutsche Geist" [From war literature: the German spirit] in *Die Furche* (Aug. 1915), 331.

17 "Zur Geschichte des christlichen Liedes" [Comments on the history of Christian hymns] in *Der Hilfsbote* (June 1916).

18 The cable probably arrived during August or September, since evidence indicates that Eberhard took up his position in October; the first issue of *Die Furche* under his editorship appeared in January 1916. Georg Michaelis (1857–1936) succeeded Graf Pückler in the leadership of the German SCM. Graf Pückler had been the co-founder of the German SCM and had served as chairman for many years.

19 Friedrich Siegmund-Schultze, the previous coeditor of *Die Furche*, had proposed Eberhard's name for consideration for the post; cf. Siegmund-Schultze's account in *Eberhard Arnold: Aus seinem Leben und Schrifttum,* 30–31.

20 "B.K., SCM, evangelizing and literary work; scholarly training and assignment, preferably work among educated people. Therefore Michaelis and Niedermeyer's offer very welcome." From Eberhard's handwritten notes for a publishing house meeting at the beginning of 1916, BA.

21 The publishing house became official on August 18, 1916. Eberhard Arnold and Heinrich Rennebach were mentioned as managing directors.

22 German title of the newsletter: *Kleine akademische Feldpost.*

23 In handwritten notes for a talk with Michaelis and Niedermeyer, BA.

²⁴ Eberhard Arnold, "Wernigerode 1916," in *DCSV Mitteilungen* (1916), 23.

²⁵ During this period a large number of songs were composed to glorify war. Some, like this one, were very gory, with a heavy marching rhythm; others attempted a mystical transformation of war into something noble and beautiful, and were sung to romantic melodies.

²⁶ Emmy Arnold, *Aus unserem Leben bis 1920,* 19.

²⁷ Regarding Steiner: *Die Furche,* (Jan. 15, 1917), 112; and regarding Buber: *Die Furche,* (Nov. 1917), 46.

²⁸ After Michaelis resigned, he was appointed Lord Lieutenant of Pomerania.

²⁹ "Repentance Day," the third Wednesday in November, was for many decades a nationally celebrated German church holiday. Today, however, it is only observed in lower Saxony.

³⁰ November 6–7, 1917 (October 24–25 according to the Orthodox calendar), marked the fall of Kerenski's provisional government in St. Petersburg and the establishment of a council of "people's commissars." On November 8 (October 26) the confiscation of property from major landowners was pronounced.

³¹ Eberhard made a full confession of guilt a few months later in his lecture "Die Herrschaft des Geistes und die Freiheit des Menschen" [The lordship of the Spirit and the freedom of man], BA:

> Who is to blame for the outbreak of war? Who is to blame for Germany's collapse? Who is to blame for the mass murder?…We pass these questions on so that they may confront every individual's conscience. It is ridiculous to assert that only the rulers are to blame, that only the prime ministers and the newspapers are to blame. Now we all need to beat our own breasts and ask ourselves how much we ourselves are a part of the way of life based on power and self-indulgence…For this is what led to war: the competition between nations for power and selfish pleasure. Whose conscience is free of this?

³² Emy-Margret Arnold, *Kindheitserinnerungen*, 36.

³³ Cf. chap. 5, n. 14.

³⁴ The introduction of *Innenland* into the production schedule of the Furche Publishing House signaled a revolutionary departure from the norm. As a comparison: in the *Kleine akademische Feldpost* of July 15, 1918, the publishers still inserted an advertisement for the new edition of the book *Munition: Bilder aus der Rüstungsindustrie* [Munitions: scenes from the armament industry], described in the blurb as "a stirring tour through the din of our armorers' workshop – 'the temple of the nation.'" Then, in the next issue:

Innenland, with the publisher's comment, "We believe that Arnold's book will fulfill a task and will have results we cannot yet foresee...Blaze the trail for this book!"

Chapter Seven

1   Germany's Youth Movement began in the early 1900s as young people all across the country sought to break down the old, rigid mores of bourgeois life. Joy in nature, hiking, music, song, dance, and in group activities were central themes among these young people who rejected what they perceived to be "ungenuine" in the older generation. The Youth Movement took shape in many different ways; various affiliated groups sprung up, representing the numerous aspects of the movement and its members. Of these, perhaps the two most noteworthy were the *Wandervogel* (see text), who first formalized the Youth Movement's aims, and the Free Germans. The latter group, of which both the Free German Youth and the Free German Union are a part, stands out in particular for the strength of its leadership and its adherence to the Meissner principles (see text). World War I affected the Youth Movement greatly, spawning cynicism among some and strengthening resolve among others. Sadly it was this same movement – these same young people who strove so hard to be completely *echt,* completely genuine – that Hitler would hoodwink and manipulate, distorting the unifying characteristics of the Youth Movement to fit his plans for the Hitler Youth.

2   This gathering took place on October 16–19, 1913. The "Festival of the German Youth" was started as a conscious replacement of, and in stark contrast to, the emotional centennial commemoration of the Battle of Leipzig (October 16–19, 1813). The *Wandervogel* movement's name means, literally, "bird of passage." It was the first group of the German Youth Movement, founded in 1896, and was known for its unconventionality and its free-spirited ideals.

3   Cf. Eberhard's essay "Über Freideutschtum und die Friedensstadt" [On the Free German movement and the city of peace], BA: "In 1917 I had the joy of being part of a genuine Free German group with a genuine feeling for life. I shared in it with profound inner participation."

4   Cf. Eberhard Arnold, *Die Religiosität der heutigen Jugend* [The religious feeling of today's youth] (Berlin: Furche Verlag, 1919).

5   *Die Furche*, no. 7 (Apr. 1918).

6   "Innere Eindrücke von der Freideutschen Tagung in Tübingen" [Inner impressions of the Free German conference in Tübingen] *Die Furche*, no. 1 (Oct. 1918), 16.

7 Quoted in *DCSV Mitteilungen*, no. 220 (May 1, 1919).

8 The other themes: "Weltleid und Christentum" [World suffering and Christianity], BA, and "Jesus und der Zukunftsstaat" [Jesus and the future state], BA. On July 2, 1919, Eberhard wrote to Otto Herpel, apparently referring to this lecture series: "Over a thousand people attended. I am in constant contact with several hundred of them. We were almost at the point of establishing a community in practice..."

9 Emy-Margret Arnold, *Kindheitserinnerungen*.

10 Eberhard Arnold to Otto Herpel, July 2, 1919, BA.

11 Emmy Arnold, *Aus unserem Leben bis 1920*, 22.

12 K. Amborn, in *DCSV Mitteilungen*, no. 223 (Aug. 1, 1919).

13 Willi Völger, in *DCSV Mitteilungen*, no. 223 (Aug. 1, 1919).

14 Eberhard Arnold to Otto Herpel, July 2, 1919, BA.

15 Willi Völger's report in the *DCSV Mitteilungen* contained a summary of the lecture, presumably taken down in shorthand.

16 In the summer of 1919; cf. Hardy Arnold, "Sannerz II," handwritten notes from June 2, 1978, BA. All that is clearly documented, however, is Eberhard's participation in the "world outlook week" *(Weltanschauungswoche)* in August 1918.

17 According to Heinrich Arnold, as related in August 1972, BA.

18 *DCSV Mitteilungen*, no. 226 (Nov. 15, 1919), 45.

19 Ibid., 47.

20 Ibid., 59.

21 Heim's lecture "Tolstoi und Jesus" [Tolstoy and Jesus] was printed and published by the Furche Publishing House, Berlin, 1920. Karl Kupisch asserted, in *Aus der Personalakte eines Schwärmers* [From the personal files of an enthusiast] and *Studenten entdecken die Bibel* [Students discover the Bible], that Karl Heim's lecture was a conscious refutation of Eberhard's bible teaching in Marburg. This is obviously false.

22 Eberhard Arnold, "Tolstoi und Jesus"; cf. *DCSV Mitteilungen*, no. 226, 55. (Eberhard and Karl Heim both chose "Tolstoi und Jesus" as the title for their respective lectures.)

23 "If by the Spirit you put to death the deeds of the body, you will live. For all who are led by the spirit of God are sons of God" (Rom. 8:13–14).

24 Karl Barth: 1886–1968. Just how unknown Karl Barth was in Germany at

271

that time can be seen from the fact that Eberhard's first letter, written on September 2 (identical in content to the one Karl Barth actually received), was mistakenly addressed to Peter Barth in Madiswil. The latter, a brother of Karl Barth, probably corrected the mistake.

25 Karl Barth's address was published by the Patmos Publishing House, Würzburg, 1920.

26 The periodical *Herrnhut* reported: "Karl Barth and Eberhard Arnold spoke on 'The Christian in Society'...the difference between the Swiss and German emphasis was particularly clear from Eberhard Arnold's words." Günther Dehn, a conference participant, observed in his notes on the lectures:

> If we come from the pietistic side, I am afraid we will not be able to bear the need of the world. The desire to cut oneself off from it, to be alone in a little circle of like-minded people, will be too strong and will win out in the end. I received this impression from Arnold's talk as well. It showed a strong desire for socialism, but it was not sufficiently down to earth...But that will have to be overcome if God's thoughts are really to have an effect on people.

Unfortunately the text of Eberhard's speech has not been preserved.

27 E.g., Günther Dehn: "Neither the founding of a religious-socialist union nor the union of socialist pastors was achieved, and I welcome this as a victory of faith," in *Geschichtsband* (collected documents 1907–1935, BA) vol. IV, bk. 1, no. 13.

28 Barth had, in fact, prepared his lecture in advance, as is shown by a letter Eduard Thurneysen wrote to Barth on September 14: "I have just read your lecture with great attention: it has real punch. It will strike our zealous and troubled German friends as exceptionally restrained and yet radical at all points."

29 Both Barth and Thurneysen, however, had virtually nothing good to say after the conference and made disparaging remarks about the German organizers, especially Otto Herpel. Eberhard did not fare much better: "Have you noticed what Eberhard Arnold writes in *Das Neue Werk* with his SCM and its belief in Christ? It seems that everything said in Tambach ran off him like water off a duck's back!" (Thurneysen to Barth, December 1, 1919). The relationship did, however, ease in the following two years; cf. chap. 9.

30 It is enlightening to read the notes Eberhard jotted in his copy of Max Strauch's book *Die Theologie Karl Barths* [The theology of Karl Barth]. Eberhard contested the idea that the relationship between God and individual people – between Creator and created being – is "only indirect, with no

possible communication." He stressed exactly the opposite: "That relationship *does* exist."

31 Eberhard Arnold to Otto Herpel, November 17, 1919, BA.

32 *DCSV Mitteilungen*, no. 228 (Jan. 15, 1920).

Chapter Eight

1 Otto Herpel: 1886-1925. Eberhard reviewed Herpel's book *Die Frömmigkeit der deutschen Kriegslyrik* [The piousness of German war poetry] (Giessen, Germany: Alfred Töpelmann) in an article titled "Der Rückgang der religiösen Welle in der Kriegsliteratur" [The ebb of the religious wave in the war literature], *Die Furche*, no. 11 (Aug. 1917).

273

2 This article has been misidentified by several authors as Eberhard's lecture on the Sermon on the Mount at the 1919 Pentecost conference of Christian academics in Marburg. But reports by participants at that conference, printed in the *DCSV Mitteilungen*, provide evidence that Eberhard's impressive lecture on the Sermon on the Mount was delivered extempore. Willi Völger's summary in the *DCSV Mitteilungen* (cf. chap. 7, n. 13, 15) preserves something of the fire and spontaneity that marked the Marburg lecture. Compared with this, "Das Gegenwartserlebnis des Zukunftsreiches" [The present experience of the future kingdom] is far more structured, more scholarly in its language, and emphasizes other points. At best it is an altered and thoroughly revised version of the Marburg lecture.

3 The title of *Der Pflug (The Plough)*, which later became a periodical and is still published today (currently in both English and German) by the Bruderhof communities, is drawn from two very similar bible quotations that were adopted as mottoes by the Neuwerk movement: "Plow your fallow ground" (Jeremiah 4:3 and Hosea 10:12).

4 German title: *Weltrevolution und Welterlösung*. Some of the proposed chapters appeared as articles in *Das Neue Werk* and in *Die Furche*. E.g., "Menschheitskultur und Christusreich" [Human culture and the kingdom of Christ], "Das Gegenwartserlebnis des Zukunftsreiches" [The present experience of the future kingdom], the lecture on the title of the book, "Weltrevolution und Welterlösung" [World revolution and world redemption], and others.

5 *DCSV Mitteilungen*, no. 229 (Feb. 15, 1920), 159.

6 Eberhard Arnold to Rev. Karl Müller, Würdenhain, April 20, 1920, BA.

7 Cf. *DCSV Mitteilungen*, no. 237 (Feb. 15, 1924), 47.

[8] Eberhard Arnold to Otto Herpel, July 2, 1919, BA.

[9] Heinrich Schultheis: 1886–1961.

[10] Georg Flemmig: 1884–1950.

[11] On January 23 Eberhard wrote to Otto Herpel, "We all welcome your dear wife especially warmly to our Fellowship of the Early Church."

[12] Emmy Arnold, *Aus unserem Leben bis 1920*.

[13] *Geschichtsband*, vol. II, bk. 1, no. 14.

[14] From Siegmund-Schultze's *Die soziale Botschaft des Christentums* [The social message of Christianity] third edition (Halle: Paul Seiler, 1921), 25f. Eberhard wrote the third chapter, titled "Sie Hatten Alles Gemein" [They had all things in common].

[15] Regarding the tolstoyans: Count Leo Tolstoy, the great nineteenth-century Russian novelist and thinker, taught that the meaning of life could be found through the literal application of Christ's teachings, especially the Sermon on the Mount. Tolstoy sought to rescue the true teachings of Christ from what he perceived to be the irrelevant, irrational doctrines of faith. He emphasized the creed of absolute nonresistance (thus, incidentally, Tolstoy made a profound impression on Gandhi). This creed included the abhorrence of physical force, detestation of legalized exploitation of the poor, condemnation of private property (because ownership was secured by force), and a rejection of government (since it existed primarily for the sake of the rich and powerful). Many of Tolstoy's followers banded into colonies, but Tolstoy himself distrusted such organized efforts, and most colonies did not last long.

[16] German title: "Familienverband und Siedlungsleben," *Das Neue Werk*, no. 20/21, 65.

[17] In Emmy Arnold's *Gegen den Strom (Torches Together)* (Moers, 1983), 32. These points are not contained in the printed version of the lecture.

[18] Eberhard Arnold to Otto Herpel, April 1, 1920, BA: "It is becoming clearer and clearer to me that we have to move to Schlüchtern, not Halle…We must draw closer together."

[19] Eberhard's plans for this appear in a letter to Normann Körber, April 29, 1920, BA.

[20] Gustav Landauer: 1870–1919. German title: *Aufruf zum Sozialismus* (the second edition appeared in 1919). The English edition (St. Louis: Telos Press, 1978) is titled *For Socialism*, as it appears in the text.

[21] Cf. Eberhard's comment during a brotherhood meeting, Rhön Bruderhof, December 1934, BA: "When we were in Berlin our intellectual and inner interests were tremendously wide-ranging...We discussed every new book on any spiritual theme."

[22] The first proponents of anarchism continually disputed whether the government-free society they aimed at could or could not be brought about by terror and force. Landauer was a pacifist and had a deep, intense loathing for violence: "Anarchism must in no way be identified with chaos and terrorism. The theorists on public law who first worked out models for an anarchistic society at the end of the eighteenth century understood anarchy to mean a society 'without public coercion, yet not without order, peace, and safety.'" Gustav Landauer, "Zur Geschichte des Wortes Anarchie" [On the history of the word anarchy] in Der Sozialist (May 15–June 6, 1909).

[23] Eberhard Arnold to Hans Thelemann, February 18, 1920, BA.

[24] Eberhard Arnold to Martin Buber, May 9, 1921, BA. The project could not be carried out due to the terms of Landauer's will and the fact that Landauer's correspondence was widely scattered and unedited.

[25] In 1920 Otto Herpel's Zinzendorf: Über Glauben und Leben [Zinzendorf: on faith and life] carried an advertisement for the "forthcoming" book Gustav Landauer in seinen Briefen [Gustav Landauer in his correspondence], which was to be published by Karl Josef Friedrich.

[26] Eberhard Arnold to Karl Josef Friedrich, November 8, 1920, BA.

[27] A few years later Helmut von Mücke became leader of the NSDAP, the National Socialist German Workers' party, in Saxony.

[28] Eberhard Arnold to Otto Herpel, April 1, 1920, BA; cf. Eberhard Arnold to Friedrich Kleemann, March 17, 1920, BA.

[29] German title: "Das Geheimnis der Urgemeinde," printed in Das Neue Werk, no. 20–21, 160.

Chapter Nine

[1] Eberhard Arnold to Dr. Pfleiderer, June 13, 1920, BA.

[2] Cf. Else von Hollander, Sonnherz-Buch [Sunheart book], unpublished manuscript, recording the communal life in notes and sketches, from the beginnings at Sannerz until the move to the Rhön, BA.

[3] E.g., Eberhard Arnold to Heinrich Euler, November 9, 1920, BA; Eberhard Arnold to F.W. Cordes, November 12, 1920, BA.

4 Friedrich Wilhelm Foerster: 1869–1966. In 1916 Eberhard obtained Foerster's services as an author for the Furche Publishing House, but Eberhard had probably known of his writings earlier. He maintained a friendly relationship with the well-known educator for almost twenty years.

5 Alfred Dedo Müller to Eberhard Arnold, March 31, 1920, BA.

6 Eberhard Arnold to Otto Herpel, April 1, 1920, BA. In September 1921 a special issue of *Das Neue Werk* came out as a "Friedrich Wilhelm Foerster issue."

7 German titles: Otto Herpel, *Zinzendorf: Über Glauben und Leben* [Zinzendorf: on faith and life]; Georg Flemmig, *Dorfgedanken* [Village musings]; Fritz Schloss, *Legenden* [Legends]; Eberhard Arnold and Normann Körber, *Junge Saat: Lebensbuch einer Jugendbewegung* [Young seed: book of a youth movement's life].

8 Eberhard Arnold to Peter Bultmann, October 5, 1920, BA.

9 Eberhard Arnold to Eva Oehlke, September 20, 1920, BA.

10 Otto Herpel to Lydia Eger, November 6, 1920, BA.

11 Eberhard Arnold to auditor Pucks, November 23, 1920, BA.

12 Friedrich Berber, *Zwischen Macht und Gewissen* [Between power and conscience] (Munich: 1986), 31f.

13 Thomas von Stieglitz's judgment (cf. *Kirche als Bruderschaft*, 148) is not tenable when he states that after the Inselsberg conference in 1919 Eberhard turned away from evangelizing and replaced the call to conversion with the call to an exodus from middle-class mammonism into a life of complete community.

14 Eberhard Arnold to Dr. Gerd Knoche, November 21, 1921, BA.

15 *Das Neue Werk*, 1921–1922, 97; cf. Michael Holzach, *Das vergessene Volk* [The forgotten people] (Hamburg: 1980), 263ff.

16 German title: "Die Hutterischen Bruderhöfer im Militärkerker von Amerika," published in *Das Neue Werk*, no. 11 (Dec. 15, 1921), 350–354.

17 Up until 1870, the Hutterites lived in Russia, where their communities were exempt from all military service. In 1871, however, the government revoked this privilege, and between the years 1874 and 1879 all Hutterites left Russia and settled in South Dakota, USA. There the majority farmed homesteads, but three groups established communities. In 1874 Michael Waldner founded the Bon Homme community. Since he was a blacksmith

(Schmied), his people *(Leut)* became known as the Schmiedeleut. Darius Walter followed with a second group, establishing the Wolf Creek community in 1875. This group took the name of their founder, becoming the Dariusleut. Lastly, Jakob Wipf, a teacher *(Lehrer)*, led an immigration in 1879 and founded the Elm Spring community. This group was then the Lehrerleut. From these three original communities have grown the more than four hundred Hutterite communities in North America today. The names of the three groups have remained unchanged, and, while all hold the same basic tenets of faith, each group has developed distinctive characteristics.

[18] Karl Barth replied that he was glad his belief in Neuwerk and Sannerz had been justified: "The ultimate is never present as a given fact, but must be striven for – again and again." In *Geschichtsband*, vol. IV, bk. 1, no. 16a.

[19] According to Emmy, the Schultheises were already in Sannerz for Advent 1921; cf. *Gegen den Strom*, 58. The text follows the account by Gertrud Dalgas in *Die Neuwerk-Krise 1922* [The Neuwerk crisis 1922], unpublished manuscript, 5, BA.

[20] Wilhelm Stählin: 1883-1975. Served as a pastor in Nuremberg. Shortly after the Wallroth conference he founded the Michaelsbruderschaft [Brotherhood of St. Michael], a ministers' association, in Berneuchen, Pomerania. From 1926-1945 he was a professor in Münster, and from 1945-1952 he served in Oldenburg as a bishop of the Lutheran Church. German title of Stählin's book: *Fieber und Heil in der Jugendbewegung*.

[21] Emil Blum: 1894–1978.

[22] Eberhard Arnold to Normann Körber, August 4, 1921, BA.

[23] The date is established by Gertrud Dalgas in *Die Neuwerk-Krise 1922*.

[24] The friendship formed with Maria Mojen lasted many years. Proof of this was shown in 1934, when Maria Mojen arranged for a friend of Eberhard to convalesce in Tessin; cf. Eberhard Arnold to Leonhard Ragaz, December 1, 1934, BA.

[25] Recorded in the minutes of the meeting held August 3, 1922, *Geschichtsband*, vol. IV, bk. 2, no. 10.

[26] Comment made by Wilm Verhulst, a guest during the days of crisis in August 1922, noted in Else von Hollander's handwriting on publishing house letterhead, *Geschichtsband*, vol. IV, bk. 2, no. 8.

[27] Only a few weeks later, Paul Hummel left the community as well.

Chapter Ten

1. In *Gegen den Strom* Emmy describes in detail the tensions in the community's atmosphere during these weeks, including the irrational outbreaks of hatred, and schemes against the members who remained.

2. German name: Gemeinschafts-Verlag Eberhard Arnold. The first reference to this name change is in a letter Eberhard wrote to Leonhard Ragaz, November 28, 1922, BA. In their "greeting to members of the Neuwerk Publishing House and to coworkers and readers of our periodical" (*Das Neue Werk*, Sept.15, 1922, no. 6, 248), Eberhard and Else von Hollander were still referring to the "Sannerz-Verlag bei Eberhard Arnold" [Sannerz Publishing House with Eberhard Arnold].

3. German name: Eberhard Arnold Verlag, Sannerz und Leipzig. Gertrud Dalgas states that the change of name coincided with the introduction of the *Renten-Mark* (stabilized currency, introduced to curb the gross inflation) in the fall of 1924; cf. Gertrud Dalgas, *Eberhard Arnold's Wirksamkeit als Verleger und Christ* [Eberhard Arnolds activity as a publisher and a Christian], unpublished manuscript, BA. (However, the first edition of *Sonnenlieder*, published in 1924, still bore the publishing house's old imprint.)

4. German titles: Max Bürck, *Vom Staatskirchentum zur Menschheitsreligion;* Julius Goldstein, *Rasse und Politik;* Eugen Jäckh, *Blumhardt-Auswahlbuch;* Eberhard Arnold, *Liebesleben und Liebe;* (for Schloss's and Herpel's books, cf. chap. 9, n. 7).

5. Eberhard Arnold to Normann Körber, August 4, 1921, BA.

6. Eberhard Arnold to Gertrud Dalgas, July 17, 1922, BA.

7. Ibid.

8. In 1926 in reply to Baron Heinrich Freiherr von Gagern, head of the Fulda district administration; cf. von Gagern in *Eberhard Arnold: Aus seinem Leben und Schrifttum*, 42.

9. September 9, 1935, quoted by Emmy Arnold, *Gegen den Strom*, 68f.

10. The periodical adopted the modified name in October 1922.

11. Gertrud Dalgas recorded a remark from Emmy that gives an indication of how serious the temptation was: "I would like to go to Jesus, together with Eberhard."

12. The picture of the sun is central in this poem too:

> Who grasps the lightning, holds the sun?
> The lightning kindles, the sun flames forth.

It appears that during Eberhard's stay in Bilthoven in July 1922 – before the crisis broke out – he had already been meditating on the essence of light and on the imagery in the prologue to John's Gospel (John 1:1–18); cf. Eberhard Arnold to Gertrud Dalgas, July 17, 1922, BA.

13 Johann Christoph Blumhardt: 1805–1880.

14 Christoph Friedrich Blumhardt: 1842–1919.

15 Cf. chap. 5, *Hermann Kutter and the Social Issue.*

16 Cf. chap. 7, *Can a Christian be a Police Officer?*

17 Eugen Jäckh to Eberhard Arnold, August 18, 1921, BA.

18 German title: *Blumhardt: Vom Reich Gottes.*

19 Johannes Harder, *Aufbruch ohne Ende: Geschichten meines Lebens* [Always on the move: stories from my life] (Wuppertal, Germany: Gudrun Harder und Hermann Horn, 1992), 103.

20 Cf. Gertrud Dalgas, *Entscheidende Schritte 1919–1935* [Decisive steps 1919–1935], unpublished chronology, BA; cf. Emmy Arnold, *Gegen den Strom*, 54.

21 The Sannerz "Statement of Faith." Judging by the circumstances, this statement was formulated by Eberhard; cf. *Geschichtsband*, vol. IV, bk. 1, no. 43.

22 Until the middle of 1921, when the community began to school its own children, Emy-Margret, Hardy, and Heinrich attended the public elementary school in the village of Sannerz.

23 Cf. chap. 12, *Distinguished Friends.* The contact between Eberhard Arnold and Kees Boeke almost completely evaporated after the "Christian Brotherhood" in Bilthoven disbanded in 1926 under circumstances very similar to those in Sannerz in 1922. Subsequently Kees Boeke gave up pacifism, the Christian ideal of community and, finally, his faith. In 1933 his express wish was to be "an educational reformer and nothing more."

24 *Das Neue Werk*, no. 3 (June 25, 1922); cf. Kees Boeke in *Wat wil libertair onderwijs?* [What is the aim of unencumbered education?] (1905): "The children must grow up to be individuals with their own wills, full of initiative, to be people with strong characters, filled with distaste for superficialities."

25 Eberhard Arnold to Siegfried Muschter, November 3, 1920, BA.

26 Cf. Gustav Landauer, *Aufruf zum Sozialismus*, 154: "Scattered here and there among all our desolation are people who are living as children, and faith and certainty are alive in every one of them..." This passage is heavily underlined in Eberhard's copy.

27 In "Aufruf für unsere Kinderarbeit" [Appeal for our work with children], *Geschichtsband*, vol. IV, bk. 2, no. 3a.

28 Eberhard Arnold, "Die innerste Wesenheit unseres Werdens" [The innermost essence of our growth], unpublished manuscript, (May 1935), 22, BA; cf. Eberhard Arnold, "Unser Weg zur Erziehung" [Our approach to education], *Die Wegwarte* (Apr. 1927), no. 7, 111.

29 Cf. Eberhard Arnold, "Unser Weg zur Erziehung."

30 German title, in full: *Sonnenlieder für Menschheitsfriede und Gottesgemeinschaft* [Songs of the sun: for the peace of humanity and God's community].

31 German song title: "Brüder, zur Sonne, zur Freiheit." In *Sonnenlieder* the original closing words of the third verse, "Holy is the last fight," are replaced by a new concluding sentence, composed by Erich Mohr: "Holy is the power of love."

32 Carl Franklin Arnold to Eberhard Arnold, May 18, 1924, BA.

33 In the summer of 1921 Heinrich Euler had conducted the first baptism in Sannerz; cf. *Gegen den Strom*.

34 Held at the Breitewitzer Mühle, near Gräfenhainichen, Saxony. The Mennonite and Baptist preacher Hans Klassen had built up the Neusonnefeld community settlement there after the original settlement near Sonnefeld in Thuringia collapsed because of internal problems. Eberhard and Emmy knew Hans and Wally Klassen even before the war; cf. chap. 4, n. 18.

35 His topic: the Sermon on the Mount; cf. Rose Kaiser in "Early memories of Sannerz and the Rhön Bruderhof," unpublished manuscript, BA.

36 Probably from Wolkan, *Die Hutterer: Österreichische Wiedertäufer und Kommunisten in Amerika* [The Hutterites: Austrian Anabaptists and communitarians in America]. J.G. Ewert had drawn Eberhard's attention to this book in 1921. Another source familiar to Eberhard at that time was Loserth's *Kommunismus der Mährischen Wiedertäufer* [The communal life of the Moravian Anabaptists]. Eberhard only heard of other Hutterite sources through Robert Friedmann in 1926; cf. *Die Wegwarte*, nos. 8 & 9, 1925.

37 According to notation by Gertrud Dalgas; cf. *Geschichtsband,* vol. IV, bk. 3, no. 13.

Chapter Eleven

1. *Wegwarte* is the German name of a small blue wildflower, also known as "bride of the sun," and introduced in North America as chicory. Some sources translate the magazine's name as *Wayside Flower*.

2. Eberhard Arnold to Adolf Braun, April 26, 1924, BA.

3. Quoted from Eberhard's "Die Lebensgemeinschaft und die Zukunft der Arbeit" [Community life and the future of our work], unpublished manuscript, (1921–1922), BA.

4. In a letter from the Neuwerk Sunheart Community to the *"werdende Gemeinde"* of Neusonnefeld, August 24, 1924, BA. "Our community household feels that its fundamental vocation is to work for the nascent community church."

5. Report about the work at Sannerz, Easter 1925, *Geschichtsband*, vol. IV, bk. 3, no. 34.

6. The quoted text is from Eberhard's article "Warum wir in Gemeinschaft leben,"*Die Wegwarte*, no. 10/11 (1925). English edition *Why We Live in Community* (Farmington, PA: The Plough Publishing House, 1995). In October 1925 Eberhard wrote a note in which he referred to the necessary reverence for *Gemeinde* and its members. *Geschichtsband*, vol. IV, bk. 3, no. 49.

7. Eberhard Arnold, "Die Lebensgemeinschaft und die Zukunft der Arbeit."

8. Eberhard Arnold to the Habertshof cooperative, February 1922, BA.

9. E.g., Hans Brandenburg, in *Die Brücke zu Köngen* [The bridge to Köngen] (Stuttgart: 1969), 76, said that "it was hardly possible to find compatibility between Wilhelm Hauer's personality and Eberhard Arnold's characteristics." Wilhelm Hauer was leader of a Köngen youth group.

10. For a brief explanation of the origins of the Free German Youth and its role in the Youth Movement context, cf. chap. 7, n. 1.

11. Eberhard Arnold to Ludwig von Gerdtell, September 7, 1920, BA.

12. For a discussion of the 1913 Hohe Meissner conference, cf. chap. 7, *Youth on the Move* and related notes.

13. Eberhard was referring to the discussion between Hermann Schafft and the Communist party functionary August Wittvogel at the Meissner confer-

ence; cf. Normann Körber, "Kampf um die Schlüchterner Jugend" [Fight for the Schlüchtern youth] in *Hermann Schafft: ein Lebenswerk* [Life and work of Hermann Schafft], 62ff. In communist terminology, the "last battle" (or "fight") refers to the final overthrow of capitalism.

14 "Der Ruf an uns" [The challenge to us], leaflet, October 1923, in *Geschichtsband*, vol. IV, bk. 3, no. 2.

15 Eberhard Arnold to Ludwig von Gerdtell, op. cit.

16 "A Christian movement that gives a united witness to Christ is not to be found here; neither is an honoring of men, which directly opposes him," wrote Eberhard in "Die religiöse Welle in der freideutschen Bewegung" [The religious upsurge in the Free German movement], unpublished manuscript (1923), BA.

17 Hans Joachim Schoeps (*Rückblicke*, 45) wrote, "A large part of us in the Free German Union consciously represented a liberal humanist attitude alongside and in contradiction to Eberhard Arnold. And we got on together very well. There was a great and generous spirit of mutual respect because anything narrow and sectarian was completely foreign to Arnold."

18 "Die religiöse Welle in der freideutschen Bewegung," op. cit.

19 According to Hans Joachim Schoeps's account (*Rückblicke*, 45): "When there were powers that opposed the Holy Spirit, powers that he sensed as coming from the world of demons, these had to be conquered. It once happened to me, when out of some dark instinct I set myself against the spirit of Sannerz and made a cynical remark, that Eberhard Arnold took thorough measures to drive out the demons from me."

20 Eberhard Arnold to the Evangelical booksellers, April 1926, BA.

21 Including apparently opposed witnesses in the project was part of the concept; cf. flyer from the Hochweg Publishing House in 1925. "Our 'Living Library' has its origin in the faith…that in the whole church the whole truth is at work. From this truth, the light of God breaks into the most varied, often humanly opposed, groups that have very clear and objective differences between them."

22 German title: *Die ersten Christen nach dem Tode der Apostel.* The 1998 English edition from The Plough Publishing House carries the title *The Early Christians: In Their Own Words.*

23 It read as follows: "The editor must express the deepest gratitude to his father. Over the years it becomes ever plainer to him how much he owes to his father's books, to his guidance in church history, his comprehensive scholarship, and his biblical and church orientation."

[24] The search for writings began with a letter to the Mennonite Publishing House in Altona, in which Eberhard asked for a collection of sixteenth-century Anabaptist songs, April 17, 1923, BA.

[25] Cf. "Warum wir in Gemeinschaft leben," op. cit.

[26] Ibid.

[27] Eberhard Arnold to Fred Sicora, January 6, 1926, BA.

[28] Eberhard Arnold to Else von Hollander, February 20, 1926, BA: "The Free Germans in Hamburg, whom I love very much, suggest the following name, which according to the ordnance map applies to the hill where the *hof* is situated: Bruderhof Botenberg [Bruderhof messenger hill]. We should become messengers for the message from the Bruderhof."

[29] Emy-Margret Arnold, *Kindheitserinnerungen*, 54.

[30] Quoted by Emmy Arnold, *Gegen den Strom*, 85.

Chapter Twelve

[1] Hans-Joachim Schoeps, *Rückblicke*.

[2] "Der Augenblick" [The moment], plans for 1929-1930. These handwritten notes were undoubtedly made at the beginning of 1929. *Geschichtsband*, vol. V, no. 52a. Regarding the "open door" principle, cf. transcript of brotherhood meeting, August 11, 1929, BA.

[3] Transcript of a discussion on January 17, 1932, BA. Here Eberhard refers to an admonition from Else Baehr during his student days in Halle: "If you don't have the humility to accept money for the Lord's service, then you cannot become a disciple."

[4] In *Gegen den Strom* Emmy gives a striking description of the Bruderhof diet: just potatoes and plenty of sauerkraut.

[5] "Erinnerungen an Eberhard Arnold" [Memories of Eberhard Arnold], tape transcript from June 16, 1993, BA.

[6] Cf. "Unser Weg zur Erziehung," *Die Wegwarte* (1927).

[7] Cf. chap. 10, *Children's Community*.

[8] "Der Kampf um die Kindheit" [The fight for childhood], *Die Wegwarte* (1928).

[9] Among these reformers, Rudolf Steiner is first and foremost. Eberhard regarded Steiner's anthroposophy as a syncretic mixture of religions in which

"a great deal that never belonged together was brought into one big muddle" (according to minutes of a talk in August 1933, BA), and therefore he could not entirely approve of the Waldorf theory of education. But Marianne Hilbert, who was a teacher at the Rhön Bruderhof from 1932 on, recalled that Eberhard found Steiner's concept of the three stages in a child's development (from ages one to seven, seven to fourteen, and fourteen to twenty-one) to be confirmed by his own observations.

[10] Eberhard Arnold to Gertrud Dalgas, May 25, 1932, BA.

[11] Eberhard Arnold, in his fundraising leaflet "Die Kindergemeinde des Almbruderhofs und ihre Erziehung" [The children's community of the Alm Bruderhof and its education] (Eberhard Arnold Verlag, April 1934).

[12] "Unser Weg zur Erziehung," op. cit.

[13] "Erinnerungen an Eberhard Arnold," op. cit.

[14] Cf. Eberhard Arnold, *Gemeinsames Leben und Kindererziehung (Children's Education in Community)* (Rifton, NY: The Plough Publishing House, 1977).

[15] Johann Heinrich Pestalozzi: 1746–1827. Swiss educational reformer, primarily concerned with the education of deprived children. Pestalozzi developed teaching methods based on concrete experience, as opposed to learning by rote. His methods still influence modern educational theory.

Wilhelm August Fröbel: 1782–1852. A German educator, he founded the first kindergarten, in Bad Blankenburg, Germany, in 1837.

[16] "Der Kampf um die Kindheit," op. cit.

[17] Friedmann was a tolstoyan. Through his studies of Anabaptist history he gradually came closer to Christian belief. For more on the tolstoyans, cf. chap. 8, n. 15.

[18] These first letters between Eberhard Arnold and Elias Walter have not been preserved; the account is based on Gertrud Dalgas's recollections in *Die Kinder im Bruderhofleben* [The children in the life of the Bruderhof], unpublished manuscript, BA.

[19] Peter Riedemann: 1506–1556.

[20] Andreas Ehrenpreis: 1589–1662.

[21] German title of the newspaper: *Rufer zur Wende.*

[22] Eberhard Arnold to Robert Friedmann, June 6, 1929, BA, regarding Hermann Buddensieg: "He goes so far as to say that the testimony of our common life and our words is the only Christianity possible for today. The

Hutterian writings, too, made an extraordinarily strong impression on him. And yet he does not see himself obliged to venture into the same life on the basis of the same witness to faith."

23 Emmy Arnold, *Eberhard Arnold: Aus seinem Leben und Schrifttum.*

24 German title: *Der Kampf um das Reich Gottes in Blumhardt Vater und Sohn.*

25 Quoted from "Erinnerungen an Eberhard Arnold."

26 Statement of the Free German Union, January 10, 1926.

27 According to Erich Mohr's words in Circular Letter no. 3 to members of the Free German Union, September 1926.

28 Hans-Joachim Schoeps, *Rückblicke:* "Although I was in a thoroughly rationalistic period of my life at the time, I could not avoid the spiritual powers at work on the Bruderhof. They streamed through Eberhard Arnold. Because of Eberhard Arnold I realized when I was quite young that Christianity is a spiritual reality that is able to transform and renew a person."

29 Circular Letter no. 5 to the Free German youth groups, February 1927.

30 After the January conference there was actually no formal decision to disband, but the number of members shrank dramatically due to a wave of resignations. A "work week" at the Rhön Bruderhof in October 1930 was a failure.

Chapter Thirteen

1 Cf. Eberhard Arnold to Elias Walter, Nov. 6, 1928, in *Brothers Unite* (Rifton, NY: The Plough Publishing House, 1988), 6ff.

2 "Ein kleiner Sendbrief an die hutterischen Brüder" [A small epistle to the Hutterite brothers], *Brothers Unite,* 24.

3 During Eberhard's lifetime eighty-nine pages of *Das Klein Geschichtsbuch* [The small history book] were prepared for publication. The book was to have had a comprehensive scholarly commentary, but the project was never completed. A.J.F. Zieglschmid's version was published in 1947 by the Carl Schurz Memorial Foundation, Philadelphia, PA, but it lacked scholarly commentary.

4 Eberhard Arnold to Robert Friedmann, June 6, 1929, *Brothers Unite,* 24ff.

5 Eberhard Arnold to John Horsch, September 14 to October 9, 1929, *Brothers Unite,* 41ff.

⁶ Cf. Eberhard Arnold to Erich Mohr, December 11, 1929, BA.

⁷ Sabatisch, Hungary, was founded by the Anabaptists in 1546 after their expulsion from Moravia.

⁸ The writing was a Christmas teaching, dating from 1652; cf. Eberhard Arnold to David Wipf, December 31, 1929, *Brothers Unite,* 44ff.

⁹ Eberhard Arnold to John Horsch, May 19, 1930, *Brothers Unite,* 51f.

¹⁰ "Schmied Michel" refers to Michael Walder, the nineteenth-century patriarch who led Hutterites from Russia to the United States and to whom the Schmiedeleut owe their name; cf. chap. 9, n. 17.

¹¹ Paul and Peter Gross to Elias Walter, March 30, 1929, *Brothers Unite,* 18ff.

¹² Quoted by Elias Walter in a letter to John Horsch, September 4, 1930, *Brothers Unite,* 220.

¹³ Bon Homme was founded in 1874 by "Schmied Michel" Waldner with the first group of emigrants from Russia.

¹⁴ Cf. chap. 9, *New Leads.*

¹⁵ Eberhard Arnold to Emmy Arnold, June 24, 1930, *Brothers Unite,* 68f.

¹⁶ Eberhard Arnold to John Horsch, May 19, 1930, *Brothers Unite,* 51ff.

¹⁷ Eberhard Arnold to Harold Bender, May 20, 1930, *Brothers Unite,* 53ff.

¹⁸ Cf. chap. 15, *The Fight for the Children.*

¹⁹ Transcript of brotherhood meeting, August 22, 1931, BA; cf. Eberhard Arnold to Elias Walter, April 12, 1932, *Brothers Unite,* 280ff.

²⁰ *Brothers Unite,* 211ff.

²¹ Quoted by Elias Walter in a letter to Joseph Stahl, August 31, 1930, *Brothers Unite,* 218f.

²² Diary entry for October 8, 1930, *Brothers Unite,* 158.

²³ "Vetter" is a Hutterian term of respect reserved for older men and ministers.

²⁴ Transcript of *Gemeindestunde* [worship meeting], Rhön Bruderhof, December 26, 1934, BA.

²⁵ Irmgard Keiderling to Else von Hollander, May 27, 1931, *Brothers Unite,* 250. Stephan Wehowsky's assumption is completely untenable when he suggests that Eberhard worked to unite with the Hutterian communities

only to save a settlement project from collapse (in *Religiöse Interpretation politischer Erfahrung* [Religious interpretation of political experience] (Göttingen: 1980, 127).

26 Irmgard Keiderling to Else von Hollander, May 15, 1931, *Brothers Unite*, 250.

Chapter Fourteen

1 Quoted by Irmgard Keiderling in a letter to Else von Hollander, May 15, 1931, BA.

2 Diary entry for July 21, 1930, *Brothers Unite*, 86ff.

3 Quoted by Irmgard Keiderling in a letter to Else von Hollander, May 15, 1931, BA.

4 In March 1931 Eberhard wrote in his diary about the reason for the Hutterites' prohibition of musical instruments: "The question at issue is simply about the way to express religion, in particular that no idolatry, including that of musical sensibility, shall take the place of faith in the Spirit."

5 Transcript of brotherhood meeting, May 27, 1935, BA.

6 Transcript of brotherhood meeting, August 22, 1931, BA.

7 Referring to the numerous old Anabaptist songs from times of harshest persecution, Arnold Pfeiffer writes in *Religiöse Sozialisten* [Religious-socialists] (Olten, 1976) that the carefree mood of the first volume has given way in the second to "a world-rejecting, mournful sound." He completely fails to realize that *Sonnenlieder II* does not replace the first volume, but rather supplements it.

8 The exact date of this diary entry is unclear, but it falls between December 19 and 25, 1930, BA.

9 According to Irmgard Keiderling's report to Else von Hollander, May 15, 1931, BA.

10 Mentioned by Eberhard in May–June 1931 in his letter to Peter Hofer, James Valley, Manitoba: "…important and urgent that our beloved David Vetter is soon sent to us from your Bruderhof." In fact David Vetter was among the first delegation of brothers to visit the Rhön Bruderhof, but that visit was not until 1937, two years after Eberhard's death.

11 Transcript of brotherhood meeting, August 11, 1929, BA.

[12] Eberhard Arnold to Elisabeth Arnold, June 18, 1934, BA.

[13] Transcript of guest meeting, June 1932, BA.

[14] Transcript of guest meeting, June 18, 1932, BA.

[15] It had actually been a call to violence against Eberhard: "Strike him dead!"

[16] Eberhard Arnold to Emmy Arnold, June 18, 1930, *Brothers Unite*, 67.

[17] John Hoyland, in his preface to *The Early Christians after the Death of the Apostles* (Wiltshire, England: The Plough Publishing House, 1939), 22, 33. (It should be noted that, although this edition carried the translated title of Eberhard's original work, it was not a comprehensive translation, and only included Eberhard's survey of the early church.)

[18] Transcript of brotherhood meeting, July 26, 1933, BA.

[19] Transcript of a talk on the meaning of Advent, December 1934, BA.

[20] *Innenland*, 174: "There are still those who point out seriously that God is quite other than man, quite other than all that man of himself wants or does. But there are very few who believe in this quite different God so really and so truly that they can see the approach of his reign and grasp it. Only these very few lend a hand in faith so that a fundamental change...actually begins."

Innenland, 176f: "God is indeed other than we are...We cannot become God. We remain other than God is. But God becomes man in order to become our God."

[21] *Innenland*, 179: "Whoever rejects faith in the intervention of God in his creation here and now as a mystical faith based on personal experience...has forgotten the gospel...Whoever wants to exalt the limited theological thinking of the human brain and elevate it as the only faith to be experienced...rejects the apostles of Jesus Christ and therefore Jesus himself."

Innenland, 210: "Whoever wants to hear, read, or experience one or the other specific thing about Christ, yet uses weakening interpretations to wipe out what he thinks is impossible, will come to grief no matter how Christian the edifice of his life seems."

[22] *Innenland*, 101: "We must never make an idol of created man or of racial instincts."

[23] *Innenland*, 112ff. "Das Gewissen und sein Zeugnis" ("The Conscience and Its Witness"). In this chapter Eberhard refers to the bible passage: "Whoever sheds the blood of man, by man shall his blood be shed" (Gen. 9:5). He writes, "Throughout all ages, the sin against the blood of a soul...has struck

man's conscience as the gravest crime, a capital crime against God and his order so that avenging it is seen as the first duty of human authority." According to Eberhard's view, the retribution administered by government contains hidden within it "a corrective justice, a justice of God's wrath." And further, "the authority of the state is meant to help and protect." When he wrote this chapter in 1931 it still seemed unthinkable to him that the state itself could commit murder, that the state could become a mass murderer, and that no one would be left to exact retribution.

[24] *Innenland,* 375: "The church receives a royal promise especially meant for the dangers of persecution: the spirit of the all-commanding Father will go with his sons and daughters to speak to his enemies through them…Under his leadership, they will be masters of any situation until the last hour comes…In the face of death they proclaim and represent the eternal truth."

[25] Today this argument has no more than theoretical value. The crimes of the National Socialists have made the swastika an enduring symbol of terror, murder, and megalomania. Any other interpretation is out of the question.

[26] *Innenland,* 330: "In the church of Christ, war and violence, law suits and legal action end…[Christ's followers] do not resist evil, but give their back to the smiters."

Innenland, 337: "The children of God's heart may not kill or go to war. They need no murderous weapons. No one who is a Christian can go to war. Whoever does, does so as an unbeliever within the order of wrath, never as a Christian within the order of love."

[27] On March 23, 1933, with the agreement of all parties except the Social Democrats, the Reichstag granted almost unlimited power to Adolf Hitler, and so in effect brought about its own dissolution. Hitler's speech in the discussion preceding the vote was full of open threats against any democratic powers and against anyone who might resist change.

[28] Transcript of brotherhood meeting, March 25, 1933, BA.

[29] Transcript of a talk for the presentation *(Darstellung)* of a new baby, Magdalena Dreher, September 3, 1933. (During a *Darstellung* ceremony, the word leader welcomes the child into the community household and entrusts the parents with the task of raising their baby with love. This blessing should in no way be confused with infant baptism.) The impressions and views of the student chaplain Kunze, as recounted in this meeting by Eberhard, add up to a deeply moving document; Kunze had anticipated with great accuracy the development of the church's struggle and had detected and analyzed in a very exact manner the National Socialists' demonic use of symbols, the suggestive force of the mass marches, the colors, and the banners.

[30] Ludwig Müller, born in 1883 (the same year as Eberhard Arnold), became bishop of the regional church in Prussia in 1933 and Reich Bishop of the "German Christians," an organization with a poorly disguised affinity to the Nazis. To resist the influence exerted by the German Christians on the church, the Confessional Church was formed.

[31] Leonhard Ragaz to Robert Friedmann, March 30, 1935, BA.

Chapter Fifteen

[1] Cf. Leonhard Ragaz to Hans Boller, August 22, 1931, BA: "Even if it should prove that the Bruderhof is not your final stopping place, this stretch of the road is undoubtedly intended and blessed by God."

[2] E.g., As Josef Stahl wrote from the Lake Byron community on March 24, 1929: "We are very glad to hear of and acknowledge your godly zeal and eager love and longing to be included in the number of God's elect… because…so-called Christians do not want to practice such self-surrender. Although many of them have heard and know about it and acknowledge that it is a work of the Holy Spirit, they go away in sorrow as the rich young man did. And they do not want to come to the supper of the Lord. And so the Lord swore in his wrath that they should not taste of it."

[3] Leonhard Ragaz to Robert Friedmann, March 30, 1935.

[4] Transcript of a talk given by Eberhard to Leonhard Ragaz and members of the Werkhof, March 11, 1935, BA.

[5] Even during the days of Sannerz, Suse Hungar had repeatedly left the community for periods of several weeks at a time and had then returned. Eberhard had a very lenient attitude to the restless streak in her character. The Bruderhof stayed in contact with her over the decades.

[6] Marianne Hilbert in "Erinnerungen an Eberhard Arnold."

[7] Robert Friedmann to Leonhard Ragaz, May 24, 1929. At Friedmann's invitation, Eberhard Arnold lectured in Vienna during November 1929; cf. chap. 13, *On the Trail of the Past*.

[8] Quoted by Robert Friedmann to Leonhard Ragaz, August 24, 1929, BA.

[9] Eberhard Arnold to Robert Friedmann, February 13, 1934, BA.

[10] Robert Friedmann to Leonhard Ragaz, March 27, 1935, BA; Leonhard Ragaz to Robert Friedmann, March 30, 1935, BA.

[11] Robert Friedmann to Leonhard Ragaz, March 27, 1935, BA: "I admit that I cannot distinguish between exactly how much of Arnold is genuine and

comes from the very depths, and how much is mixed with all-too-human influences."

12 Cf. chap. 12. During the years 1929–1935, Ragaz was obviously torn between sympathy toward and appreciation for the Bruderhof, and mistrust and criticisms against it. Hans Meier, for example, reports in *Solange das Licht Brennt* [As long as the light burns] (Norfolk, CT: Hutterian Brethren, 1990), 45, that in December 1933, Ragaz wrote a letter of recommendation for him to Thomas Masaryk, the President of Czechoslovakia, a personal friend. Shortly before this Ragaz had acknowledged that Eberhard, in a meeting of the FOR in Bad Boll, had established the connection between the questions of property and nonviolence.

13 The Nazis' winter relief *(Winterhilfe)* program was a compulsory charity instituted to provide aid in the form of food and clothing, especially in winter.

14 Transcript of brotherhood meeting, November 1, 1934, BA.

15 The Confessional Church began in 1934, emerging from the Pastors' Emergency League, in opposition to the "German Christians" and the Nazi-instated "Church of the Reich." In response to what it called the "state of emergency" within the church at large, the Confessional Church formed its own emergency church structure, which completely rejected the validity of the Church of the Reich. Many members of the Confessional Church were persecuted for their beliefs. Some, such as Dietrich Bonhoeffer, became involved in the political resistance against the Nazis.

16 Cf. Hans Meier, *Solange das Licht Brennt*, 43ff. Their route lay through Switzerland and Austria to Prague, where Hans Meier made inquiries whether it might eventually be possible to take over an old Hutterian "Haushaben" [communal settlement] in Moravia.

17 Cf. *Brothers Unite*, 318f.

18 Although several foster children had to remain in Germany, the majority of the foster children in the Bruderhof's care traveled to Switzerland, after receiving permission from their mothers or guardians; cf. *Gegen den Strom*, 152f.

19 As seen in various references in letters to Hardy Arnold. On January 19, Eberhard wrote that he was still hoping to find a place for another Bruderhof "in Appenzell or…in Waadt Canton." On January 22, Emmy wrote of the possibility of another Bruderhof, "preferably in Switzerland."

20 According to recollections by Gertrud Dalgas. There is an interesting historical parallel. In the sixteenth century the princes of Liechtenstein were also manor lords of Nikolsburg in Moravia. They provided refuge for fugitives,

forced to hide because of their faith, from the whole of Europe, among others for the Tyrolean Anabaptist Jakob Hutter.

[21] Julia Lerchy came to the Bruderhof a few months later; she was taken into the novitiate in October of 1934 and into the brotherhood at the beginning of 1935. She remained with the Bruderhof communities until her death in 1991.

[22] Dietrich Bonhoeffer: 1906–1945. Eberhard knew the Bonhoeffer family from Breslau, where Dietrich's father had been a professor of psychology and neurology.

[23] Guests were no longer allowed to stay overnight. Only people who intended to stay six months or longer with the community could be accommodated, and these only for a limited period; cf. *Gegen den Strom,* 153.

[24] The German word *"Einstimmigkeit"* (used in reference to the community), for example, does not translate as "unity" but as "unanimity." As remembered by Winifred Bridgwater.

[25] Cf. Eberhard Arnold to Karl Born, November 2, 1935, BA:

> Vegetarianism and the theosophical theory of evolution shift animals into far closer a relationship with human beings than was ever recognized by the prophets and apostles…We cannot hold to an evolutionary theory that regards animals as higher than plants. Instead we believe that people should be regarded as of greater worth than both animals and plants. What should horrify and distress Christians today is the contempt for and murder of people.

[26] Kathleen Hamilton, "Erinnerungen an Eberhard Arnold."

[27] Edna Percival, "Erinnerungen an Eberhard Arnold." Edna Percival joined the Bruderhof in the summer of 1935.

Chapter Sixteen

[1] In 1933 about twenty adults joined the brotherhood, about ten in 1934, and about fifteen more in 1935.

[2] One customer was the last Hohenzollern emperor, who lived in exile near Utrecht, Holland. He had ordered books and writings from the Eberhard Arnold Publishing House ever since the early twenties.

[3] Transcript of a brotherhood meeting, end of July 1934, BA.

[4] Karl Keiderling to Alfred Gneiting, July 5, 1935, BA. The sales and fund-

raising trips were as problematic as they were necessary. Several Swiss cantons refused to issue entry permits for the traveling brothers. And among fellow Christians in Switzerland, there was at times a failure to grasp the desperate plight of the Bruderhof. Typical of this is Leonhard Ragaz's totally exaggerated criticism in March 1935: "His aim" – meaning Eberhard's – "is the ruthless financial exploitation of the whole religious-socialist movement in Switzerland...It is simply a fact that Arnold's community would have collapsed long ago if we had not again and again supported it."

5 Eberhard Arnold to Ellen and Gerbrand Dekker, February 21, 1933, BA.

293

6 "Die schwierige Lage der Christen in der Krisis Mitteleuropas" [The difficult situation of the Christians in the crisis in central Europe], lecture in Edinburgh, April 23, 1935, BA.

7 Eberhard Arnold, "Werbeschrift für den Almbruderhof Silum" [Appeals for the Alm Bruderhof, Silum], May 1934, BA.

8 Eberhard Arnold, "Weihnachtsbrief" [Christmas letter] from the Rhön to the Alm Bruderhof, (December 1934), BA; cf. transcript of brotherhood meeting, December 5, 1934, BA.

9 According to Hans Meier in *Solange das Licht brennt,* 50. According to Gertrud Dalgas, the young men did not leave the country until March 18; cf. *Entscheidende Schritte.*

10 Gutenberg is a castle on a prominent cliff in the Rhine valley at the southern extremity of the principality of Liechtenstein.

11 "Die schwierige Lage der Christen in der Krisis Mitteleuropas," op. cit.

12 Reported by Hardy Arnold, May 1, 1935, BA.

13 Eberhard Arnold to Hans Zumpe, April 18, 1935, BA.

14 It was from the circle associated with Leyton Richards that Arnold and Gladys Mason came to the Bruderhof. Richards had visited the Rhön Bruderhof at the end of February and the Alm Bruderhof at the beginning of March 1935.

15 The Dutch Mennonites gave the community speedy and generous aid after the Rhön Bruderhof was dissolved by the National Socialists in 1937.

16 Transcript of brotherhood meeting, October 22, 1935, BA.

17 Later known as the Cotswold Bruderhof in Ashton Keynes, Wiltshire.

18 Eberhard Arnold to Emmy Arnold, December 25, 1930, BA; cf. *Brothers Unite,* 186.

[19] "Werbeschrift für den Almbruderhof Silum," op. cit.

[20] Shorthand notes of a report of a journey, November 1, 1934, BA.

[21] From letters during the England journey; cf. Eberhard Arnold to Hans Zumpe, April 1935, BA.

[22] Eberhard Arnold to Hans Zumpe, April 20, 1935, BA.

[23] E.g., In a letter to Alfred Gneiting written on July 5, 1935, BA, Karl Keiderling reported that Eberhard had made jokes throughout the midday meal.

[24] As remembered by Winifred Bridgwater.

[25] Transcript of brotherhood meeting, June 25, 1935, BA.

[26] Most probably June 13–14 at the Alm Bruderhof; this is shown by dates in several old shorthand notebooks, BA.

[27] According to Hans Meier's recollection in "Hans Meier Tells His Story to a Friend," printed pamphlet (Rifton, NY: The Plough Publishing House, 1979), 44; cf. *Solange das Licht brennt,* 108.

[28] He had already announced this step in a letter to Hans Zumpe on November 2, 1935, BA.

[29] Transcript of a talk on November 9, 1935, BA.

[30] Eberhard Arnold to Emmy Arnold, November 13, 1935, BA.

[31] Eberhard completed the final chapter of *Innenland* in the last weeks before his death. He had several different proposals for its conclusion and left the final editing to his son Hardy. The new edition of *Innenland* was printed in 1936 on the Alm Bruderhof.

[32] *Innenland,* "Der Gottes Friede" ("The Peace of God"), 274.

[33] Winifred Bridgwater, "Erinnerungen an Eberhard Arnold."

[34] John Hoyland, from the English edition of *The Early Christians.* John Hoyland had visited the Rhön Bruderhof in July 1935.

Time Line

Major Events in the Life of Eberhard Arnold

1883 **July 26** Born in Königsberg as the third child of Carl Franklin and Elisabeth Arnold.

1899 **July** Stays at the home of "Uncle" Ernst Ferdinand Klein in Lichtenrade. Experiences a decisive inner change.

1900 Plays active role in a Breslau bible study group and in the YMCA.

1901 Helps with preaching efforts of the Breslau Salvation Army.

1902 Encounters Ludwig von Gerdtell for the first time.

1905 **Spring** Passes his final high school exam in Jauer, Lower Silesia. Begins to study theology at Breslau University.
Fall Moves to Halle an der Saale.
Enrolls as a student of theology at the Royal Martin Luther University.

1906 **May** Elected chairman of the Halle chapter of the Student Christian Movement (SCM).

1907 **March 4** Meets Emmy von Hollander for the first time.
March 29 They become engaged.

1908 **April** Receives permission to take theology examination for his doctorate.
October 2 Permission revoked over issue of baptism.
Enrolls in the philosophy faculty in Halle.
October 25? Gotthelf Müller baptizes Eberhard.

1909 Studies at Erlangen University.
November 30 Passes his examination, summa cum laude.
December 20 Marries Emmy von Hollander, and they move to Leipzig.

1910 Serves as secretary of the SCM in Halle; Lectures in Dessau and Oranienburg.
July 1 Receives his doctorate in philosophy from Erlangen University.

1911 Lectures in Magdeburg, etc.

1912 Lectures in Halle and Erfurt, etc.

1913 **February** Suffers from tuberculosis of the larynx.
April Arnolds move to Oberbozen, Tirol.

1914 **August 2** Eberhard is called up for military service, but is released for health reasons after three weeks. He returns to Halle.

1915 **Fall** Appointed as the SCM's literary advisor and as media relations manager with the Furche Publishing House. Arnolds move to the Berlin suburb of Wilmersdorf.

1918 *Innenland* is published by the Furche Publishing House.

1919 **Easter** Family moves to Berlin district of Steglitz.

Summer – Fall Lectures in Marburg, Bad Oeynhausen, Saarow, Tambach, Hamburg, and Rostock.

October 28 Resigns as business manager of the publishing house but continues as editor, co-publisher, and literary advisor of *Die Furche* and as SCM secretary.

1920 **Spring** Lectures in Berlin, Bückeburg, and Schlüchtern.

April 1 Leaves the editorship of *Die Furche*, but remains on the SCM executive committee.

June 21 Arnolds move to Sannerz.

August 28 or 29 Injures his left eye, which eventually goes blind.

1921 Lectures in München, Düren, Sannerz, Vienna, Göttingen, Pappenheim, Mannheim, Schlüchtern, and Frankfurt am Main.

1922 **July** Arnolds visit Boekes in Bilthoven, Holland.

After their return, the Sannerz community suffers crises, and many people leave. Only seven members remain.

Fall Lectures in Schlüchtern, Breslau, and Frankfurt am Main.

1923 **August 30 – September 2** Speaks at a youth conference on the Hohe Meissner, and is a co-founder of the Free German Union.

Fall Lectures in Hannover and Stuttgart.

1924 **Spring – Summer** Lectures in Nordhausen / Harz, Stuttgart, Chemnitz, Dresden, Leipzig, and Döbeln.

1925 Lectures in Dresden and in Lichtenstein, Saxony, etc.

1926 Eberhard's book *The Early Christians after the Death of the Apostles* is published as Source book I of the *Quellen* series.

1927 **May** Arnolds and Sannerz household move to the Hansehof, near Fulda (this will later become the Rhön Bruderhof).

1928 **Spring** Lectures in Hannover, etc.

1929 **June** Visits Johann Loserth in Graz to discuss publishing the Hutterites' *Das Klein Geschichtsbuch*.

End November Gives lecture series in Vienna and in Graz.

Visits historical Hutterian settlements in Hungary.

1930 **May 30** Embarks on journey to United States and Canada.

Mid-June – August Visits the Hutterian colonies in South Dakota.

August – December Visits the Schmiedeleut colonies in Manitoba, then travels on to the Dariusleut and Lehrerleut colonies in Alberta.

December 9 Accepted into the *Gemeinde* of the Hutterian Brethren by the elders of the Dariusleut, Lehrerleut, and Schmiedeleut.

December 14 Ordained as "servant of the Word."

1931 **January – Mid-April** Revisits the Hutterian colonies in Alberta, Manitoba, and South Dakota.

April Lectures at the University of South Dakota and at Goshen College.
May 10 Returns to Germany.

1932 Works on a new edition of *Innenland*.

1933 **End October** Breaks his leg. The complicated fracture requires an operation in Fulda.

1934 **End February–Early March** Journey to Switzerland, then on to Liechtenstein. Supervises the building up of the Alm Bruderhof.
Mid-May Returns to the Rhön; undergoes a second operation on his leg in Fulda.
July–September Makes his second visit to the Alm Bruderhof.
October Appointments with various government ministries in Berlin.

1935 **March 1–9** Visits the Alm Bruderhof for the third time.
March 11 Meets in Zürich, Switzerland, with Leonhard Ragaz and representatives of the religious-socialist movement.
March 25–May 6 Journeys to England and Scotland. Lectures in London, Edinburgh, Glasgow, and Birmingham.
May 13–June 5 Fourth visit to the Alm Bruderhof.
June 13–July 31 Fifth visit to the Alm Bruderhof.
September 27–October 5 Sixth visit to the Alm Bruderhof.
November 12 Leaves the Rhön Bruderhof and travels to the Elisabeth Hospital in Darmstadt.
November 16 Dr. Zander performs a lengthy operation.
November 22 A second operation is carried out to amputate Eberhard's leg. Eberhard Arnold dies the same day at around four o'clock P.M.

Select Bibliography

Arnold, Christoph et al. *God Fulfills His Promises: Meetings in Memory of Arno Martin.* Rifton NY: Plough, 1978.

Arnold, Eberhard. *Am Anfang war die Liebe: Die ersten Christen nach dem Tode der Apostel.* Wiesbaden: Coprint, 1986.

——. *Aus der Arbeit unter den Gebildeten.* Eilenburg, 1907.

——. *Das inwendige Leben.* Moers: Brendow, 1994.

——. *Der Kampf des Gewissens.* Moers: Brendow, 1994.

——. *Der Krieg: Ein Aufruf zur Innerlichkeit.* Gotha, 1914.

——. *Die drei Bücher im Felde.* Gotha, 1915.

——. *Die Revolution Gottes.* Stuttgart: Radius, 1984.

——. *Die Religiosität der heutigen Jugend.* Berlin, 1919.

——. *Gemeinsames Leben und Kindererziehung.* Rifton NY: Plough, 1977.

——. *Innenland.* Berlin, 1918.

——. *Innenland.* Unchanged reprint of 1918 ed. Sannerz, 1923.

——. *Innenland.* Revised and enlarged edition, Liechstenstein, 1936.

——. *Lebensbeweise lebendiger Gemeinden.* 1913. Reprint Rifton NY: Plough, 1973.

——. *Liebesleben und Liebe.* Schlüchtern, 1922.

——. *Love and Marriage in the Spirit.* Rifton NY: Plough, 1965.

——. *The Early Christians after the Death of the Apostles.* Foreword by John Hoyland. Wiltshire: Plough, 1939.

——. *The Individual and World Need.* 2d ed. Farmington, PA: Plough, 1993.

——. *Salz und Licht: Über die Bergpredigt.* Moers: Brendow, 1982.

——. *Sendbrief vom Almbruderhof zum Rhönbruderhof, 1934;* reprint, Rifton NY: Plough,1976.

——. *Urchristliches und Antichristliches im Werdegang Nietzsches,* Eilenburg, 1910.

——. *Zu Gottes Reich: Worte gebundener Rede.* Rifton NY: Plough, 1969.

Arnold, Eberhard and Emmy. *Seeking for the Kingdom of God: Origins of the Bruderhof Communities.* Rifton NY: Plough, 1974.

Arnold, Eberhard and Emmy, and Arnold, Johann Heinrich. *The Heavens are Opened.* Rifton NY: Plough, 1974.

Arnold, Eberhard and Körber, Normann, eds. *Junge Saat, Lebensbuch einer Jugendbewegung.* Schlüchtern, 1921.

Arnold, Emmy. *Gegen den Strom: Das Werden der Bruderhöfe.* Moers: Brendow, 1983.

Arnold, Emmy, comp. *Sonnenlieder.* Sannerz and Leipzig, 1924.

——, comp. *Sonnenlieder II.* Fulda and Leipzig, 1933.

Arnold, Emmy et al. *Eberhard Arnold – Aus seinem Leben und Schrifttum: Ein Zeugnis für völlige Gemeinschaft.* Bridgnorth: Plough, 1953.

Balders, Günter, ed. *Ein Herr, ein Glaube, eine Taufe: 150 Jahre Baptisten-Gemeinden in Deutschland.* Wuppertal, 1984.

Barth, Karl. *Der Christ in der Gesellschaft.* Würzburg, 1920.

Berber, Friedrich. *Zwischen Macht und Gewissen: Lebenserinnerungen.* Munich, 1986.

Bergmann, H. A., ed. *Onderwijskundigen van de twintigste eeuw* [Educators of the twentieth century]. Amsterdam / Groningen, 1983.

Beyer, Werner and Dressler, Johannes. *Ein Leib sind wir in Christus: Evangelisches Allianzwerk 1886–1986.* Bad Blankenburg, 1986.

Beyreuther, Erich. *Der Weg der Evangelischen Allianz in Deutschland.* Wuppertal, 1969.

Brandenburg, Hans. *Die Brücke zu Köngen.* Stuttgart, 1969.

Dehn, Günther. *Die alte Zeit, die vorigen Jahre: Lebenserinnerungen.* Munich, 1962.

Delf, Hanna and Schoeps, Julius H., eds. *Gustav Landauer – Fritz Mauthner, Briefwechsel 1890–1919.* Munich, 1994.

Finney, Charles G. *Lebenserinnerungen.* Düsseldorf, 1902.

Foerster, Friedrich Wilhelm. *Jugendseele – Jugendbewegung – Jugendziel.* Erlenbach/ Zurich, 1923.

Furche-Verlag, ed. *Denken – Glauben – Handeln: Almanach zum 50. Jubiläum des Furche-Verlags.* Hamburg, 1966.

Gerdtell, Ludwig von. *Die Revolutionierung der Kirchen,* Berlin, 1921.

———. *Rudolf Euckens Christentum.* Eilenburg, 1909.

Giese, Ernst. *Und flickten die Netze: Dokumente zur Erweckungsgeschichte des 20. Jahrhunderts.* Marburg, 1976.

Harder, Johannes. *Aufbruch ohne Ende, Geschichten meines Lebens.* Edited by Gudrun Harder and Hermann Horn. Wuppertal,1992.

Heim, Karl. *Tolstoi und Jesus.* Berlin, 1921.

Herpel, Otto. *Zinzendorf: Über Glauben und Leben.* Schlüchtern, 1920.

Holzach, Michael. *Das vergessene Volk.* Hamburg, 1980. Eng. ed. *The Forgotten People: A Year among the Hutterites,* Sioux Falls, SD: Ex Machina, 1993.

Hüssy, Gertrud. *A Joyful Pilgrimage: Emmy Arnold 1884–1980.* Rifton NY: Plough, 1980.

Hutterian Brethren, trans. and ed. *Brothers Unite: An Account of the Uniting of Eberhard Arnold and the Rhön Bruderhof with the Hutterian Church.* Rifton NY: Plough, 1988.

Jordy, Gerhard. *Die Brüderbewegung in Deutschland, Band 2: 1900–1937.* Wuppertal, 1981.

Kempen, Thomas von. *Von der Nachfolge Christi.* Stuttgart, 1965.

Kindt, Werner, ed. *Hermann Schafft – Ein Lebenswerk.* Cassel, 1960.

Kupisch, Karl. *Studenten entdecken die Bibel: Die Geschichte der DCSV.* Hamburg, 1964.

Kutter, Hermann. *Sie müssen! Ein offenes Wort an die christliche Gesellschaft.* Jena, 1910.

Landauer, Gustav. *Aufruf zum Sozialismus.* 1911. 4th ed. Cologne, 1923.

———. *Rechenschaft.* Berlin, 1919.

Loserth, Johann. *Der Anabaptismus in Tirol von seinen Anfängen bis zum Tode Jakob Hutters.* Vienna, 1892.

———. *Der Anabaptismus in Tirol vom Jahre 1536 bis zu seinem Erlöschen.* Vienna, 1892.

Meier, Hans. *Solange das Licht brennt.* Deer Spring Bruderhof, Norfolk CT / Michaelshof, Birnbach, 1990.

Merz, Georg. *Wege und Wandlungen*. Munich, 1961.

Mow, Merrill. *Torches Rekindled: The Bruderhof's Struggle for Renewal*. 3rd ed. Rifton NY: Plough, 1991.

Müller, Alfred D., ed. *Friedrich Wilhelm Foerster und die wirkliche Welt*. Zurich, 1928.

Pfeiffer, Arnold, ed. *Religiöse Sozialisten*. Olten, 1976.

Rathmann, August. *Ein Arbeiterleben: Erinnerungen an Weimar und danach*. Wuppertal, 1983.

Riedel, Heinrich. *Kampf um die Jugend: Evangelische Jugendarbeit, 1933–1945*. Munich, 1976.

Schoeps, Hans Joachim. *Rückblicke*. Berlin, 1963.

Siepmann, Heinzfried. *Brüder und Genossen*. Cologne, 1987.

Spemann, Franz. *Landeskirche oder religiöse Freiheit?* Berlin, 1907.

Stählin, Wilhelm. *Fieber und Heil in der Jugendbewegung*. Hamburg, 1921.

Stieglitz, Thomas von. *Kirche als Bruderschaft: Das hutterische Kirchenbild bei Eberhard Arnold aus heutiger katholischer Sicht*. Theological dissertation, Paderborn, 1991.

Strauch, Max. *Die Theologie Karl Barths*. Munich, 1927.

Ströver, Ida C., and Arnold, Eberhard, ed. *Der Heliand: Darstellungen aus dem Leben Jesu im Lichte altgermanischer Anschauung in 7 Tondrucktafeln*. Berlin, 1916.

Susman, Margarete. *Eberhard Arnold*. Special printing of the periodical *Neue Wege*, 51. Jgg., Zurich, October 1977.

Vollmer, Antje. *Die Neuwerkbewegung 1919–1935: Ein Beitrag zur Geschichte der Jugendbewegung, des religiösen Sozialismus und der Arbeiterbewegung*. Ph.D. dissertation, Berlin, 1973.

Wehowsky, Stefan. *Religiöse Interpretation politischer Erfahrung: Eberhard Arnold und die Neuwerkbewegung als Exponenten des religiösen Sozialismus z.Z. der Weimarer Republik*. Göttingen, 1980.

Zumpe, Hans et al. *Eberhard Arnold: Sein Leben für die Bruderhöfe*. Liechtenstein, 1935.

Index

Other Titles from Plough

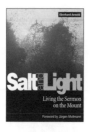

Salt and Light
Living the Sermon on the Mount
Eberhard Arnold

Talks and writings on the transformative power of a life lived by Jesus' revolutionary teachings in the Sermon on the Mount.
$15.00 / £10.00

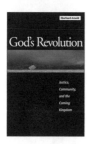

God's Revolution
Justice, Community, and the Coming Kingdom
Eberhard Arnold

Topically arranged excerpts from the author's talks and writings on the church, community, marriage and family issues, government, and world suffering.
$15.00 / £9.00

Why We Live in Community
with two interpretive talks by Thomas Merton
Eberhard Arnold

A time-honored manifesto that adds a fresh, engaging voice to the vital discussion of the basis, meaning, and purpose of community.
$8.00 / £5.50

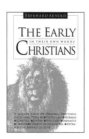

The Early Christians
In Their Own Words
Edited by Eberhard Arnold

A topically arranged collection of primary sources that provides a guide and yardstick for Christians today. This is a book that all students, priests, librarians, and history lovers will want on their shelves.
$25.00 / £16.50

Discipleship
Living for Christ in the Daily Grind
J. Heinrich Arnold

A collection of thoughts on following Christ in the nitty-gritty of daily life. Includes sections on love, humility, forgiveness, leadership, community, suffering, salvation, and the kingdom of God.
$16.00 / £10.50

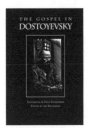

The Gospel in Dostoyevsky
Edited by the Bruderhof

An introduction to the "great, God-haunted Russian" comprised of passages from *The Brothers Karamazov, Crime and Punishment,* and *The Idiot.*
$15.00 / £10.00

The Violence of Love
Oscar Romero
Comp. and transl. by J. R. Brockman, S.J.

In Romero's words we encounter a man of God humbly and confidently calling us to conversion and action. Those who let his message touch them will never see life in the same way again.
$14.00 / £9.50

The Plough
A Publication of the Bruderhof Communities

A quarterly journal with articles on issues and new items of interest to seekers for whom social justice and the call of the gospel are one and the same.
$10/year   £7/year

To order or to request a complete catalog, call 800-521-8011 (US) or 0800 269 048 (UK). Visit our website at www.plough.com.